Monetary Stability and Economic Growth

Monetary Stability and Economic Growth

A Dialog between Leading Economists

Edited by

Robert A. Mundell

Professor, Columbia University, New York City, USA

and

Paul J. Zak

Professor, Claremont Graduate University, Claremont, California, USA

Edward Elgar
Cheltenham, UK • Northampton, MA, USA

Published by
Edward Elgar Publishing Limited
Glensanda House
Montpellier Parade
Cheltenham
Glos GL50 1UA
UK

Edward Elgar Publishing, Inc.
136 West Street
Suite 202
Northampton
Massachusetts 01060
USA

A catalogue record for this book
is available from the British Library

Library of Congress Cataloging in Publication Data
Bologna-Claremont International Monetary Conference (15th : 1999 San Miguel de Allende, Mexico)
    Monetary stability and economic growth ; a dialog between leading economists / edited by Robert A. Mundell and Paul J. Zak.
        p. cm.
    Proceedings of the 15th Bologna-Claremont International Monetary Conference, held in San Miguel de Allende, Mexico, 1999.
    Includes index.
    1. Monetary policy – Congresses. 2. Economic development – Congresses.
    I. Mundell, Robert A. II. Zak, Paul J. III. Title.

HG230.3 .B655 2003
332.4'6--dc21

3 2280 00772 7902

2002068818

ISBN 1 84064 998 4

Typeset by Manton Typesetters, Louth, Lincolnshire, UK.
Printed and bound in Great Britain by Biddles Ltd, *www.biddles.co.uk*

Contents

Figures   vii

List of participants   ix

Foreword   xi
By Steadman Upham

Preface   Monetary stability and economic growth in unstable times   xiii
By Robert A. Mundell and Paul J. Zak

1   The Sixth Lord Robbins Memorial Lecture: Reform of the
    international monetary system   1
    By Robert A. Mundell

2   The state of the world economy   24
    Introduced by Paul A. Samuelson

3   The euro in Europe and the world   38
    Introduced by Christopher Johnson

4   Monetary policy and economic growth in Latin America   59
    Introduced by Robert L. Bartley

5   Monetary policy in the NAFTA area and the possibility of
    monetary union   78
    Introduced by Herbert Grubel

6   Randall Hinshaw Memorial Lecture: Exchange rate policy in
    Latin America   88
    By Arnold Harberger

7   Is monetary stability possible in Latin America?   101
    Introduced by Michael Connolly

8 Monetary policy and economic performance in Mexico 117
  Introduced by Judy Shelton and Abel Beltran Del Rio

9 Economic policy in Japan and East Asia 137
  Introduced by Jeffrey A. Frankel

10 The future of the international monetary system 153
  Introduced by Robert Solomon

Index 169

Figures

6.1   Exports, imports and tradables   89
7.1   Unemployment and prices   102

Participants

Fausto Alzati, Executive President, Centro Intercional Lucas Alaman para el Crecimiento Economico (CILACE), Mexico

David M. Andrews, Professor of International Relations, and Director, European Center of California, Scripps College, USA

Sven M. Arndt, C.M. Stone Professor of Economics, and Director, Lowe Institute of Political Economy, Claremont McKenna College, Conference Moderator, USA

Armando Baquiero, Economist, Banco de Mexico, Mexico

Robert L. Bartley, Editor, *The Wall Street Journal*, USA

Abel Beltran Del Rio, President and Founder, CIEMEX-WEFA, USA

Michael Connolly, Professor of Economics and Chair, University of Miami, USA

Jeffrey A. Frankel, James W. Harpel Professor of Capital Formation and Economic Growth, Kennedy School of Government, Harvard University; Former Member, President's Council of Economic Advisors, USA

Herbert Grubel, Professor Emeritus of Economics, Simon Fraser University, Canada

Arnold Harberger, Professor of Economics, University of California, Los Angeles, USA

Christopher Johnson, UK Advisor, Association for the Monetary Union of Europe, UK

Robert A. Mundell, Nobel Laureate in Economics; University Professor of Economics, Columbia University, Conference Director, USA

Roberto Salinas-Leon, Director of Economic Strategy, TV Azteca, Mexico

Eduardo Sojo, Director of Economic Planning, Government of Guanajuato state, Mexico

Paul A. Samuelson, Nobel Laureate in Economics; Professor Emeritus of Economics, Massachusetts Institute of Technology, USA

Judy Shelton, Professor of International Finance, DUXX Graduate School of Business Leadership; Board Member, Empower America, USA

Robert Solomon, Guest Scholar, The Brookings Institution; Former Advisor to the Board of Governors of the Federal Reserve, USA

Paul J. Zak, Associate Professor of Economics, Claremont Graduate University, USA

Steadman Upham, President, Claremont Graduate University, USA

Foreword

By

Steadman Upham, President of Claremont Graduate University

Every president should have the opportunity to address such a distinguished group of scholars. The Bologna–Claremont International Monetary Conferences have a tradition of excellence and intellectual rigor, bringing together the very best and brightest economists for frank, probing dialogs of economic issues of foremost current concern. The participants are carefully chosen to represent a wide range of views, the better to stimulate thought and discussion. Each of the last fourteen conferences was edited and published as a book derived from the discussions. The previous volume, entitled *Currency Crises, Monetary Union and the Conduct of Monetary Policy* was edited by Claremont Graduate University Professor Paul Zak and published in 1999 by Edward Elgar. The 1997 conference upon which that book is based included four Nobel Laureate economists.

This year the participants are no less distinguished, and the intellectual work produced by the attendees and the discussion of the group serves as another element in the important legacy of this conference and of its founder, Claremont Graduate University Professor Randall Hinshaw. The 1999 Mexico Conference, while adding to this legacy, marks both a change in venue away from Europe and the United States, and an important opportunity to focus on the United States' new economic relations with Mexico and Latin America.

Since the passage of the North American Free Trade Agreement, Mexico and the United States have vastly strengthened their trading partnerships. The lowering of tariffs and the opening of the U.S.–Mexico border to trade have dramatically increased opportunities for individuals and businesses in both countries. In July of this year alone, the U.S. and Mexico engaged in trade valued at over sixteen billion dollars. This mutually beneficial trade relationship has led to stability in U.S.–Mexico border areas.

As demonstrated by the Asian tiger economies, trade openness and government stability are fundamental components of sustained development. In the future, the United States and Mexico will become further integrated economically. The economic stimulus will lead Mexico to become the economic engine of Latin America. Let me close by inviting you to Claremont for further discussions of economic issues and continued contributions to the Bologna–Claremont International Monetary Conference legacy.

Preface   Monetary stability and economic growth in unstable times

By

Robert A. Mundell and Paul J. Zak

For more than thirty years, the Bologna–Claremont International Monetary Conferences have generated spirited and engaging debates on international monetary policy. They have brought together top experts in international economics to debate and put into context leading issues facing the world economy, recorded for posterity in conference proceedings. This volume falls in the same tradition of its predecessors and reports the proceedings of the fifteenth conference, held in San Miguel de Allende, Mexico, October 1–4, 1999, on the subject "Monetary Stability and Economic Growth in Unstable Times."

The conference had two interesting sequels. One was that nine days after the conference it was announced that Robert Mundell, the conference director, was awarded the Nobel Memorial Prize in Economic Sciences. The other was that nine months after the conference, its major sponsor, Vicente Fox, Governor of the State of Guanajuato, was elected President of Mexico.

The 1999 conference was the first to be held outside the U.S. or Europe, and has resulted in a greater – and welcome – emphasis on developing countries in general and Latin America in particular. There were of course extensive discussions about the "tequila effect" that hit Latin America after the Mexican currency crisis in December, 1994, the "Asian flu" that infected parts of Southeast Asia but left other countries curiously immunized, as well as the Russian bond default in 1998, and the Brazilian devaluation of 1999.

This book does not only report the history of monetary (mis)management, but extracts important policy lessons from this history. Among the issues tackled: How does monetary stability affect economic growth? Which monetary institutions are most and least susceptible to crises? How can countries best achieve monetary stability? When is monetary union desirable? Which anchors for monetary stability are likely to be most effective? How will the advent of the euro affect financial markets and the international monetary system? Will the euro become a rival to the dollar? Should the exchange rates among the three largest currency blocs be managed? Is international monetary reform possible and what direction should it take? These subjects provoked lively discussions among the participants. Also recorded are questions and comments from the audience, who attended the conference. When audience members identified themselves their names are included in the text.

Two of the highlights of the conference this year are the Robbins Lecture and the Hinshaw Lecture. The Robbins Lecture was named in memory of Lord (Lionel) Robbins, the important British economist who acted as Director of the Conferences from their inception in 1968 until his death in 1984; the Robbins Lecture this year was delivered by Robert Mundell.

The Hinshaw Lecture, inaugurated at this conference, is named in memory of Randall Hinshaw, the international economist from Claremont Graduate University who managed the entire conference series and edited the proceedings from the beginning in 1968 until his death only last year. The Hinshaw Lecture was delivered by Arnold C. Harberger, Professor Emeritus at the University of California at Los Angeles and former President of the American Economic Association.

We were honored to have Vicente Fox, former Governor of the State of Guanajuato to speak at the adjourning dinner.

It is our pleasure to acknowledge the sponsors of the conference in San Miguel de Allende. They include CILACE, the government of Guanajuato, Ixe, Casa de Bolsa, CEMEX, Cementos de Mexico, Banamex, the Technologico de Monterrey, Claremont Graduate University and the Bologna Center of the Johns Hopkins University.

1. The Sixth Lord Robbins Memorial Lecture: Reform of the international monetary system

By

Robert A. Mundell

I am deeply honored to present this Robbins Lecture. Lord (Lionel) Robbins was a great economist who, from the time I first met him at the London School of Economics in the fall of 1955, I came to admire and respect and love. He had a great influence on the economics profession and, from the time these Bologna–Claremont conferences began in 1968, he was our conference chairman and set the tone for and influenced the agenda of each of its meetings over the years. It is a special pleasure to present this lecture in the presence here in San Miguel de Allende of members of his wonderful family.

My lecture is on "Reform of the International Monetary System." This is a subject in which Lord Robbins himself had a lifelong interest. He was always a staunch advocate of a fixed exchange rate monetary system and in the 1960s he became an eloquent advocate of a European currency. Had he lived to this year he would have been gratified to see the euro come into being and he would have added his powerful voice to those in Britain who wanted that important country to join the euro area. Yet, at the same time he would not have accepted a world of large currency areas as a final solution but would have put his shoulders behind attempts to restore a truly international monetary system.

A CENTURY OF TURMOIL

The imminence of the millennium encourages a longer run view of events. We can now look back on the entire twentieth century. At once we can see it as the century of the greatest innovation in human history. How else can we acknowledge the significance of such a bewildering number of revolutions: electricity, the automobile, the aeroplane, the telephone, radio, the phonograph, tank warfare, antibiotics, radar, atomic fusion and fission, atomic war, jet travel, rocket ships, the space age, DNA, ICB missiles, the missile shield, the computer, fax machines the Internet, genetic revolutions, cloning and more? The dark side of the century must also be recognized: population explosion, world wars, ideological fanaticism, monetary instability, hyperinflation, depression, genocide, environmental degradation and terrorism.

Behind these scientific and political events, the international monetary system tells a story. Political events in the twentieth century were very much influenced by the international monetary system, just as the international monetary system was rocked by important political events. The international monetary system provides a thread to guide us over seemingly unconnected economic and political events.

The thread can be seen if we divide the century into three almost equal parts. The first third of the century was occupied with the international gold standard, its breakdown during World War I, its abortive restoration in the 1920s, and its collapse again under the pressures of deflation and the Great Depression in the early 1930s. Over this period, gold was the basic international standard of value.

The second third of the century started with the new price of gold established by President Franklin D. Roosevelt in 1934 and ended in a series of moves that started with the crisis of the gold pool in 1967, proceeded through the "two-tier" system established in 1968 and the demise of the Bretton Woods arrangements in 1971, culminating in the movement to generalized floating in 1973. For most of this second period of this century, other currencies were tied to the dollar and the dollar, up to 1971, was tied to gold. In this era the 1944 U.S. dollar – "as good as gold" – was the basic standard of international value.

The last third of the twentieth century was taken up by flexible exchange rates. It began with the breakdown of the postwar Bretton Woods arrangements in 1967–71 and the movement to generalized floating in 1973. It came to an end in 1999 with the creation of the euro and the movement toward a tripolar system. Over this period the dominant unit of account was the U.S. dollar, no longer linked to gold.

Is there a unifying theme connecting these thirds? The answer is, yes. It is the role of the United States economy, an economy that already in 1913 – before the war and when the Federal Reserve System was created – was three times larger than its nearest rival, larger than the British, German and French economies put together.

Before 1913, however, lacking a central bank, the monetary power of the United States was dissipated and dispersed. It was the act of creating the Federal Reserve System in 1913 that changed fundamentally and forever the operation of the international monetary system. Upon its creation, it was the most important central bank in the world. Henceforth, the working of the gold standard would be determined principally by the policy of the Federal Reserve System. Soon after the World War began, the dollar succeeded to the position of the pound sterling as the most important currency in the world.

Keynes was the first economist to notice how the creation of the Federal Reserve and World War I undermined the operation of the international gold standard:

> But the war has effected a great change. Gold itself has become a "managed" currency…Consequently gold now stands at an "artificial" value, the future course of which almost entirely depends on the policy of the Federal Reserve Board of the United States…The value of gold is no longer the resultant of the chance gifts of Nature and the judgement of numerous authorities and individuals acting independently…convertibility into gold will not alter the fact that the value of gold itself depends on the policy of the Central Banks…In truth, the gold standard is already a barbarous relic. (Keynes 1923: Ch. 4)

The postwar price level was about 40 percent higher than the prewar level, and this reduced the real value of gold reserves. There was sufficient gold for the system insofar as most countries had not returned to the gold standard. But the generalized return to gold in the late '20s put pressure on gold reserves and led to a scramble for it that brought on the great deflation of the early 1930s. Gustav Cassel's prediction, that a return to the gold standard with prewar conventions about the use of gold in reserves and in circulation would create "a serious shortage of gold leading to a progressive appreciation of its value" was exactly vindicated.

Deflation did come and by 1932 the price level in the United States had come back down to its prewar level. Higher tariffs and taxes in the United States, coupled with tighter monetary policies, brought in its wake, mass unemployment, bankruptcy and depression. With morale and economic strength in the democracies undermined, the road was laid open for fascist aggression and World War II.

All the major countries succumbed to the deflation of the early 1930s; it was very clearly an appreciation of gold against commodities. Price declines averaged around 35 percent. Many economists blamed the gold standard for the deflation. But the correct view is that World War I forced countries to violate the rules of the gold standard and engage in deficit finance and inflationary policies that raised the general price level above prewar levels. Restoration of the gold standard in the 1920s simply restored the gold standard equilibrium that had prevailed before the war. Economists like Gustav Cassel of Sweden, Ludwig von Mises of Austria, Charles Rist of France and John Maynard Keynes in England understood that deflation could be the consequence of a return to the gold standard and predicted it. That they were correct is confirmed by the fact that the deflation of the 1930s brought the dollar price level back to the level it had been in 1914.[1]

Two paths were open to avoid the deflation of the 1930s. One would have been to give up the idea of returning to the gold standard, and living with a system in which the world price level was more or less managed by the Federal Reserve System. That in fact was the solution at Bretton Woods: the U.S. managed gold and the other countries managed the dollar. But no European country was willing to concede that position of leadership to a new and untried central bank of a country that, however dominant, was not even a member of the League of Nations.

The other way of avoiding the deflation would have been to render it unnecessary by increasing gold liquidity by enough to match the increased gold requirements of the new system. Had the dollar price of gold been raised in 1930 – when the deflation was just getting under way – to the price it was raised in 1934, i.e., $35 an ounce, there would have been no need for a 35 percent fall in the dollar price level. But no economist proposed such a policy, and the United States – which did not foresee the economic disaster it was facing – would not have listened. The traditional U.S. gold price of $20.67 an ounce was sacrosanct.

The United States floated the dollar early in 1933 but after a year, President Franklin D. Roosevelt devalued the dollar, raising the price of the gold to $35 an ounce. The dollar was now at the center of the system and gold had become a mere passenger. Keynes's view was that monetary policies would not be governed any longer by the requirements of gold convertibility whenever this conflicted with the new goals of monetary management.

Under the new arrangements, the United States fixed the price of gold and most other major countries fixed their currencies to the dollar. Initially, in the late 1930s, gold was overvalued and the dollar was as good or better than gold, reflected in the very low interest rates prevailing at the time. This was a period that began what came to be known as a period of "dollar shortage" and it would last into the early 1950s. The bulk of the world's monetary gold reserves were concentrated in the United States (70 percent in 1948).

As long as the United States had gold reserves in excess of what was legally required for a reserve against Federal Reserve liabilities, the United States could conduct its policies without concern for its balance of payments. But the apparently invulnerable U.S. gold position was becoming undermined by changes in the U.S. price level. During World War II and the immediate postwar period, the U.S. price level more than doubled, halving the real value of gold reserves. From 1950 until 1970 the price level rose by another 50 percent, again lowering proportionately the real value of gold.

Apparently the U.S. constraint of gold convertibility was not preventing inflation. Gold was losing its role as an anchor. The system that now emerged was therefore close to the system Keynes had predicted would emerge in the 1920s.[2]

The ever-upward movement of the price level meant that US monetary policy was on a collision course with the fixed dollar price of gold. If the dollar price of gold were in equilibrium in 1934, it could not be in equilibrium in 1971 after the dollar price level had more than tripled.[3] It was just a matter of time before the United States would have to end its commitment to sell and buy gold at $35, and with the end of that commitment, the Bretton Woods era would be over.

In retrospect, the international monetary system should be seen as conferring benefits and costs on the United States and the rest of the world. But the division of those benefits and costs between the United States and particularly Europe were changing rapidly. Europe began its drive for monetary union in 1969 at a summit meeting of European leaders at The Hague. Once Europe had become committed to European Monetary Union, it needed the international system and the fixed exchange rate link to the dollar as its instrument of economic convergence. By 1970, however, the United States had decided to "benignly neglect" the drive toward European Monetary Union and no longer saw the fixed exchange rate system as a major benefit to the United States. The excuse for breaking it up came in the middle of August 1971 with some European requests for large conversions of dollars into gold. President Nixon took the dollar off gold, and in 1973 all the major countries moved to generalized floating.

The last third of the century was taken up with the problems raised by the absence of an international monetary system, the role of the dollar and flexible exchange rates. The biggest problem was the breakdown in monetary and fiscal discipline. Gold and oil prices soared and the dollar price level increased at rates never before seen in peacetime. The United States itself suffered three back-to-back years of two-digit inflation at the end of the 1970s. Only with the change in the policy mix in the early 1980s, to tax cuts to spur the economy and tight money to stop the inflation, did the United States get its economy back on track.

Meanwhile, Europe fretted under U.S. leadership during the Vietnam era, the U.S. balance of payments deficit, the weak dollar and at the same time the increasing use of the dollar as the international money. A European currency was one possible antidote, that would at the same time be an important step in completing the Common Market. The flexible exchange rate system made it harder to achieve convergence. By the end of the Cold War followed by German unification in 1990 the urgency of the project led to the signing of the Treaty of Maastricht in 1991, the most important component of which was the blueprint for a single European currency, which emerged as the euro in 1999.

SIGNIFICANCE OF THE EURO

The significance of the euro for the international economy lies in its ability to change the power configuration of the international monetary system. When the euro was created it became at once the second most important currency in the world with enormous potential for growth.

What about the three EU countries that qualified for the EMU but exercised their option to stay out? Although leaders have said that entry is only a matter of time, the electorates in Denmark, Sweden and Britain have doubts that the benefits of monetary union exceed the costs, doubts that have been fanned by desultory leadership. The three countries have some things in common. They were part of EFTA [European Free Trade Association] rather than the EEC [European Economic Community], they are each wary of being pressured into increased fiscal harmonization and political integration, they are all proud of their history and story-book parliamentary monarchies, and all three have left-of-center governments. But these similarities mask a fundamental difference. The clue to the difference lies in the very different shares of government spending in GDP. In the two Scandinavian countries government involvement in the economy is much above the European average, whereas in Britain it is much below it. The Scandinavian countries fear that tax harmonization will force them to diminish their lavish welfare state programs, whereas the British fear the opposite. But demography is on the side of the British case: population aging and drastically lower ratios of workers to pensioners is going to force a cutback and even some privatization in the Scandinavian welfare states. Britain's position is closer to what is a sustainable average for all Europe than the other countries. In any case, my own view is that all three countries will join the euro area in the next few years.

The euro area is certainly expanding outside the EU itself, and quite rapidly. First, 13 countries of the CFA franc zone in Central and West Africa were automatically attached to the euro, through the French franc. Second, another ten or 12 countries have been slated as "accession countries," eligible, if they meet the prerequisites, to join the European Union and therefore also the euro area. Although I realize a decision has not yet been made on the subject, my own view is that countries eligible for accession should be required to join the euro area.

With the three outs eventually in, along with Greece and the inaugural EU-11, there will be 15 members plus 13 African countries plus up to 12 accession countries for about 40 potential countries in the euro zone. I have little doubt that at least another ten countries in the Middle East, Eastern Europe, Africa, South America and Asia will also choose to tie their currencies to the euro. We can therefore expect the euro zone to comprise upwards of 40 to 50 nations over the next decade, with a population near to 500 million and a combined GDP that is higher than that of the United States.

By, say, 2010, it is likely that the euro and dollar will be on equal terms and that central banks will want to keep their reserves about equally in each currency. Making some extrapolations that involve substantial guesswork, we might assume the stylized facts shown in Table 1.1 approximate the international reserve position in 2010. If this scenario approximates reality, demand for dollars for use in central bank reserves and in international portfolios will be at best sluggish over the next decade, while demand for euros will be high. Trade balances and exchange rates will have to reflect this shift in portfolio preferences. Unless offset by changes in capital movements, the U.S. deficit will of necessity become smaller and the dollar weaker, with the opposite happening in Europe. A strong euro is a likely consequence after the transition period is complete.

Table 1.1   Foreign exchange holdings (trillions of U.S. dollars)

	1998	2010	Change
Dollars	1.2	1.2	–
Euros	–	1.2	1.2
Other	0.4	0.8	0.4
Total	1.6	3.2	1.6

Of course the other currency areas will not stay put. The dollar area itself may continue to expand. It is possible that if Japan solves some of its macroeconomic problems, it could become the center of one or two foci (with China) of an Asian currency bloc. It is conceivable that a Latin American currency bloc initially tied to the dollar might develop. Alternatively, the four nations of Mercosur – Brazil, Argentina, Uruguay and Paraguay – might try to form their own currency bloc. Similar possibilities exist in Africa.

The euro has forced us to change our view of the international monetary system. In place of a world where each nation-state floats its currency and tackles inflation problems on its own, we enter a world of currency combinations, dominated at the present by the dollar, euro and yen areas. In the near future the world will become less dependent on the dollar, and power in the international monetary system will be distributed differently. This change will bring to the fore new and more meaningful ideas about reform of the international financial architecture. The euro promises to be a catalyst for reform.

THREE ISLANDS OF STABILITY

Today we have in the dollar, euro and yen areas three large currency areas that together account for 60 percent of world output. The exchange rates among these currency areas constitute the most important prices in the world. Any kind of reform of the "international financial architecture" has to deal with exchange rates among the "G-3" currencies.

The international financial architecture under the gold standard included mechanisms for: (1) fixing exchange rates; (2) achieving a high degree of price stability; (3) achieving equilibrium in the balance of payments; and (4) establishing a world currency. When each country designated its currency by a specific weight of gold, free trade in that commodity ensured fixed exchange rates. Because money supplies were linked to gold and gold was scarce, inflation was kept under control. Gold flows between countries altered money supplies and thus kept the balance of payments in equilibrium. And the common use of gold in currencies came close to the creation of a world currency.

The last decade of the twentieth century has been a decade of price stability. In this sense it is like the first decade of the century. But there the similarity ends. Price stability was achieved in the first decade through a highly efficient international monetary system, the international gold standard, a system that also provided the world not only with fixed exchange rates but also with the bonus of a world currency. The last decade provided the core regions with price stability but with extreme volatility of exchange rates, and no trace of a world currency. In that sense, the last decade is in deficit to the first decade on two accounts: the absence of fixed exchange rates, and the absence of a world currency.

The idea of a world currency today seems a long way off. But opposition to large currency areas or a world currency among modern economists is in sharp contrast to the opinion of all the great economists of the past – without exception. The ideal system for economists of the past would be a single money for the world, the very apotheosis of fixed exchange rates. A single money would maximize the properties of money as a unit of account, a convenience in exchange, a measure of value, a unit of deferred payments (especially if it were a stable money!), and information and transactions costs.

The dollar, euro and yen areas have each achieved a high degree of price stability. Why between such areas of price stability is it necessary to have exchange rate changes? We have seen the euro drop to lows that have exceeded 25 percent from its starting point against the dollar, and this in less than two years. Can this instability be expected to continue? One way to try to answer this question is to look at the predecessors of the euro, the ECU and its bulwark, the Deutschmark. Think of the instability of the DM–US$ rate over the past 25 years. In 1975, the dollar was about DM3.5. Five years later, in 1980, it was half that, at DM1.7. Five years later, in 1985, it had doubled to DM3.4. And then in the ERM crisis in August 1992, the dollar had gone down below DM1.4. Today the dollar is above DM2. If these tremendous fluctuations occurred in the dollar–euro rate, it would crack euroland apart!

Nor is a look at the history of the yen–dollar rate comforting. For a quarter century after 1948 the dollar was 360 yen; in 1985, before the Plaza Accord, it was around 240 yen; ten years later it had fallen to 79 yen. And then three years later, in June 1998, it had soared to 148 yen, bringing on the Asian crisis; and then suddenly it came down 105 yen, only to rise again toward 125 yen. Instability of this type destabilizes financial markets, disrupts trade and neighbouring countries, and creates extremely difficult conditions for the rest of Asia. At the time of the historic Bretton Woods meeting in 1944, the architects of the IMF realized that exchange rates – and especially the exchange rates of the major countries – were a matter of multilateral concern and had to be managed for the benefit of all countries, a concept that has been lost in recent years.

In passing, one should recognize the culpability of the instability of the dollar–yen rate as a cause of the so-called Asian crisis. I do not like to call it an Asian crisis because it was really restricted to four countries: Thailand, Malaysia, Indonesia and South Korea. The crisis in these countries had ripple effects in the rest of Asia. But at least five countries escaped the brunt of it: Singapore, China, Hong Kong, Taiwan and Japan. These countries had three things in common: a precise target for their monetary policy, more than ample foreign exchange rate reserves, and relatively low debt ratios. The countries that were subjected to shocks did not handle the appreciation of the dollar against the yen between April 1995 and June 1998 in a way that was transparent to the market. Note that the more successful countries had quite different monetary targets: Hong Kong had a currency board; China had a fixed exchange rate with capital controls; and Singapore, Taiwan and Japan sought to stabilize a commodity basket.

I mentioned earlier that virtually all of the great classical economists believed strongly in fixed exchange rates. Keynes was no exception. In the 1920s Keynes wrote a book called *A Tract on Monetary Reform*. In it he argued ably that countries would have to choose between stabilizing their price level or their exchange rate, when the price level in the rest of the world (he was thinking also of gold) is unstable. In that case the country should give priority to stabilizing its internal price level. But if the rest of the world was also stable, then the authorities should have a secondary goal of stabilizing the exchange rates. Keynes was quite insistent on it and I believe he was completely right, as he was when he supported the gold-based fixed exchange rate system at Bretton Woods.

There have been many attempts to paint Keynes as an inflationist and as an opponent of gold. He was neither. He never said that "gold is a barbarous relic." In his *Tract* he said that "the gold standard is already a barbarous relic," by which he meant that the gold standard of the 1920s was nothing like the gold standard before the war because now (i.e., the 1920s) its effectiveness depended on the policies of a few central banks. He was here making the brilliant and original observation that the vast size of the U.S. economy had changed forever the way the gold standard would work.[4]

A G-3 MONETARY UNION

An international monetary system based on fixed exchange rates is as possible today as it was in Keynes's day. Leaving aside for a moment the question of gold, we need to move towards a system that would try to stabilize the dollar–yen and dollar–euro rate. I want to make the case for establishing such a system under today's institutional conditions.

Economists know that when a central bank wants to ease monetary conditions, it has to expand its balance sheet, which it can do in one or both of two ways: it can buy domestic assets (typically bonds) or foreign assets (typically foreign exchange or gold). Alternatively, to tighten up the money supply, it has to contract its balance sheet, and sell either domestic or foreign assets. Which policy – domestic or foreign asset transactions – is better?

The answer may depend on the situation of the country. Two corner solutions can be considered. A monetary authority that uses a currency board system changes its money supply only by intervention in the foreign exchange market. These economies are usually – but not necessarily – small, open economies heavily dependent on foreign trade and international capital transactions. The success of the currency board system in maintaining stability will depend on the stability of the anchor currency.

At the other extreme is a closed economy, such as the world economy with a single currency. Here there is no alternative to the use of domestic assets simply because there are no "foreign" assets. Very large currency areas – if they existed – would also find it convenient to follow this corner solution path.

But our world of currency areas is not like that. The largest currency areas, the dollar, euro and yen areas represent at most 25, 17 and 12 percent of the world economy. For these economies to ignore the foreign sector would like a large open economy ignoring its balance of payments. The European Central Bank and the Federal Reserve have this bizarre notion – never demonstrated as a correct proposition in economic theory – that intervention should be restricted to changes in domestic assets, while not touching – heaven forbid! – foreign assets. Why should these areas hold a third of the world's currency reserves and two-thirds of the world's monetary gold stock if they are never to be used for monetary purposes?

Monetary officials in the modern world who ignore the foreign exchange rate are putting their heads in the sand, preventing themselves from ingesting important information, and a central bank that abjures intervention in the foreign exchange market as a matter of principle is fighting with one hand tied behind its back. It is the wrong principle.

When a currency overshoots in, say, a downward direction and monetary tightening is called for, it is preferable to sell foreign assets rather than domestic bonds. The sales have equivalent effects in restricting the supply of liquidity, but the sale of foreign assets also defends the currency.[5]

It should be noted that this prescription represents an application of the principle of effective market classification: instruments should be paired with the targets they influence most directly (see Mundell 1968: 169–70).

What about the belief of many who say:

> Intervention in the foreign exchange market doesn't work. Turnover in the market amounts to $1.5 trillion a *day* and any likely central bank intervention is just a drop in the bucket. Experience with intervention in the past – e.g., in the winter of 1978–79 when the United States borrowed $30 billion from its partners to try to arrest the fall of the dollar – has been completely unsuccessful.

A closer and more comprehensive look at experience with intervention, however, shows precisely the opposite. The entire history of the international gold standard was a history of successful intervention. Over two decades of experience with the Bretton Woods arrangements kept that fixed exchange rate system in place. Currency boards have long used automatic intervention to fix exchange rates for decades. More recently, intervention to fix the exchange rates of the euro area has been completely successful, ending within the euro zone virtually all speculative capital movements. Whenever intervention has been intelligently conducted, it has been successful.

There are four principles of successful intervention: (1) intervention should have a clearly-stated purpose; (2) it should not be sterilized; (3) it should occur in both the spot and forward markets; and (4) it should be concerted. In the 1978–79 example, the Federal Reserve dumped foreign exchange on the market but then turned around and bought an equivalent amount of government bonds, preventing the intervention from having any effect on U.S. monetary policy.

Exchange rate instability is a major threat to prosperity in the world today. Instability of exchange rates brings with it instability of financial markets and capricious changes in real debts, tax burdens, interest rates and wage rates. The emerging-market countries of Asia will never be able to completely restore confidence until they stabilize their currencies.

But how should we go about getting more exchange rate stability? Both the European Central Bank [ECB] and the Federal Reserve System have become champions of inflation targeting and of "benign neglect" of the exchange rates.

The difficulties of fixing exchange rates among the G-3 countries are much exaggerated. An extreme step would be to adopt the euro model as it will be in its final form and move toward a *single*-currency monetary union of the G-3. I am not recommending that. The U.S. would not want to give up the most important currency in the world. Europe would not want to give up the euro after three decades of struggle to achieve it. And Japan would not give up the yen if the other areas kept their currencies. What I am proposing is not a G-3 single currency monetary union, but a G-3 *three*-currency monetary union. A G-3 three-currency monetary union would not be more difficult than the monetary union already achieved by the countries making up the euro area, i.e., European Monetary Union (EMU) before the final step of the transition to the single currency.[6]

How could such a monetary union come about? Europe has already pointed the way with the progress it has made toward an 11-currency monetary union. The EMU required a common agreement on (1) the targeted inflation rate; (2) a common way of measuring the inflation rate (Eurostat's Harmonized Index of Consumer Prices, HICP); (3) redistribution of the seigniorage (in proportion to equity in the ECB); (4) a pivot for locking exchange rates; and (5) a centralized monetary policy. Europe has already implemented those steps inside the euro area. Why should it be more difficult to do it between, say, the United States, Europe and Japan? The rates of inflation and the inflation targets are close enough, why not just lock exchange rates, organize a common monetary policy and make an agreement on seigniorage? It would be administratively and institutionally easy and the politics would not be more difficult than a monetary union between France and Germany.

It is very convenient to have a division of responsibilities along comparative advantage lines. Suppose the ECB and the Bank of Japan were assigned the task of fixing the euro and the yen to the dollar; purchases and sales of foreign exchange would determine their contributions to monetary expansion and contraction. If then a Monetary Policy Committee, composed of policy makers in all three areas, made decisions about monetary policy, the monetary union would be in full swing.

TOWARD AN INTOR

If a G-3 fix and policy union could be achieved, it would be a comparatively simple additional step to expand it to the other members of the IMF. The G-3 currency union could be used as the platform for a world currency. A common unit of account could be established that could have a fixed and stable relationship to the G-3 currencies, and which could become the official unit of account for the IMF and World Bank. At long last, an international financial architecture would come into being.

A strong case can be made for making provisions for widening, extending and generalizing the monetary union to other countries. First, the other countries would benefit from stability of exchange rates among the three largest currency areas. Second, all countries would benefit from the adoption and use of a global unit of account. Third, larger countries outside the G-3 may resent a kind of G-3 dominance in which they have no voice. Fourth, a world currency is in the nature of a "social contract" in which every country, however, small, should have a juridical stake.

The Board of Governors of the International Monetary Fund represents a broad-based international monetary authority in which, with few exceptions, all countries have votes. The adoption of an international currency with a name like INTOR, sanctioned by the Board of Governors, freely convertible into dollars, euros and yen at fixed exchange rates, would mark a great step forward in the creation of an international financial architecture.

What unit of value should the INTOR be? I would tentatively choose a basket of the G-3 currencies, say 40 percent dollars, 40 percent euros (counting Britain, Sweden and Denmark) and 20 percent yen.[7] As relative GDP's change, these weights could be adjusted.[8]

There is no reason why a limited number of INTORs could not be printed and allowed to circulate. INTORs could be made acceptable and yet each country could retain its own currency, freely convertible into INTORs.[9] The anchor for the INTOR system would initially be the G-3 currencies, designated as the agent of the Board of Governors, but subject to periodic review. A separate Department of the IMF could be set up to monitor the actions of the G-3 Monetary Policy Committee. In the long run, of course, the composition of the G-3 itself may change.

The basic plan for a new international currency could be implemented in three stages:

Stage I   Transition to stable exchange rates in the G-3
Stage II   The G-3 Monetary Union
Stage III   Creation of an international currency

Stage I would be inaugurated with steps preparatory to the G-3 Monetary Union. A gradual process could start with fixing wide bands around a central parity. The determination of the central parities and the bands would, of course, depend on the date of introduction. Suppose, to fix ideas, that a central parity of US$1 = €1 were decided upon with a wide margin on either side of parity, say, a lower limit on the euro of $0.85 and an upper limit of $1.15. Similar rates could be put around a central parity of the yen, say $1 = 125 yen, with lower and upper bands around the dollar of about 110 yen and 140 yen. These are very wide bands that would permit very substantial fluctuations until the central banks had adapted their working procedures and achieved consensus about the central parities. In subsequent steps the bands would be narrowed.

Stage II would involve the five steps outlined above: the fixing of targets and definitions of inflation; the establishment of a joint Monetary Policy Committee; the arrangement for the division of seigniorage; and the mechanism for locking exchange rates.

Stage III would commence after the second phase has been completed. It would involve the selection of the name and value of the international currency unit, the mechanism and agency by which it will be introduced, the system and criteria for controlling its quantity, its backing in terms of currency or gold reserves, and the location of its central authority. Once a specific plan had been agreed upon and ratified, a Constitutional Convention similar to that convened at Bretton Woods in 1944 could be inaugurated.

CONCLUSIONS

The achievement of an international currency may seem remote today. Yet it is surprising how quickly events can overcome inertia. It would have been hard to imagine the Bretton Woods Articles of Agreement before World War II, but the shock of that War brought it about. It would have been hard to imagine the creation of the special drawing rights, the embryo of a world currency, in the early 1960s, but it was agreed to at the IMF meetings in Rio di Janeiro in 1967. It would have been hard to predict the formation of the European Monetary System but it came about, under the pressure of a weak dollar, in the late 1970s. The next big crisis might be the occasion for a reconvening of a Bretton Woods type conference to establish the conditions for a new international monetary system.

The idea of a world currency is actually an old one. Julius Caesar set up a Roman monetary standard in 46 BC based on a 12:1 bimetallic ratio, monopolizing and overvaluing gold. That arrangement was to last through its successors in Constantinople for over twelve centuries, with the Roman *aureus, solidus, nomisma* or *besant* fulfilling the role of universal unit of account over the reaches of that great empire.

The Italian merchant and banker, Gasparo Scaruffi (1519–84), published in 1582 an impressive work on money that contained a viable proposal for the establishment of a universal mint, the adoption of one uniform coinage through-out Europe, with the same shape, weight and name in every country, "as if the world were one city and one monarchy." At that time, as now, the interna-tional monetary system was in a state of great confusion, owing to alterations in the values of coins, multiplicity of coins, bad coinage and other abuses. His work was called *Alitinonfo*, a name derived from the Greek meaning "true light," and taken from his desire to spread true light on the subject of money. He did spread true light but centuries later the monetary system was still in a state of great confusion and it was said, in the nineteenth century, that Italians had the best writers on money and the worst coins!

Later in the nineteenth century, at the Paris conference of 1867, presided over by Prince Jerome Napoleon, a plan for a world currency linked to gold coins in multiples of five gold French francs was widely discussed. Several international conferences followed up on this idea. However, it never achieved the agreement of Britain, already the world's leading financial power. A common theme throughout monetary history is that the top financial power has a stake in rejecting international monetary reform because it reduces its own monopoly.

Less than a century later, by the time of the Bretton Woods conference, a world currency figured in both the major plans for the post-war world mon-etary order. The British plan – essentially Keynes's plan – envisaged a world currency called "bancor." Note the change in the British view. When sterling was top dog, Britain rejected an international currency. Now that the dollar had become top currency, Britain accepted the idea!

One would have expected the United States to be cool to the idea of a world currency at Bretton Woods. Surprisingly, the official American plan – essentially White's plan – made provision for a world currency, to be called "unitas." But in the negotiations leading up to Bretton Woods, the Americans cooled to the idea. Belatedly, perhaps they came to realize – or believed that the U.S. Congress would realize – that a world currency would be at the expense of the use of the dollar.[10] The United States then used its dominating position at the conference to bury the world currency idea and base the Bretton Woods arrangements on gold and the dollar. Another reason might have been that the organizational technology required for managing a fiat currency at the global level had not been developed.

Does the role of the United States today as the sole superpower foreclose the possibility of an agreement to create an international currency? I think there are grounds for optimism. First of all, as a consequence of the frequent currency crises of recent years, there is growing recognition that international monetary arrangements are in a state of crisis. Second, the advent of the euro has changed the power configuration of the international monetary structure and diminished the monopoly position of the dollar. In the future, the dollar will have to compete for seigniorage and control with the euro even in the absence of reform. Under these circumstances, the United States may see that its self-interest as well as the rest of the world lies in the direction of a reconstructed international monetary system.

A world currency would level the playing field for big and small countries alike. As Paul Volcker has aptly put it, "A global economy needs a global currency." Why not make one?

QUESTIONS

AUDIENCE QUESTION: I'm an undergraduate student from Universidad Anáhuac del Sur in Mexico City and this is my question. You talked about the weaknesses and the possible flaws that the euro may face. What do you think the obstacles are that the dollar could have in the future?

ROBERT MUNDELL: Thank you for the question, it's a very good one. The dollar is likely to have problems in the future. Let's suppose that ten years in the future, the euro area includes the EU 15 and about five other countries. It's now as big or bigger than the dollar area. By the year 2010, people are going to want to keep their assets – financial assets and central bank assets – about equal between dollars and euros. At the present time there are very few euros out there, but a lot of dollars. Presently there's about 1.6 trillion dollars in foreign exchange reserves. Let's take a very conservative estimate and suppose that there's going to be $3.2 trillion in the year 2010. If at that time people want to divide their assets between the two, there's going to be almost no room for growth of dollar assets, and almost all the growth is going to take place in euro assets. Once that process begins, there'd be a change in trade balances or capital flows that would have to adjust. The threat to the dollar is that if a process begins where there's not just steady growth of dollars, say 100 billion dollars a year, but diversification into the euro, then there could be a tremendous run on the dollar of exactly the same kind that occurred in 1978 and 1979, when bankers were going around the world saying the new word is diversification and getting into the European currencies. It's going to be more important, because now it's not ten or 15 European currencies, but it's one big European currency. If this occurs, there'll be a big depreciation of the dollar, a big increase in the price of gold in terms of dollars, and there might be a crisis that will have to be managed in some way. Is this scenario likely? I don't believe it's likely until there is some help from the business cycle. What I mean by that is when the current boom, which is getting long in the tooth, slows, U.S. interest rates, which would normally fall, will probably actually rise on the expectations of increased inflation in the United States, and there's going to be a movement out of the dollar into the euro. So I see a transition coming. I don't know when it'll come, probably in the next two or three years. This process requires very careful thinking about the dollar to euro rate and how that's going to be managed.

AUDIENCE QUESTION: You mentioned that in order to establish a currency board, a period of preparation is needed to reach fiscal balance, control over the money supply, reduction of inflation, and stability of the exchange rate. What would you say to those that think that on top of those elements, a country also needs a free flow of capital, as with NAFTA, and also a free flow of labor?

ROBERT MUNDELL: A country doesn't particularly need to have a free flow of capital. A currency board can function with no capital movements whatso-ever. You still get price stability. The important thing about the currency board is that it is not subject to speculation. Indeed, with a currency board, the rate of return between New York and California is identical, so there are no capital movements. The problem with the systems that we've had is that capital often goes the wrong way. A system like that in Mexico had a huge influx of capital, maybe 80 billion dollars over three or four years in the early 1990s. Then after some doubts about the system, expectations change and a big outflow of capital occurs, triggering a crisis. You're not going to have that with a currency board, because the exchange rate is permanently fixed.

AUDIENCE QUESTION: Professor Mundell, are there any problems with us-ing a single currency throughout all or most of the world?

ROBERT MUNDELL: We could certainly have the same money all over the hemisphere if it were the U.S. dollar. Countries could always dollarize by working out the exchange rates and how much that would cost and whether the gains in stability would be worth it. There's a tremendous advantage to having a common currency – even a currency board doesn't provide the advantages of a common currency. One of the advantages is simply the transparency of pricing. You immediately know the price of a shoe in Mexico, the price in Alaska, and in all the areas which use that currency. Similarly, wage rates are known in each area, and this is a tremendous advantage, because people can make comparisons. I should note that this is not always an advantage in two areas where per capita income and wage rates are enormously different. In this case it may create envy and frustration that would lead to a desire to emigrate toward the high-wage region.

Another issue is corruption; I think that every country has to work hard against corruption. When I was in Argentina, there was a historic case where, for the first time in five years, someone had been put in jail for tax evasion. It was because he had millions of dollars of tax evasion. People ask me if I am in favor of enforcing the tax laws and putting people in jail if they don't pay their taxes. I have to say I'm not sure, given the high tax rates in Argentina. It would be much better if the value-added tax was lowered to 12 percent or 10 percent and then enforced. That is possible to do. People will submit to laws only when they're reasonable. Corruption by people elected to govern is a terrible thing. Every country has some elements of it, but in most countries it's the exception rather than the rule. But in a few countries, it's the rule rather than the exception and to reduce corruption requires a change in the culture. To the extent that a common, stable currency provides transparency, it reduces the opportunity for corruption.

AUDIENCE QUESTION: I'd like to pose two questions. One is regarding your evaluation of what happened in Mexico in late 1994 and early 1995 with the peso devaluation. The Mexican central bank was unable to defend the currency and therefore there wasn't really much to do to prevent the devaluation. That is what seems to be understood about it. If we look at purchasing power parity right now at 9.50 pesos to the dollar and the stability that has been prevailing for the Mexican peso for the last few months, you would have to say that 9.50 would be an equilibrium rate between the Mexican peso and the U.S. dollar. I would like your considerations regarding this. The second question I have is, what is your view of what's going to happen in the European community over the next ten years, if the membership goes up to, say, twenty? I would like your opinion on the fact that the countries that are participating in the union right now had to go through a lot of stages beginning, say 25 years ago, stages like the EMS [European Monetary System], like the Plaza Accord, like the Louvre Accord, etc. How could you say that in just ten years the euro area could grow to such an extent without the additional countries going through those phases of monetary restriction and fiscal control?

ROBERT MUNDELL: Let me answer the second question first. The Europeans went through stages in the 1960s and advanced toward monetary union. Nothing much came of it, though they had more cooperation. Then they had the Hague Summit in December, 1969. They had a plan for a fixed exchange rate arrangement, but then the whole international monetary system changed. The early phase was easy for them because they were already fixed to the dollar. But after the floating began, it became several times more difficult to get fixed rates in Europe, so the whole thing fizzled. The impetus for European monetary union varied with the dollar cycle. The weak dollar, which produced big balance of payments deficits in the late 1960s, led to the Hague Summit. The Europeans wanted to have a monetary system that would be somewhat free of the dollar. After floating began, that took the edge off that. They couldn't talk anymore about dollar overhang, because if they didn't want the dollars they could sell them, but they chose to hang onto them. Then in the late 1970s, with a big run up of U.S. inflation that led to the Bremen meeting between [German Chancellor Helmut] Schmidt and [French President] Valéry Giscard d'Estaing and the European Monetary System and that was a big help. Then with Reaganomics, the dollar soared. The dollar went from 1.7 marks in 1980 to 3.4 at the end of 1984. At that point, nobody wanted to think about monetary integration in Europe. But after the cycle turned, the dollar went weak again, then you've got the Delors Report and the unification of Germany.

Europe is an island of stability with a GDP that's over 7 trillion dollars, and potentially much more. It's easy now for countries in the Baltics, the Czech Republic, Slovakia and others to fix their exchange rates to the euro using currency boards. It's easy for them, because a currency board to the euro gives them a taste of what monetary discipline is going to be like when they actually are part of the euro zone, when they have no chance of getting away from it. If you operate a currency board, you can operate in a monetary union. The potential impact on the EU is marginal now. These countries are all small relative to the euro area GDP, so adding countries to the European Monetary Union won't affect its stability.

The other question is about Mexico. For the next 50 years people will talk about what Mexico should have done in November 1994. And everybody, I'm sure, is going to have a different take on it. I think the worst thing that happened wasn't just letting the exchange rate float down to four, its lower limit, from 3.5, it was when the Mexican minister of finance came to New York and made a presentation without saying anything about the fundamentals of monetary and fiscal policy. It was a disaster and it led to the crisis. But what I would have done in hindsight was suggest a currency board for Mexico in 1992–93. Suppose, as [MIT Economics Professor] Rudi Dornbusch said, that the peso exchange rate was overvalued so Mexico could devalue to four, or, if you want to err to the conservative side, to 4.2 to the dollar. I don't think anybody would have suggested more than that, but the cost of going too high is that you get a little more inflation at the new equilibrium. But go to 4.2 and announce then that you're going to have a currency board. After that everybody will know exactly what the exchange rate is all the time, and more importantly, they'll also know exactly what monetary policy in Mexico is going to be from then on. A currency board would have prevented the move-ment down to 9.5.

You said that on a purchasing power parity basis, you think that the exchange rate seems to be about right, but look at the excess inflation that Mexico has had over the past couple of years. Think of the devastating impact that it has had on capital markets in Mexico and the uncertainty that's involved. People don't know whether the inflation rate is going to be 3, or 4, or 5 percent, or as in previous times 35 percent. There's no direction to policy. The man in whose honor I'm lecturing tonight, Lionel Robbins, always said that without an exchange rate system, the economy is like a sailboat without a rudder. The balance of payments gives you a rudder for monetary policy, while a fixed exchange rate gives you the price level of the currency area to which you are fixing.

AUDIENCE QUESTION: In Mexico we need insurance for our money. Wouldn't it be better to have five years with a silver peso and then decide on a currency board?

ROBERT MUNDELL: I'm reminded of a situation that occurred in 1944 at the IMF Bretton Woods meetings. The countries had more or less decided on gold as the basis for their currency. But then the Cuban delegation proposed that sugar be included as one of the commodities for stabilization. A country can go on a metallic standard if they believe they're going to have a good price experience from it. If you think the price of silver is going to be stable enough to be a better guide than either the euro or the dollar, then silver would be a good standard. I am uncertain about silver because of the instabil-ity of silver prices. In 1980, silver prices went up to 50 dollars and then came back down. It would be terrible to be on a silver standard at that time because the currency would appreciate whenever the price of silver went up. If there's volatility in silver, a country wouldn't want to fix to it.

I believe that the system we're moving toward is three monetary areas. One of them is certainly going to be the U.S. dollar, another is going to be the euro area, and there might be a gold area out there. It's the only commodity that could be used as a monetary metal. Gold serves as a hedge against inflation-ary policies in the two major areas, so I think that would be the case. Now you could argue that silver would also do this. I wouldn't recommend this to Mexico, though. The fact that a country produces a commodity doesn't mean that would make a good standard for it. South Africa produces a lot of gold, more gold than anybody else, but it doesn't mean that stabilizing to gold would be a good policy for South Africa. You want to do the thing that's going to be best for the economy. It's not inconceivable that you'd have the dollar and the euro and maybe the yen and gold and maybe silver out there, who knows what would happen? But, silver's very different from gold because there are huge stocks of gold in existence. There are 120 000 tons of gold that have been dug out of the ground and a third of that is in jewelry, and maybe a third is in speculation, and another third is with central banks. So, there's a huge stock outstanding, and what gives gold an element of stability has been that annual supply increments and annual changes in demand are a very small proportion of the total stock outstanding. There's no big outstanding stock of silver that would be the counterpart to the stock outstanding of gold hordes.

NOTES

1. Using Jastram's index of wholesale prices in the United States, with 1930 = 100, the prices indexes for selected years were as follows: 1912: 80.0; 1913: 80.7; 1914: 78.7; 1920: 179.7; 1921: 113.0; 1927: 110.5; 1929: 110.1; 1930: 100.0; 1931: 84.3; 1932: 75.3; 1933: 76.2.

2. The full significance of this change in the operation of the system was not fully realized at the time. Under the historic gold standard there was a feedback mechanism that, even if it acted very slowly over long periods of time, would eventually make the price of gold an equilibrium price. When there was a gold shortage, money would be restricted and prices and wages would tend to fall, lowering costs of production and raising profits in gold mining and eventually leading to increased exploration and gold production; similarly, when there was a gold surplus, prices and wages would rise and gold production would he reduced. Periods of inflation tended to cancel out periods of deflation and in the long run prices remained steady. Thus you could find, over hundreds of years, periods that, despite being centuries apart, would register the same price level. For example, approximately the same price levels prevailed in the United States in the years 1804, 1819, 1863, 1916, 1930 and 1941, and again in the years 1824, 1835, 1853, 1880, 1909, 1914, and 1933. In Britain, prices were approximately the same in 1646, 1660, 1673, 1691, 1702, 1736, 1852, 1884, 1910 and 1933, and again in the years 1652, 1694, 1709, 1724, 1742, 1758, 1784, 1835, 1845, 1880 and 1936. Over these long periods gold possessed a long-run stability because there was an adjustment mechanism for keeping it stable.

   This period of stability ended abruptly in the 1930s with the transition into the second third of the twentieth century. After 1934, there was no longer an "international" gold standard. Only the United States was committed to convert gold at a fixed price, and only for the "monetary purposes" of foreign central banks. Gold no longer circulated; Americans were prohibited from holding gold outside of decorative and industrial uses; and gold clauses in contracts had been rendered null and void by the Supreme Court. The requirements of gold convertibility exerted only a very loose discipline on U.S. monetary policy. Long gone were the days when long periods of inflation were succeeded by periods of deflation. Since the 1930s the direction of prices has been inexorably upward.

3. Wholesale prices in 1971 were 3.35 times wholesale prices in 1933. See Jastram (1981: Table 21).

4. Keynes himself was critical of newspapers that always tried to stereotype him as an opponent of gold. The following letter to *The Economist* in 1933 makes it clear that he was not opposed to a gold-based international monetary system that he would later endorse at Bretton Woods:

   I do not know that what you call "the evolution of my ideas" is particularly important. But for the sake of accuracy I should like, in thanking you for your leading article on March 18th, to remind you that my recent advocacy of gold as an international standard is nothing new.

At all stages of the post war developments the concrete proposals which I have brought forward from time to time have been based on the use of gold as an international standard. The qualifications which I have added to this have been always the same, though the precise details have varied; namely, (1) that the parities between national standards and gold should not be rigid, (2) that there should be a wider margin than in the past between the gold points, and (3) that if possible some international control should be formed with a view to regulating the commodity value of gold within limits.

You will find that this was my opinion in 1923 when I published my *Tract on Monetary Reform* (see chapter 5) and again in 1930 when I published my *Treatise on Money* (see chapters 36 and 38), just as it is today, as set forth in my articles in *The Times* and in my pamphlet *The Means to Prosperity*. I apologize for occupying your space. But since there are people who deem it creditable if one does not change one's mind, I should like to get what kudos I can from not having done so on this occasion!

5. To be sure, the intervention may be a small proportion of market transactions, but it sends a signal that has wider implications as an announcement of intentions.

6. In fact, it might be sufficient if any two of the three currency areas agreed to form or initiate the monetary union. The dollar, euro and yen areas have monetary masses that are more or less proportionate to their GDPs, say about $10 trillion, $7.0 trillion, and $5 trillion respectively, collectively making up perhaps 60 percent of world GDP. A monetary union of any two of the areas – Europe and Japan, or Europe and the United States or the United States and Japan – would make it the dominant currency area and thus an attractive area for the third to join.

7. Should the new INTOR be linked to gold? There would be much opposition to overcome. But a link to gold would have several advantages. First, gold is still the second most important international reserve, second only to the dollar. Second, gold is not the monopoly of any country. Third, a gold INTOR coin that was overvalued and circulated would give tangible expression to the idea of a universal unit of account and popularize the idea of an international currency. Fourth, gold backing of the INTOR would give the latter a fallback value and build confidence in it. Fifth, the use of gold as an exhaustible resource would be an ever-present reminder that global resources are finite. And finally, it would be a bridge from the monetary system that characterized the world economy for more than two thousand years before 1971 and the future.

There are, nevertheless, difficulties associated with integrating gold into the international monetary system that did not apply when gold circulated freely as money. As long as gold is less liquid (exchangeable) than money, any permanently fixed relation between gold and INTORs would fall victim to Gresham's Law, and lead to mass dumping of gold stocks.

8. For historical reasons, a case could be made for using Special Drawing Rights (SDR) as the unit for the INTOR. The weights of the G-3 in the SDR – counting the UK's share in the euro – were not very different as of January 1, 1999: 39 percent for the dollar, 43 percent for the euro, and 18 percent for the yen. Two years later, however, on January 1, 2001, as a result of the appreciation of the dollar, the weights were changed to 45 percent for the dollar, 40 percent for the euro, and 15 percent for the yen, a formula which, in the long run, unduly exaggerates the weight of the dollar.

9. The interconvertibility of INTORs and national currencies would require that part of the demand for money in each country would be satisfied by INTORs and therefore that national central banks would have to keep the supplies of national currency short of the demand for money.

10. See Mundell (1995) for a discussion of this issue.

BIBLIOGRAPHY

Jastram, Roy (1981), *Silver: The Restless Metal*, New York: John Wiley & Sons.

Keynes, J.M. (1923), *A Tract on Monetary Reform*, London: Macmillan.

Mundell, R.A. (1968), *International Economics*, New York: Macmillan.

Mundell, R.A. (1995), "The international monetary system: the missing factor," *Journal of Policy Modeling* 17(5): 479–92.

Robbins, Lionel (1930), "On the elasticity of demand for income in terms of effort," *Economic Journal*, reprinted in *Readings in the Theory of Income Distribution*, Philadelphia: Blakiston Company, 1946: 237–45.

Robbins, Lionel (1932), *An Essay on the Nature and Significance of Economic Science*, London: Macmillan.

Samuelson, P.A. ([1947], 1983), *Foundations of Economic Analysis*, Cambridge, MA: Harvard University Press.

2. The state of the world economy

Introduced by

Paul A. Samuelson (via satellite)

I will begin by discussing inflation, monetary stability and growth in the world economy.

I've lived a long life. And that means that I have witnessed a number of new ages and new final paradigms, the end of history, and I don't think that right now we're in a new revolutionary improvement in the behavior and expected future behavior of the mixed economy. A number of problems are behind us. But in economics, what goes around comes around. It's possible that when you've cured that last case of smallpox in Somalia, that smallpox goes into the history books. The problem of inflation control isn't like that at all. It's more like the containment of weight of an adult in an affluent society. Eternal vigilance is not only a price of liberty, but it's also the price of a slim figure. There are remarkable things going on in the economy because of computers. This has profound micro influences on economic history. When micro influences become large enough and bunch together, you have macro effects. However, even when you make corrections as best we can, for the inadequacy of our tools to measure productivity in what has become a largely service economy, there is not a sea change in the U.S. GDP statistics. The same is true for most of the world.

Similarly, I like to read the *Atlantic Monthly*, but I don't believe, when I look at the last issue, that the Dow-Jones is 33 percent undervalued compared to its fundamental value. The equity premium, no doubt, will decline over time, but the equity premium, like Tobin's q, will both rise and fall over time. So, we have been lucky, we have been more than lucky, because by a combination of unpredictable circumstances, we have at the head of the Federal Reserve a skillful and non-dogmatic, powerful chairman, and he has helped our luck. For a variety of political reasons, we've also had great luck in the U.S. economy. Nevertheless, by several different measures the private sector saving rate has been declining substantially since 1980, with a similar trend at the corporate level. By chance and by what I have to call good fortune, this is offset by a public sector surplus.

The U.S. economy, which I've followed very carefully edition by edition in my textbook, in my judgment behaves more nearly like a dream economy than used to be the case when the first edition was being written. I also think that the oligopoly power of the Fortune 500 U.S. corporations has ebbed away and has had profound effects upon corporate governance and the status of the union movement. So, America, and now I must give the credit to the American people, not to policy, have shown an amazing flexibility, being willing to accept new types of jobs. I attribute much of America's recent prosperity to this sea change in attitudes and behavior. But in my judgment, that is a fragile thing. It is something which has built up nicely in the 1980s and the 1990s, but is also something which can seep away in an overheated economy. That is why I've been a bit on the wrong side in the advice that I've been giving the U.S. authorities. It's advice, by the way, worth every penny that I've received in return for it, but I've been saying that one should be on the austere side in monetary policy. This, not because I've lost my do-goodism idiocies, I've still got them all, but because, what I'm trying to maximize is the sustained average of the performance of the economy, not just for today and tomorrow, but over the next five years. Well, mostly I've been wrong in that caution. I really can't say that it's a worse world because they didn't listen to me in this particular case. But, what I'm emphasizing is what does not exist in Germany today, for profound historical reasons, what does not exist in France, what does not exist in Spain, and what does exist in America, are profound sociological and political reasons for our economic performance. One of the worst dangers is that we ought not to risk losing this temporary agreeable behavior to generate a little extra current output. It's not a new paradigm. It's an approach toward an older paradigm which only imperfectly prevailed anywhere in economic history.

QUESTIONS

ROBERT MUNDELL: Paul, I'm glad to see you in such good form. I want to ask you a question about exchange rates. We have seen extremely high volatility of the dollar–yen rate, when the dollar went down to 78 yen in 1995 and then went way up to 148 yen. Now it's down again to not much more than 100. But we have also seen big changes in the dollar–euro rate and my question is about that and the future of the euro. When the U.S. expansion starts to slow down – and you've noted that this is one of the longest expansions on record and might be the longest when it is finished – the dollar should weaken, and speculation could lead to substantial diversification from dollars into the euro. Coupled with a very large build-up in the U.S. net debt position, combined with the current account deficit, do you think that there's going to be some need for management of the dollar–euro rate? Would you support a proposal for more explicit management of the dollar–euro rate?

PAUL A. SAMUELSON: First, a couple of points. I have to confess that I was completely accurate on the behavior of the euro after January 1, 1999 when it started. What I predicted was that nothing revolutionary would happen, but there would be a slow trend in one direction. Unfortunately, the algebraic sign which I predicted was wrong, because I thought there might possibly be a honeymoon effect that many people had hoped for. Italian interest rates came down towards German interest rates and so I thought there could be a psychological element favoring that movement. Well, that didn't happen. However, the fact that there should have been, over a period of nine months, that kind of fluctuation in the dollar–euro rate, to me is not surprising. Henry Wallich, who I thought was one of the best people that ever served on the Federal Reserve, asked me about the surprising instability of the post-Bretton Woods exchange rates. I said to him that I wasn't convinced it was surprising. When Baron Rothschild was asked what the stock market was going to do, he said it would fluctuate. Similarly, I said to Wallich that things fluctuate. What is a normal standard deviation to put in a Black–Scholes formula for option contracts on the euro–dollar rate? I expect there to be instability. There is no natural tendency for stability in exchange rate behavior, where the new rate would be some kind of fundamentally predictable real level, based on the terms of trade between countries. Further, terms of trades have fluctuated more than any of the writers that I was familiar with thought 30 years ago.

You ask is there going to be a need for management. That is an entirely different question. Interventions, you know from experience, but also could know from working out the numbers, that a nation can lose in three weeks, reserves that are substantial compared to what it's built up over years in trying to fight market forces. That's part of inescapable macro-inefficiency. So, I would be skeptical that, because, let's say the Japanese, for their recovery, would like the yen to depreciate. And let's suppose that [Treasury Secretary Robert E.] Rubin's policy is still in effect, but a strong dollar occurs because of the strong American economy. I always thought that at best, that was a little bit like King Canute blessing the incoming tide at the time, and I don't suppose that such a doctrine can be embedded in stone. I don't think that with fundamental forces going against the yen staying where it is, the yen may not depreciate. All the goodwill between two sub-cabinet people in the Japanese and American governments can muster up, even if they have the ear of the executive, are unlikely to make any lasting change. So interventions are very difficult.

Now, economists can dream up solutions to some of the worst problems in the world. And naturally, it will occur to them that in some situations we should go back to capital controls. I'm eclectic. I've been eclectic only part of my life. I was once very impatient with my teacher back in Harvard and I said, "Professor, the trouble with you is that you're so damned eclectic." And Gottfried [Haberler] said in his slow, humorous way, "Paul, how do you know mother nature isn't eclectic?" And there was my road to Damascus. Ever since, my credo has been, I've got to be as eclectic as the facts call for, but to be more eclectic than that, I need to remind myself that an open mind can be an empty mind. So there could be a time when some temporary recourse to capital controls would, after it's all over, been judged to have done more good than bad. I can tell you those times will be very rare. The good news from capital controls comes in early. The bad news and the bill, comes in after-wards. So for now, I don't want to get into the sliding peg. There is something of a contradiction in a perfect market where it is supposed that people can count upon daylight savings time, they've advanced on a putative future basis more or less known to everybody, and that this eases the disequilibrium and makes it a quasi-equilibrium situation. I think that sliding pegs stimulate all sorts of bets. A lot of the cleverness of the huge hedge funds comes from government. It's all a zero sum game, but it's always the government that's in the poker game, ready to lose a lot of money. Hedge funds can be pretty sure, over a certain interval, that they know the direction the next move will take, so the risk is generally minimal. I don't want to be dogmatic, but I think that anyone who is deeply skeptical about floating exchange rate systems and the few large currency blocks in the world and he thinks sliding pegs will in-crease stability, I think that that faith might be exaggerated. I could be wrong, though.

AUDIENCE QUESTION: I wonder if you could elaborate a bit on your sug-gestion that financial markets are very efficient at the micro level, but very inefficient at the macro level. This certainly has an appeal as an intuitive explanation of events that we observe. On the other hand, on the theoretical level, it's not easy to see why the correct valuation of 30 underlying stocks should add up to an incorrect valuation of the average of them.

PAUL A. SAMUELSON: According to economic history, with the phenom-enon of cumulative self-fulfilling prophecies, asset markets have bubbles. It's not a question anymore, the stock market is in a bubble. There's every theoretical reason, in terms of expectations, that if a movement gets started in one direction, either away from equilibrium, somehow defined, that that movement will continue. We know so much about bubbles, but the vital, single fact that we want to know, is the actuarial odds of how long it will last. And we have absolutely no handle on the theory of how long it will last, because it can always last as long again as it has already lasted. People think that the history of Ponzi schemes is brief. There are only a certain number of new suckers in the world. That's profoundly wrong, because the old suckers who have been paid off, come back in as new suckers. And they're right to do so. I will tell one true story to illustrate this.

In the late 1970s, my dear colleague Franco Modigliani wrote an article where he argued that the Dow Jones index is grossly undervalued. It was about 750, and should be at least 1400. Well, you can't sell the Brooklyn Bridge unless you are a good story-teller, and Franco had a good story. He knew why the market was grossly undervalued. He said only an Italian would understand this. It's because people in the market do not understand the proper correction that should be made to price–earnings ratios for inflation. They think that stocks and bonds are essentially the same thing. As a result, anybody can tell you confidently when an upswing in inflation takes place what that will do to the yields of bonds. If you apply that same line of reasoning to stocks, then the 750 level in the late 1970s, when I was getting 18 percent on my Fidelity Investments overnight fund, and Milton Friedman was only invested in bonds, undervalued the stock market. Franco said what people don't realize is that price–earnings ratios implicitly appreciate with inflation. When you make that correction, then at least a doubling of the Dow Jones is justified.

Well, Paul Samuelson, always ready to be the helpful colleague, said to Franco: "Yes Franco, you're right, and it might even be that you're right for the right reason, but you know Franco, you could lose your shirt buying the Dow Jones, because it ought to be at 1400, but it's only at 750. When everybody is insane, it's folly to be wise." That's the difference between a macro attempt to correct a perceived inefficiency and a micro. And Franco said to me improperly, "Paul, you don't have to teach me how to suck eggs, I know that, I'm not going out and investing my Grandmother's portfolio in stocks because the market's making this mistake." So, I think there are profound reasons why macro efficiency doesn't assert itself, and why perhaps there isn't even a trend towards it becoming more relevant.

Consider the Thai situation in the middle part of 1997. Earlier, every credit rating agency, Standard & Poor's, Moody's, and so forth, had given Thailand a very good rating. The previous year, the economy had grown in real terms at 6 percent. The previous five years, it had averaged nearer to 8 percent. Everything looked sunny. That's when the money was coming in. For a variety of reasons, and we don't really need to look for profound reasons, because we're dealing now with the economics of avalanches. It is a pistol shot in the Alps that causes a village to be submerged, or more correctly, the piling up of the snow which had been occurring and was present, made this possible. But for whatever reason, including the competition of the Chinese, the new guy on the block, in competition with the other emerging markets in the trade area, suddenly there was a change, and the money went the other way. South Korea, which had been growing well by imitating exactly every virtue and every fault of the Japanese system. They had deep pockets, they had new technocratic bankers, they had the influence of not disinterested bureaucrats, and they were heavily invested in short-term borrowing. Of course the pistol shot in Thailand reached them. So, I don't consider it a mystery that the macro markets are capable of misbehaving. Rather, it seems to me that that's in accord with the realities of economic law, though it's different at the micro level.

This isn't the place to moralize, but somebody should be thinking about Long-Term Capital Management's investors – how it was that the best and the brightest, who thought they were making thousands of quasi-independent bets, hedged as well as is possible, ended up trying to balance a baseball bat as tall as the Empire State building. In fact, it was just a number of people making essentially the same big bet. Of course when the word got around that LTCM was in trouble, they even had to ask for money, it wasn't hard to figure out exactly what the trouble was and all the bids to them dried up and a lot of vultures made money on their distress.

AL HARBERGER: Paul, I think the audience here would be very interested in your telling us your secret of eternal youth. You both look and sound very much the same as you did 20, 30, 40 years ago, and I think it's just wonderful.

My substantive comment is the following: some considerable time back, people thinking about macroeconomics thought in terms of structural models. We had little, mid-sized, and big structural models and they were a very important part of the way people viewed the world. What I seem to perceive, both in much of the profession's thinking and certainly in terms of policy authorities, both in the Fed and elsewhere, is a trend toward thinking of policy as a kind of a servomechanism. That we have an accelerator and a brake and a steering wheel, and we look at all of the evidence that's coming in day by day and week by week, and the policy authorities come to decisions about is this the time to use one, two or three of these instruments. Do you agree with this perception of a change in attitude? That's the first question. My second question is do you see any dangers for the future in this servomechanism type of behavior?

PAUL A. SAMUELSON: Let me think aloud. First let's talk about short-term forecasting purposes, and now I'm talking about what is a very dull business. At the non-profit organization and finance committees that I sit on, we don't even let people go through the process of briefing us on the outlook for the next 12 to 18 months. We all know pretty much what there is to be known.

Most of the banks have actually fired their short-term forecasters and they can subscribe to the modern equivalent of DRI and know what the simple odds favor. Those forecasts are not bad. They are better than Wall Street analysts. They are better than gypsy tea readers. But, what they tell you is not useful. I can remember, a few years ago I went to hear a representative of Citibank from London at a Copenhagen meeting and he told the inside story of what they expected to happen. I opened my *Wall Street Journal* and I looked at futures on the interest rates, and everything, and everything that he told us was already priced in the market. A very few people who I know, and it is surprisingly few, can over a long time period by their wits, good timing, and momentum make money investing.

Experience has shown that these eight massive models are not "M" [monistic] models. Citibank got burned badly. There was a brief time in the early 1970s when monistic monetarism, for a time didn't do too badly. But the reality which had staggered like a drunken sailor into the gunsights of that model moved and in this technological change in the financial securities markets and institutions, the constancy of any velocity of money figure (the ratio that measures what I have in my jeans and dictates my spending) to the level of nominal income flow, that has to be, now and forever after now, a much more volatile thing. This kind of simple-minded, almost Neanderthal model did pretty well for a time, but these forecasts all turn over together, that's the only thing we can be sure about, and what they're sure about is why they were wrong on previous occasions. So I don't think there is anything in the technical advances that have been made in the macro literature, such as rational expectations and random walks [unpredictability] in technological progress which have useful lessons for the financial markets and for policy purposes. Maybe that's reassuring, because it means that we're not subject to a new regime we didn't have before. I do think that the easily accessed professional trading systems, that allow me to turn my portfolio over in an afternoon, literally is like putting a new powerful cannon in the hands of children. You know in the old days, if you had a demented kid on the farm, all he could do is torture the dog or do a little harm. Today, he just puts together a little fertilizer and he can blow up a huge skyscraper. When I go before St. Peter I'm going to have to answer for some of these financial advances.

Does online trading make markets more volatile? We don't know. We really do not know what happened on that Tuesday morning in 1987, a day after Black Monday [October 19, 1987]. There was an hour when essentially every market was closed down by the circuit breakers, and then the markets opened up again. Someday Alan Greenspan will write his memoirs and he'll reveal what he said to Banker's Trust and the other investment banks, but the 1987 crash is a very important element. I heard Alan Greenspan say in a private dinner at the Boston Federal Reserve that the market crash was just to cool things off a little. So I asked with so many people worried, why the Fed didn't raise margin requirements? This would be a shot across the bows of the ultra-bulls. Greenspan responded, "Paul, we don't know whether that'll end up doing good or otherwise." He added that how things worked out in the aftermath of the 1987 crash may itself have added 3000 points to the present value of the Dow Jones Industrial Average, because a lot of people learned a lesson that the cowardly people who sold after Black Monday ended up with big losses. I think I'd better stop there.

CHRISTOPHER JOHNSON: Hello Paul, this is Christopher Johnson of the Association for Monetary Union of Europe. I would like to put a question to you about the U.S. balance of payments. There's a rather disturbingly large deficit in the current account. Should we not be looking at this just as much in terms of the capital account, where of course mathematically there has to be a corresponding surplus in the capital account. The U.S. has always been known as one of the world's major capital exporters. A country like Mexico has a lot of investment from U.S. multinational companies. But, the inflow of capital into the U.S. is very much greater than the outflow. And this, of course, has turned on its head all the traditional views we used to learn in economics, maybe in earlier editions of your textbooks, that rich countries were capital exporters and the poor countries were capital importers. Well, the U.S. is certainly not poor. It's the world's richest country and the biggest importer of capital. One can see this as having pushed the rate of the dollar up. Everybody wants American assets, either factories or shares, and this of course has driven the current account into deficit. But, should we worry about this? Is this a natural and self-sustaining situation, a virtuous circle, where as long as Wall Street goes up, the U.S. can import capital, and people are very happy to hold dollars? In addition, does this mean that the risk of a Wall Street correction is going to be amplified by a reverse flow of capital as the world's investors take their profits and seek solace elsewhere in the euro, the yen or whatever? Maybe Mr. Greenspan is aware of this and that's why he doesn't want to be blamed for bringing about the correction on Wall Street by putting interest rates up too high. So, is this virtuous circle or is it really a precarious and worrying situation? Have we discovered perpetual motion, at least in the U.S. economy, so that it could go on forever being the world's fastest-growing economy and continue to import capital on the basis of that rapid growth, which will thereby be further fueled and encouraged?

PAUL A. SAMUELSON: One of the ways of saying things that are interesting is to say things that excite and scare people, and I consider that a cheap popularity which I should eschew. But, I do say all the time, and not to shock, that no country is too big to be immune to a run. I have written a lot for

Japanese, Korean and some Latin American newspapers, saying things there which I think should be said for them, but I'm really picky when I say things about the U.S. I don't think that it was an irrational view toward the end of the 1950s when more and more people abroad piled up assets here, because this was a safe haven with the U.S. dollar an undervalued currency. But there should become a point at which the flow could begin to go the other way. I can well imagine a situation, fortunately it's not realistically imminent, where a serious correction in America could become an algebraic down bubble. History is replete with them. When foreigners want to take more and more money out, maybe because the economy has recovered, or just for reasons of diversification, that's exactly the time when American money will flow out, too. If the euro is a better deal prospectively a year and a half from now, to financiers from Zurich and Frankfurt, it will also be a better deal for San Francisco and Chicago. And so yes, I think there is a potential problem.

I'm also confessing my arrogance, as one of my former students wrote a paper which was very well received by the assembled central bankers at the Kansas City Federal Reserve meetings. What was said there, and said more than once, was that the Federal Reserve should stick to one goal, the requisite price level stabilization, and not have an interest in the stock market. If they added that to the Federal Reserve charter it would be a very good rule. I don't think that in Japan in 1985, you could properly address those topics with my methodology and say, who cares about the speculative land boom and who cares about the speculative stock market boom because everybody was making money. That's why we should be concerned. I don't think the Federal Reserve must follow every sparrow that falls to earth, but they must follow the economy because the U.S. is not immune to a currency run. Now, that's a different thing from doing what I've heard criticized, that we're not on an M [money supply] standard anymore, we're on a stock market standard and the Fed appears to have a new duty to keep the stock market up. I don't think that's the actual duty, but they're interconnected. And when I examined that paper, which defended the view, every one of its theoretical simulations, that we should have a balance sheet approach on what debt growth does to lending, I agreed with it. But my spin on it would be that this makes it a problem, at least in the backrooms of the central banks of the world, to be worried about.

ROBERT SOLOMON: Paul, in your initial remarks when you used the term "capital controls" various people around the table here whom you can't see frowned. I thought perhaps you'd like to think about what is being discussed among those who are considering this so-called "architecture" of the international monetary system. The device that's being talked about most commonly is what's been used in Chile – a tax on short-term capital flows. This seeks to discourage volatility of short-term capital, but not to discourage capital flows in general, particularly long-term flows. This device has been supported by a man who used to be Undersecretary of the Treasury, he's now Secretary of the Treasury and I think you have a certain acquaintance with him. Do you have any comments on that?

PAUL A. SAMUELSON: In the first place, my acquaintanceship is a distant one. The Secretary of the Treasury [Lawrence H. Summers, who is Samuelson's nephew] was an undergraduate at MIT. He scrupulously avoided every course I ever gave and I scrupulously avoided giving him any advice on any matter, so there was a so-called Chinese wall between us. But I'll turn to me. I have a certain skepticism of "Tobin taxes" [taxes on short-term capital flows] to handle what some people might consider excessive turnover in mutual fund investing management. Putting a little sand in the gears, a little friction, a Tobin tax on transactions – I'm against that. Among other reasons, it's not that it's a crime, but it's a blunder, because this moves markets overseas. If in New York markets there's a tax on transactions and if American citizens are still free to go to any market in the world, you can be very sure that substitute markets will open up. Where Chile is concerned, this could be a more enforceable thing – a tax on short-term movements. Bob, you remember that for many years Switzerland paid very low interest rates on transitory balances and Switzerland was a safe haven for political and other reasons. And so there were in effect, some impediments of that kind.

The role that I would envisage as possible, and with something that could be salutary about it, would be like the recourse to circuit breakers in the stock market. We're not sure whether circuit breakers and up-tick rules for short sales make things better or worse. But, assuming that in the peak of the worst gale, they make things better, some short-term moratoria standstill fiats could be useful. The trouble with fiats, and I speak with good credentials as a liberal in the modern sense, is that they increasingly spring leaks. People learn the ways around them. They increasingly create inefficient allocations of resources and so they fall of their own weight, and when you do the post-mortem, there's no law of conservation of harm – everything you gain from the capital controls, you lose – but, it could be worse than that.

Let's take the case of Malaysia. My teachers were always looking for controlled experiments performed by economic history. You know I'm very good at criticizing my teachers, because I was so preoccupied with them for a long time in my life. Belgium originally, after World War II, was a more open economy and you could get white flour rolls there, whereas Holland was controlled. And see how much better Belgium did in the late years of the 1940s than Holland did. Well, those are not good controlled experiments. But in my journalism, I've tried to see whether a strong case could be made that those countries which have followed the IMF, Thailand for example, and South Korea, followed them full force. In comparison with those that have resisted, it's a no-brainer, less control was better. There are time periods when that's so and then there are time periods when it's going the other way. At the moment, the head of Malaysia believes that he can document that they are better off [with controls]. I think we should reserve judgment until nature tells us more.

JUDY SHELTON: Hello, Paul. I would like to go back to some comments you made about the Asian situation. You referred to the Thai baht in 1997, and I think the same analysis might apply to the Philippines, or Malaysia, or South Korea or Indonesia. I thought you were suggesting that a lot of very smart foreign investors, who thought they were putting money into productive opportunities in these countries, suddenly got wise and decided that they were not going to be productive and generate revenues so they pulled back. To me, that is in keeping with the idea of crony capitalism – suddenly realizing that these were not good investment decisions. To what extent would you say that the collapse in the exchange rates for those countries, the currency meltdown, contributed to the subsequent economic problems? That is, which was the driving force – did the currencies reflect these sudden changes in the economic expectations, or did they cause it? I wouldn't want to suggest speculators were villains, but maybe they were taking advantage of a very flawed system – a very unstable global currency system – and that also contributed to the economic downfall of these countries.

PAUL A. SAMUELSON: First, I have to say that the inextricably intercon-nected are foolish mistakes by speculators and investors, and structural flaws in the way of doing business. You all recall the degree to which we were preached to by the successful Japanese in the late 1980s, who had gone way beyond the Harvard Business School where you had to have a plan, an investment project, you had to have a stream of income. Under the business school system, nine out of ten potential projects are scratched and you pick the better ones. Well, instead of that, in Japan, decisions were made by consensus – a new, wonderful thing in a corporation.

I know how this wonderful decision by consensus worked. At one of our previous meetings in Claremont, California, an executive of a large Japanese automobile company was at the reception dinner. Probably his company had provided part of the funds. He told me that he was a very good head of this Japanese company because he was a person of two cultures. He said, "I am a Mexican, but I am an American executive and so I'm better prepared to deal with the Japanese." And I said, "You're the man I need then, you're an outside observer. Tell me how this decision making by unanimity and by consensus works." He said, "Here's how it happens: call all the people in the room and tell them what you're discussing, and they spend three or four hours trying to guess how I want it to come out. Finally, I get tired of that and so I tell them how it's going to come out and that's what decision making by consensus is." Now, I only jest to make a point. Japanese companies have deep pockets, and are unconcerned about their stock market value. That sounds like a good thing. But deep pockets, without detailed, rational business school kinds of calculations about investment projects, means you can make big mistakes and you can persist in those big mistakes for a very long time. And so, when people speak about Asian crony capitalism, the only thing that's wrong about that is to make it exclusively Asian, and also to make it exclusively capitalism. For example, in the Korean case, the government bureaucracy and politicians, and not necessarily disinterested politicians, with an independent banking system, are encouraging large corporations with no comparative advantage in innumerable diverse operations, to go deeply into debt, be deeply leveraged, on ephemeral projects that have no real reason to be active.

Now, to take Judy's question, in Thailand, there were a lot of marginal projects which made some economic sense and were profitable. Things looked great when money was coming into the country and the general availability of capital was strong. By the way, the money coming into the country came from the whole Western world and especially emerging market mutual funds. But investors weren't particularly well informed. What they were well informed about was the total return for the previous eight quarters of similar projects. A lot of projects that had some merit, lost merit alongside of those which never really had merit and would only in the end survive by being pooled with other things. This is evidence of a bubble economy, and it becomes pervasive. Then drastically between day and night, the bubble burst. Now, that's an over-simplified picture, because it isn't simply a bursted bubble and a return to equilibrium. The system is also always subject to [internal and external] shocks.

FAUSTO ALZATI: Hello Professor Samuelson. Neoclassical growth theory, essentially established by Robert Solow, predicts long-run convergence in per capita incomes between poor and rich countries. Now, we also know from historical evidence, that when countries share common economic rules, as let's say between the north and the south of the U.S. after the Civil War, that convergence takes place. Poor countries and poor regions grow faster and the gap between rich and poor tends to close. Now, if that is the case, wouldn't a movement towards unified currency areas, and eventually a single global currency, be a better solution for promoting growth than, let's say, floating exchange rates? If you agree with that proposition, what measures should be taken in the short run to promote this?

PAUL A. SAMUELSON: At the beginning, let me say that I don't think that it is a crucial matter whether a region or the world is on a single currency or whether you have coexisting, floating currencies for the basic problem of development. To an economic historian, the key feature of the last half of the twentieth century is the catch-up of much of the rest of the world with the primary position of America. My back of the envelope calculation when peace broke out in Europe and Japan in 1945 was that the U.S.A. had almost 50 percent of world GDP. Europe was devastated, Japan was devastated. In the next 25 years, the U.S. fraction of world GDP dropped from 45 percent to 40 to 35 percent to 30 to 25 percent to perhaps 20 percent of the world. This convergence didn't happen after World War I. And we economic theorists should be asking ourselves why Austria was such a basket case after World War I and contrast it with post World War II. That catch-up is not inexplicable. We speak of "miracles" and we can work out econometrically how much is due to the inputs, human capital, and to technological innovation. But we picture it as a bicycle race. The frontrunner, or a few frontrunners, break the wind for the rest. This is all in accord with Schumpeter's theory of innovation. It is to be noted that there isn't a single one of the bicycle riders in the back who had notably forged toward the front, and towards the very beginning, who had broken out. We need to keep that in mind in understanding why an emerging market like China can be growing the way it has been growing, that there will be a time when we suddenly discover that the trees don't grow to the skies.

Consider the history of Argentina. Argentina has a currency board and can even formalize that and use the U.S. dollar as its currency. I would not add, in a guess of growth rates in Argentina, a half of one percent per year extra growth catch-up on the U.S. because of its currency board. I don't think that the rational things which can be done in Argentina, in quasi-imitation of the best things that are done in America and in Japan, are there under either a floating exchange rate or dollarized system. It is a question of the advantages and disadvantages of each system.

Now I'm going to talk about the euro. It's worked out about as the American skeptics thought would be the case. Europe is not one country. The situation in Ireland, in Denmark, in the Netherlands, and maybe even Spain is different from what the situation is in Italy, which is more like the situation in France and Germany. But Italy, which has in my judgment benefited a lot in its budget and a lot of other things by being a European Union member, but the price of that is that the central bank in Frankfurt isn't doing anything for the developing Italian situation and couldn't be doing the same right thing for Ireland, which, for example, may be overheating. This should not surprise anybody. That's what happened under the gold standard, and that's part of what a single currency system is like.

Take for example the U.S. 12 Federal Reserve districts that use a single currency. When [MIT Economics Professor] Olivier Blanchard studies business cycles, he doesn't find that West Virginia cuts its prices relative to the rest of the country and attracts industry that way. He finds an important part of the picture is differential migration. Few Americans live near where they were born. I exaggerate. But in Europe, I can go 12 miles and run into two dialects and maybe a different language and I don't see that there has been any special new equilibrating migratory behavior in the short nine months under the currency union. Over time, there may be. There are both economic laws operative in things as well as country-specific effects.

ROBERT MUNDELL: Paul, thank you from all of us at the conference for joining us. In thanking you, I am speaking in the role that would ordinarily have been performed by [deceased Claremont Graduate University Economics Professor] Randall Hinshaw, in whose honor and memory we are holding this conference. We thank you very much for an excellent contribution and we're all very pleased and happy to see you in such great form and wish you many more happy and fruitful years ahead.

3. The euro in Europe and the world

Introduced by

Christopher Johnson

In previous Bologna–Claremont conferences, I've been one of the few representatives of the old continent of Europe and thus I've had a heavy responsibility. Though I've been outnumbered, I've always been plugging this strange animal called the euro. I was always greeted with a certain amount of skepticism by my American friends, especially the distinguished Nobel prize winners. Many people predicted that the euro would appreciate in the markets and indeed a lot of people lost a lot of money betting on that. In fact, the euro has been weaker than expected. It not yet fallen to one dollar and it has recently recovered a bit in the markets. This has been quite a good thing for Europe, because European exports have thus become more competitive against American exports. The weak euro has not had any deleterious effects on price stability. The inflation rate in Europe remains at about 1 percent, which is lower than in the United States.

Before I move on to some of the other points I want to make, I would just like to tell you all, regrettably, that Britain has not yet joined the euro. But nothing succeeds like success, and the British are just waiting to make sure that the euro is successful. So far, so good, but it's only been around for nine months. When it's been around for two or three years, the British will suddenly realize they made a mistake in waiting to jump on the bus and that they must get on before it's moving so fast that they can no longer jump onto it. This may not happen until about 2002 or 2003.

Having got Britain out of the way, I will talk about Europe as a whole and about the Euro-11 – these are the 11 countries which are in the euro, including France, Germany, Spain, Italy and therefore, a great majority of the 15 European Union countries. The first issue is the importance of the euro in the world economy vis-à-vis the dollar and the yen. This is an aspect that has sometimes been neglected but it's very important. As well as looking at the euro internally, we need to look at it externally as an international currency. What we come to is that the role of the euro is more important than that of the Euro-11 in terms of GDP or trade. The Euro-11 is now 14 percent of world

GDP, compared with 19 percent for the U.S. If Britain and the remaining European Union countries joined the Euro-11, this bloc would be almost equal in terms of proportion of world GDP to the U.S. So we can say, broadly, Europe carries the same weight as America in terms of production. In terms of world trade, Europe is more open to trade than the United States and it already accounts for 17 percent of world trade, compared with 14 percent for the U.S. That 17 percent would go up to 22 percent with the membership of Britain, Sweden and other countries. In terms of international bank loans, the euro represents 20 percent of the world market, the dollar is 36 percent – almost twice as much. In terms of bond issues, the euro is a bit more, 24 percent compared with 45 percent for dollar-denominated bonds. That's the international market. In the domestic market, the U.S. is much bigger, because of all the Treasury bills and corporate bonds which have been issued to domestic U.S. investors, so the U.S. accounts for 48 percent of GDP compared with 21 percent in Europe.

In terms of foreign exchange markets, the dollar is nearly half the total, the euro about a quarter. And in world currency reserves, the dollar is even more important, about 70 percent compared with about 11 percent in Europe. This is the case because a lot of the market before the euro was formed has now been consolidated out; European countries holding each other's currencies like the deutsche mark as reserves are no longer foreign exchange reserves, they have become domestic holdings. The same is true for quite a lot of the bank and bond items that were cross-holdings within the Euro-11, they have dropped off the books.

If we look at invoicing and world trade, and this is one of the most important dimensions of the currency, we can see that for a long time the dollar has been even more important than the share of the U.S. in world trade. We have something called the internationalization ratio, which is the ratio of the currency used in world trade to the ratio of the share of the country in world trade. The dollar is used in about 45 percent of world trade, so that's an internationalization ratio of about three times the 15 percent share of the U.S. in world trade. The ratio of the yen is slightly lower than one, in other words, the share of the yen doesn't even equal the share of Japan in world trade. The euro accounts for about 28 percent of invoicing compared with Europe's share of world trade, an internationalization ratio of 1.7. What we conclude from all this is that the euro has become, overnight, a major world currency. It's certainly second to the dollar and well ahead of the yen, but it has a lot of ground to make up before it can look the dollar in the face and be regarded as equal to the dollar in either invoicing or financial markets. But the share of the euro would be increased quite remarkably if Britain and other countries were to join the monetary union. Importantly, the share of the euro is increasing rapidly, particularly in bond markets, where the rate of increase in euro transactions has been 25 percent just in the first six months of this year, compared with only about 6 percent for the dollar. And these developments have been, to some extent, concealed by the rise in the dollar against the euro, which has made the dollar's share appear not to have changed. But, comparing in terms of constant exchange rates, the share of the euro has increased remarkably and will be seen to increase much more clearly if the dollar again falls against the euro. So that's a quick sketch of where the euro is vis-à-vis the dollar.

The second issue is the effect of the euro–dollar exchange rate on each economy. The relationship seems to be a rather volatile one, which a lot of people like [Director of the Institute for International Economics] Fred Bergsten were predicting. This is where all the action is now in the foreign exchange markets. It's not between the deutsche mark and the dollar. The deutsche mark doesn't exist for that purpose anymore, nor does the French franc. The euro–dollar exchange rate is volatile. A 10 percent shift in the euro against dollar exchange rate produces something like a one percentage point shift in the domestic price level. When we're talking about inflation rates of only 1 or 2 percent, another 1 percent makes a very big difference. So I would say there is certainly a need to take this relationship seriously. Benign neglect may be the only attitude central bankers know how to take, but the neglect may turn out not to be so benign at all in view of the short-term volatility and medium-term misalignment to the economies on both sides of the Atlantic.

The more difficult question is, can we control this relationship in any way? Should we seek to manage it by means of exchange rate bands, as was done under the Louvre Agreement, or by means of intervention in foreign exchange markets, or by modifying domestic policies on interest rates? An interest rate policy at the current time would mean the U.S. would need to have a lower interest rate, while Europe would need to have a higher interest rate. Interest rate differentials are now about 2.5 percent between dollars and euros, therefore the dollar should be allowed to fall. I think we should manage a fall in the dollar of that extent, 2.5 percent over the coming year. I'm afraid this is a rather idealistic vision, because we all know that currencies can change 2.5 percent in either direction in a single day. So, I think we're looking here at a kind of medium-term orientation, rather than the prescription for day-to-day exchange rate management. But, it's a problem we shall need to take seriously.

In the final section of this report, I'd like to note that the euro can play a role as an anchor for other currencies. For countries intending to join the European Union within the next five years – for example, the Czech Republic, Poland and Hungary – the euro can play the role the exchange rate mechanism played in an earlier stage for western Europe. It can also be used as a peg by some of the countries in the Far East which have been caught out by pegging to the dollar, and the dollar only, when the dollar was strong.

We may need to rethink the whole idea of exchange rate pegging. [U.S. Treasury Secretary] Larry Summers thinks it's a bad idea and we shouldn't try to do it anymore. But I think Korea or Thailand or Hong Kong or China cannot simply neglect their exchange rates because they don't know how to peg it. An exchange rate is an important policy variable over which you may have no control. It may be an important policy weapon if you can exercise some control over it. In terms of foreign trade, as I've explained, the euro is as important as the dollar and countries need to look at the mix of their foreign trade when deciding which currency to use. Is it the dollar or the euro or the yen? Or is it some kind of basket of all of them? I've never made any secret that I regard the euro, as being one stage towards some kind of world currency union. Bob Mundell just pointed out to me a passage in a book written before the Second World War by my late father-in-law Lionel Robbins, who of course used to be a major figure at these meetings, which said that the ideal would be a world currency. And just to show you it's nothing new, there was a world currency reform conference in 1867 where the world was on the verge of agreeing to a currency union between the dollar and the French franc and the British pound and German mark. We didn't quite make it, because the Americans and the British couldn't align their exchange rates by the 2.5 percent which would have been needed at the time. Well, that opportunity came and went. If another such opportunity comes, we should seize it. Meanwhile, the progress of the euro I think is a very good test case for whether it is possible to have a monetary union between politically independent countries. I believe that it is. We don't need a world government in order to have a world currency and most of us perhaps don't want a world government, but some of us might think a world currency is still a good idea.

DISCUSSION

SVEN ARNDT: Thank you very much, Christopher. The first comment is by Michael Connolly.

MICHAEL CONNOLLY: I'd like to ask Christopher to address the internal rules of the game to ensure policy consistency between monetary policy, financing of fiscal deficits within the euro, the issue of seigniorage, and procedures for the sharing of seigniorage. At the same time, if you could discuss open market operations – who will conduct them, are they to be conducted by the European Central Bank, and will the Bundesbank play a role? Lastly, would you discuss monetary independence and interdependence within the European Monetary System.

ROBERT SOLOMON: Christopher's last statement talked about a world currency union as perhaps a substitute for a world political union, if I understood it correctly. I think it's important to point out in that context that the major impetus for the integration within Europe, including the common currency, has been political, not economic. This starts with [French economist] Jean Monnet right after World War II and then you had a whole series of integrating steps among European countries. The European Community, European Union, European Monetary System – I won't go through it all. But each one of these was based on a desire on the part of France to embrace Germany and a willingness of Germany to be embraced.

MICHAEL CONNOLLY: What are the main lessons, Christopher and Bob, that you think can be gained from the long European process of unification that led to the euro? What are the main do's and don'ts for other countries and other regions in the world, especially for this region [Latin America] in which we are now?

CHRISTOPHER JOHNSON: First, let me answer Mike Connolly's question about the internal rules of the game. One rule of the game is that the same interest rate has to be accepted throughout the European monetary area. Now, if we didn't have the European Monetary Union, some countries who are expanding very rapidly like Ireland and Spain, would probably think they needed higher interest rates, and other countries like Germany and Italy, which are not expanding so rapidly, might want lower interest rates than they have now. The drawback of having a monetary union – a 'same size fits all' monetary policy – is meant to be overcome by fiscal policy. The Irish already have a big budget surplus and it's likely to get even bigger, so it's important they should do nothing to relax that tough fiscal position which is offsetting the monetary position. Similarly, countries which are less economically robust, like Italy, need to be allowed to have a higher budget deficit. The Italians, in fact, originally thought they would need a higher budget deficit, still within the ceiling of the 3 percent, which is the maximum allowed under the guidelines of the monetary union, but they now think that they won't need a higher budget deficit. Thus, there is an obvious relevance of fiscal policy to offset the uniform monetary policy. There are also micro interventions which countries can make, for example, the taxation of housing.

ABEL BELTRAN: Could I inquire about sanctions, for instance, if a country deviates in its deficit and doesn't satisfy the European Monetary Union rules? Are there specific sanctions within the European system, for example, fines and penalties that they must pay to Brussels as a result of deviating from the internal rules?

CHRISTOPHER JOHNSON: There are indeed sanctions for deviating above a 3 percent fiscal deficit. But the decision whether to apply them is a political one and therefore, well, we ain't seen nothing yet. Nobody has infringed on the 3 percent and many countries are, in fact, in surplus. Michael Connolly raised a rather technical question about the sharing of seigniorage. Seigniorage revenues are not going to be all that great because the inflation rate is very low. On the other hand, there is a seigniorage factor, based on the number of notes and coins which a country has in issue. Germany is a country that uses cash to a much greater extent than any other country in the monetary union. When the deutsche mark is removed from circulation in notes and coin form, which they will have to do at the beginning of 2002, the German Treasury will not get as much seigniorage from their share of the euro, which is based on the capital they put in, which is more or less proportional to the size of the economy. So there's a problem which may require some delicate negotiation.

Michael's other question was, who would actually conduct the monetary policy. It's clearly the responsibility of the European Central Bank that has governors from each of the national central banks, so it's a European system of central banks in which each country has a say and can advocate an interest rate change based on its own domestic conditions. European central bankers are accountable to the European Parliament and they have discussions with the European finance ministers which created a certain amount of tension at a recent meeting of the European 11. Somebody asked me what the telephone numbers are that the U.S. has to ring to talk to Europe. First of all, you would ring the European Central Bank and its President, Mr. [Wim] Duisenberg and then you would ring the President of the European Council of Finance Ministers, [Finnish Finance Minister] Sauli Niinisto. Countries that haven't joined the European Monetary Union, like Britain, are out of this loop. Bob Solomon's point is that European monetary integration has a political impetus, but there is no impetus to create a single European state. It is an impetus to get closer politically – close enough to be able to make coordinated economic decisions, close enough to avoid the kind of economic disagreements which have led to wars in the past. That is a much more modest ambition than creating a single European government, which very few people in Europe want – not even the Germans. So, when we say political, we have to know what we're talking about.

Abel Beltran asked about the main lessons of European integration, and I think the main lesson is don't try to do it during a world economic and financial crisis, because that will blow you off course. The movement toward monetary integration in Europe has been going on since 1970. We were blown off course by the oil shocks in the early 1970s. We were blown off course again by both the second oil shock in the early 1980s and then by the shock of German reunification in the early 1990s. These three things all happened when European monetary integration was actually on the cusp of taking place. In each case it led to a postponement, but finally we have a clear sky and we're not anticipating any further shocks of that kind until the integration process is complete in 2002 when euro notes and coins begin to circulate. What we have now is financial market integration only.

ROBERT SOLOMON: I want to make a point of clarification on terminology. The European central banking system – the European System of Central Banks – includes all 15 members of the European Union. The term that's used to designate the central banking system of the euro zone – the 11 countries – is "Euro System." It's easy to remember that, because it sounds like Federal Reserve System. And it has a certain similarity to the Federal Reserve System. There's a central bank and there are the individual national central banks that are now in a position similar to that of the Federal Reserve banks in the U.S. The Euro System is the term that's used in the euro zone. The European System of Central Banks includes even the non-members. Confusing, but important to understand the distinction.

CHRISTOPHER JOHNSON: There are two institutions within the European Central Bank. One is the Governing Council, which consists of the 11 countries and the central banks of those countries, which, as you say, is the Euro System. There is also the General Council, on which all 15 countries are represented, including Britain, Sweden, Denmark and Greece. This is a less important body.

ROBERT MUNDELL: Christopher, I want to first thank you for that excellent introduction to the euro. Then I want to raise the question of expansion of the European Monetary Union. Let us explore first the political situation in the UK. We all know that the [former] head of the Conservative Party, [William] Hague, has come out adamantly against the euro and issues connected with it, and I would like your assessment of the possibility of a change in that position, particularly given the influential role played by [Chairman and Chief Executive of News Corporation] Rupert Murdoch.

The other issue concerns the entry of new countries. I'm not talking now about other EU members like Denmark and Sweden and Greece, but rather the Central and Eastern European countries that have been invited to join the European Union. To what extent is it the responsibility of the European Central Bank to work with those countries, for example, helping them, for example, to set up currency boards that would help them achieve the required Maastricht convergence conditions. After these countries are formally invited to join the EU, what will be the process that will assist them in achieving the convergence conditions? I understood, for instance, that France and the Banque de France were actively involved in promoting relations with Poland. Is there going to be a unified policy on the expansion conditions for the euro area?

CHRISTOPHER JOHNSON: I'd be glad to deal with these important questions, Bob. The second one is easier, so I'll begin there first. The position of the European Union is that new member countries, which probably won't become members for another five years at least, cannot join the exchange rate mechanism of the euro until they have joined the European Union itself. When they've joined the exchange rate mechanism, then they can quite quickly qualify to join the euro area. But nothing prevents them in the meantime from pegging their currencies to the euro, but they are not guaranteed the support of the European Central Bank in doing so. The important thing about being a member of the European Union and the exchange rate mechanism is that you get a two-way agreement – the European Central Bank supports these currencies, but the countries have to pass tests for joining the European Union, like low inflation and a low budget deficit. These countries may be more likely to use the euro as a kind of crawling peg, though they are likely to have to devalue from time to time. I needn't draw a diagram for our Mexican friends [after the 1994 peso crisis], but such a system is supposed to work. It can sometimes end in disaster, but in these countries we hope that it won't.

The British have an option to join the euro and that is something that was negotiated in the Maastricht Treaty by John Major's Conservative government. The position of [Prime Minister Tony] Blair's government has not changed all that radically, so there is an option to join. The British have not yet decided whether or when to exercise it. But there's nevertheless a difference. The Conservative Party is committed against joining the euro for the next ten years. This is the advice of William Richard Fetcher, who says that Britain should withdraw from the European Union altogether. That's a radical position which has some sympathy on the right wing. Tony Blair's [Labour] government, in principle, would like to join the euro, but they have two obstacles. One is that public opinion is against it. Bob Mundell mentioned Rupert Murdoch, who controls two of the important newspapers [*The Times* of London and *The Sun*]. Conrad Black, who is a Canadian millionaire, controls another [*The Daily Telegraph*]. I'm encouraged by the fact that Rupert Murdoch recently had lunch with the current head of the European Commission, Romano Prodi. So maybe if Murdoch is given an Italian television station, he will drop his opposition to Britain joining the euro. Nevertheless, there is public opposition which the Blair government has to conquer. It hasn't really begun to try to persuade people yet and it may not do so until after the next election, most likely in 2001. Blair wants to be a two-term or three-term Prime Minister. He doesn't want the unpopularity of the euro to rub off on him, though he's still very popular. But after the next election, the British are likely to proceed to a referendum and a government campaign in favor of the euro. By then, I think it will be evident the euro is such a success that Britain cannot stay out of it, for both political and economic reasons. I believe Britain will join the euro in 2003 or 2004.

SVEN ARNDT: I want to raise an issue that came up in Bob's excellent Robbins Lecture [Chapter 1] which I think I'd like to hear more discussion on. That is the question as to how the euro, as it becomes an established currency, will affect the dollar as a reserve currency. On one hand, one hears that this is a zero sum game – any tendency by world central banks to accumulate euros would mean a deccumulation of dollars. At the other extreme is the position that the accumulation of euros will actually come out of growth rather than from other currencies. Central banks holding deutsche marks, for example, and Swiss francs would reduce these holdings and pick up euros. Bob didn't come all the way over to the zero sum game side, but was pretty pessimistic and concerned about what this would look like, and I'd like to have some discussion on that.

JEFFREY FRANKEL: Let me first attempt an answer to Sven's question before I say what I had planned. Until recently I was in the U.S. Administration [as a member of the President's Council of Economic Advisors] and I formulated a response to the issue of the effect of the euro as a reserve currency depending on whether the euro or the dollar would be strong. My preferred answer is that both currencies are going to be strong. That might sound like a contradiction, but if you think of the strength of currencies in terms of purchasing power, then to the extent that both the European Central Bank and the Federal Reserve follow appropriate monetary policies, both currencies could be strong by the measure that makes the most difference. That's not a complete answer to your question, but it's an important part of it.

I also want to propose a thesis regarding the odds for the long-term success of the European Monetary Union, and it consists of a couple of parts. One is a classic optimum currency area theory, which Bob Mundell invented. The classic optimum currency area criteria determine whether a group of countries, such as European countries, are good candidates for giving up their currency independence and includes the extent of integration as measured by trade, the extent of labor mobility (which was Bob's criterion in his original article), the extent of fiscal and political integration, and the symmetry of shocks (or the synchronization of the business cycle). Let me say overall, I think EMU is a good thing, but Europe, even the EMU-11, do not qualify by these criteria as well, for example, as the states of the United States. But the first of two or three points I want to make is that these factors are endogenous, they change over time. Trade and labor mobility and other measures of integration, as well as symmetry of shocks, are increasing within Europe as a result of the European Union and as a result of EMU itself, so it's endogenous.

The other component to the thesis I am putting forward has to do with shocks. Christopher Johnson pointed out that in the past the plans for EMU have been disrupted or postponed several times because of shocks, and he trusted that that wouldn't happen again, but of course it could happen again. On average, we have a major shock in the global economic system roughly once per decade – the oil shocks of the 70s, Reaganomics in the 80s, German unification in the 90s. There's no way of saying what the next shock will be, but it seems likely that there will be one eventually. So here's my thesis. If it happens that there are no serious shocks in the next ten or 20 years, or that the shocks that occur affect all European countries in roughly the same way, then European Monetary Union will survive. By 20 years from now, I think the amount of trade integration, labor mobility, fiscal integration, political integration, and shock correlation within Europe will be so high that members will be able to weather whatever happens from then on. But if there is a major asymmetric shock over the next ten or 20 years, then I would worry about EMU survival, particularly if it comes during a transition period when the UK or some of the other countries that aren't currently in are joining.

HERBERT GRUBEL: Christopher, I would like to raise another interpretation of the role of politics in the European Monetary Union. It's not necessary in Mexico to talk about the role the central bank has played in creating economic instability. I think most of the economic instability in Latin American countries, and in many European countries, was caused by the misbehavior of central banks. The central banks themselves are not to be blamed, because the ultimate cause is politics. For example, politicians use monetary policy to get themselves re-elected and provide favors to their friends. I believe that, and it is supported in the research by Professor Neils Segerson of the University of Copenhagen. He had a company that consulted with the central banks of Europe examining why the Bank of Italy and the Parliament of Italy were willing to give up the power that they have had to influence economic conditions in Italy, thus increasing their chances of being re-elected. He discovered a profound answer: every once in a while politicians have pangs of conscience and they say, have we really been doing the best thing for our country? Has it been really in the interest of Italy to have had a bank that could play games for the politicians? I think the politicians and the central bankers have ultimately realized that they have had their fun during the postwar years and it hasn't worked. Because of this, they designed a new central bank that is going to be removed from this kind of a political influence. And that is why I think they were willing to join the European Central Bank.

But this immediately raises a question for Christopher Johnson. If the governing bodies of the European Central Bank are eventually captured by analogous political influences, being so much bigger, will they not play havoc for the entire region and maybe for the world, than the Bank of Italy was able to do? Therefore, in my judgment, one of the most crucial issues facing the European Central Bank is the question of true political independence. One way to do this is to have them only obey rules and operate on principles which will stand the test of time. For example, I think the European Central Bank should no longer be responsible for maintaining full employment, that price stability should be the only target. Even this is not politically neutral. Ultimately, human organizations and agreements must have some accountability. In a democracy, the people ought to have an opportunity to say, enough is enough. So the conundrum is that if we give the European Central Bank a very strong constitution that isolates them from politics, they can then go off and do the craziest things. Maybe the European Central Bank is controlled by somebody who has studied economics at MIT. We don't know, you see. So, what is the basis for accountability? I'm sure Christopher has thought about this, and I would like to hear about the tension between politics and economic outcomes.

CHRISTOPHER JOHNSON: That calls for an answer. I'm not quite sure whether Herb is casting the politicians or the central bankers in the role of crazy men. In the first part of his question, it was the politicians who could do no right, and in the second part it seems the central bankers may be just as bad, but I don't think so. I'd just like to retell his stylized facts about Italy a bit differently, because this is illustrative of what's going on in Europe today. The Italian politicians were unable to control the country's fiscal deficit. The central bank actually had to come in, rather against the wishes of most politicians, and clean up the mess by having tight monetary policy to offset loose fiscal policy. But that increased the deficit still more because the high interest rates in Italy raised interest payments on the debt.

What has happened in Italy now is that because people trust Italy to be a good member of the monetary union, it has reduced its fiscal deficit and then it has had the added reduction in interest rates that reduced the deficit still more, so Italy at the moment is in a virtuous circle. But I think the attitude of the Italian central bankers was that they had a thankless task. They had to be the bad cop while the government was being the good cop, and nobody always likes playing the bad cop role, so I think they were quite glad to hand that over to the European Central Bank. Italian central bankers are losing power, but they didn't enjoy having to exercise power in the way they did.

Now as Herb says, the European Central Bank is guaranteed its independence. It is more independent than either the Fed or the Bundesbank whose status could be changed by an act of parliament. The European Central Bank has its independence given to it by treaty. It's absolutely entrenched. But, having said that, as I've said about Italy, central bankers don't like to be unpopular, so the first thing they do is to encourage governments to behave themselves fiscally, which they are doing, and which the governments are doing anyway, for good reasons. The other thing is that they have to be sensitive to issues like unemployment and growth. This is also in the Maastricht Treaty. The Central Bank has to operate within the wider economic policy objectives. So while its principal objective is price stability, it is not the only one.

DAVID ANDREWS: On the issue of the political independence of the European Central Bank, Christopher Johnson is quite correct in asserting that constitutionally the European Central Bank will be more independent than the Bundesbank. But of course, what's really important is the influence of the Central Bank and the dialogue that takes place with political authorities. The Bundesbank's influence in the German policy dialogue was not rooted solely in its constitutional mandate. There was tremendous public support for the Bundesbank. Many people point to Germany's terrible historical experiences with inflation. I'm more inclined to believe that Bundesbank officials were terribly clever at playing the political game in Germany.

The European Central Bank has a much more difficult game to play in managing political dialogue with 11 national systems. Let me just give a very simple example. The vehicle language for work in the European Central Bank is English. It was the working language for a short while, but the French objected to the term "working language" so it's now the "vehicle language." English is, of course, the language of only Ireland of the Euro-11, so everything the European Central Bank does has to be translated into several languages. Indeed, the ongoing complex series of negotiations within Europe is much more complex than the Bundesbank ever faced.

AL HARBERGER: I think I'm pretty much on the same wire as Jeff Frankel in this story. Fixed exchange rate systems, first of all, have functioned many times quite well for extended periods of time. And fixed exchange rate systems have also broken down and had difficulties many different times. I think there's a general agreement among economists that small shocks are not a problem. Big shocks are the problem. When the big shocks are positive, reserves are flowing in, the expansion of money takes place, the price level rises, there is an endogenous adjustment that is easy for countries to go through, and basically no problem.

It's the negative shocks that create the trouble. Negative shocks reach adjustment by pressing the prices and wages of the country down. It seems that almost regardless of the institutional arrangement, economies resist this kind of negative pressure on the general price level and wages. Argentina has been going through this type of deflationary process since at least 1994, and it still has not achieved an equilibrium. But Argentina is a very special case and I don't want to go into its details. Before coming to this meeting, I anticipated this issue and I picked up my statistical abstract and I looked at the problem of Appalachia in the United States. Appalachia was a problem in the 1930s. It has never ceased to be a problem. In the 1990s, Appalachia is one of the two leading locations with high unemployment. It is by far the leading area for welfare recipients and other measures of poverty. This has persisted in spite of considerable migration of capital over the years and a very considerable migration of people out of the state. So, I think it's a problem. I was at a meeting about a year ago, at which [former President of France] Valéry Giscard d'Estaing was present and this very issue came up. He was called upon and had a very patrician answer: we have great mobility of labor within Europe, we have Spaniards going here and Turks going there and goodness knows what. Mobility of labor will take care of everything. Well, I really don't believe that, but I am interested in learning what, in the deliberations within the euro mechanism, people think about this problem.

ROBERT BARTLEY: I want to make a few observations on why the politicians in Europe were willing to give up an element of sovereignty in constituting a common currency. If you look at it from a politician's viewpoint, the main advantage of monetary sovereignty is the electoral use of money illusion. That is, if monetary expansion affects the real sector before it is offset by inflation in the financial sector, if you can guess that lag correctly and expand money at the appropriate moment before an election, when the election occurs you're getting the real sector effects, not the financial sector effects.

What's happened, I think, is that money illusion is vanishing, that this lag is shortened with the exposure of the public to the inflation of the 1970s, with the increasingly efficient cross-border financial markets, and due to computers and communication advances. Monetary sovereignty has become much less politically valuable to the people involved, and in a Public Choice view of their role, they decided that they were better off without it. I think that's the explanation. And if that's so, it may be a good omen for further currency unifications as politicians in the rest of the world learn this same lesson.

On a somewhat separate issue – the question of accountability – the Bank of Japan has just recently been declared independent. I, and a lot of people around, think that Japanese monetary policy, at the moment, would be better if they weren't so independent.

QUESTIONS

AUDIENCE QUESTION: There is a somewhat different political issue that has more to do with the state of public finance in the euro zone. Many analysts have suggested that a lot of the member countries, both the core countries and the non-core countries, are meeting the convergence criteria through creative accounting. As a result, deficits have been coming down because of lower debt service. But at the core, there are many lingering problems which apparently have not been tackled, which have a lot to do with the welfare policies to which these European countries are committed. Once the effect of lower debt service wears off, countries will have to face some very tough decisions, and I wonder if there has been any progress along those lines.

AUDIENCE QUESTION (Lane David of Universidad Ibero-Americana):   My question is not quite in order, but interest rates serve as a signaling mechanism for the allocation of resources and with the increasing divergence that we're going to see in the European Union as the newer members join, how is that going to affect the flow of capital within?

PAUL J. ZAK: I want to tie all these pieces together by telling you what Christopher Johnson told me at dinner last night. Christopher expects the euro zone to include 20 or more countries in the next ten to 15 years. This brings enforcement of European Central Bank rules to the forefront. If Jeff Frankel is right and shocks become asymmetric, the probability of a violation of the rules becomes greater as the number of countries rises, and particularly as the diversity of countries – the Polands, the Czech Republics – increases. This suggests two issues. One, can national institutions merge so that we have true uniformity without creative accounting? Second, what are the mechanisms that allow countries to opt out? Have those mechanisms been built in so that at some point if a country faces a very large shock, it has the ability to opt out of the EMU? The institutions should not make that too likely, but should make it available. There's got to be flexibility built into the system. I don't think a world currency solves this problem. Indeed, it could be dangerous because then every country would absorb shocks with purely internal adjustments. This is a very delicate matter which I think summarizes the core issues of the last three or four arguments.

ROBERT MUNDELL: On Paul's recent point, and related to Jeffrey's, if there is a big shock, say in three years, it'll be interesting to know how a country could opt out, since it does not even have its own currency. So there's an institutional problem on the mechanism for opting out. Should an individual country be hit by a very big shock, it wouldn't have, at that point, a currency of its own to seek refuge in. The Delors Committee wanted the single-currency plan to be almost irrevocable.

HERBERT GRUBEL: Well, I believe that the extremely large shocks of the past were endogenous to the world system that adopted the wrong economics that came from Paul Samuelson. For example, the reaction to the oil shock. My main answer is, at least for smaller shocks, the availability of flexible exchange rates or the ability to change the exchange rate in response to a shock, has allowed the political system to delay the necessary real adjustments. For example, suppose unions are too strong in a country, but politicians can't afford to take them on. They can take them on indirectly by committing themselves to a fixed exchange rate system, because if the unions then have excessive wage demands, they will learn that the central bank and the exchange rate is no longer going to bail them out. There is a whole range of ways in which floating an exchange rate is a way of avoiding the real adjustments necessary to get to a more efficient economy and better economic growth. That's my answer. We'll talk about it at length this afternoon.

ROBERT MUNDELL: Sven raised the issue of how important the euro is going to be in the world economy. I don't intend to make an argument about that now. I did it a little bit last night and I've written so much on this that I don't want to repeat myself. What I do want to ask, though, is this: when eleven currencies are going to be replaced by one new currency, what does that do to the stability of a flexible exchange rate system? What does economic theory have to say about this? The answer is that economic theory doesn't say anything about it. It's an unsolved problem. Just imagine that you take a world of 200 currencies and then collapse them into currency areas so you get maybe 150 odd currency areas floating. Let us suppose this "Walrasian system" is dynamically stable. Now suppose you take some subset of these currency areas and form a monetary union. Will the system still be dynamically stable? That's a problem in mathematical economics that has not been solved yet, and I just want to raise it so that those here who are mathematicians can try their hand at finding the solution.

Herb Grubel raised the issue of politics, and I agree with a lot of what he said. I think that one of the great benefits to at least half of the countries that are joining the euro system is that they are going to have a much better monetary policy than they had before. This certainly applies to Portugal,

Spain, Italy, and Greece. If those countries had adhered to a deutsch mark zone throughout this period, they would have had much better monetary and fiscal policies. Italy is a good example. It had a fixed exchange rate for 22 years – 1949 to 1971. Then when it moved toward flexible exchange rates, it completely lost monetary discipline, and the lira lost half its value. Then Italy joined the European Monetary System, and with a great struggle recaptured monetary stability. Unfortunately, the restoration of monetary stability was associated with the development of a most absurd fiscal instability, in which public debt shot up from 50 percent of GDP to over 100 percent.

I believe that, for all the countries going into the euro system, monetary policy will be much better, with the possible exception of Germany. But even Germany may gain from getting away from a deutsche mark that was too prone to overvaluation.

Jeff Frankel raised the question of optimum currency areas, and I'm usually credited or blamed for introducing this notion. One of the issues is the problem of asymmetric shocks. There's a vast literature now on asymmetric shocks. It generally shows that if countries are going to be affected differently by shocks, then it creates a problem when they give up the exchange rate as a weapon of adjustment.

I disagree with the general tone of this literature. If you read my article carefully, it was essentially an attack on the idea of flexible exchange rates. Its major thrust was to say that, given the arguments that were then made for flexible exchange rates, they would not accomplish what they were intended to do unless currency areas were based on regional rather than national lines.

The literature has tried to see if there exist important "asymmetric shocks." But in Europe at least most general shocks affect all or most countries. Very few can be identified as nation-specific. Indeed the most important kind of nation-specific shock derives from changes in national exchange rates. If a small country devalues, that affects that single country uniquely. But monetary union would rule out that kind of shock so it is irrelevant.

There are other kinds of asymmetric shocks. Consider a terms of trade shock. The oil shocks have been terms of trade shocks but, at least for Europe, with the possible exception of Britain as a result of North Sea oil, they are not really asymmetrical. But suppose half the European countries produced oil and the other half didn't. In that case the oil shock would be asymmetric. Half the countries in Europe would be better off while the other half would be worse off. One could argue, as a digression, that monetary union could be an advantage because the oil shock would be neutral for Europe as a whole, as far as its effect on Europe's standard of living was concerned. But the main issue is whether exchange rate changes are appropriate in these circumstances. Why would exchange rate changes help countries to offset basic changes in their terms of trade?

The fact is that exchange rate changes cannot compensate for changes in the terms of trade. A change in the terms of trade alters the relative price of exports and imports, a real change. An exchange rate change alters the prices of both exports and imports to the same degree as the devaluation, a purely nominal or monetary change. If the price of oil doubled, lowering the real wealth of the oil-importing countries, why should the latter compound their difficulties by raising the price of oil and all other commodities even more?

The idea that you can use the exchange rate to offset a change in the terms of trade is a fallacy that would be enough to flunk any graduate student in an examination. But the fallacy has a perverse durability. The 1990 Bank of Canada annual report was written at a time when [then governor of the Bank of Canada] John Crow had been trying to achieve zero inflation, and he was being successful in lowering it, but at a terrible cost in terms of unemployment and the current account. The exchange rate had appreciated enormously over this period, and the Bank of Canada supported its policy with the false argument that exchange rate changes could offset changes in the terms of trade. Upon raising this issue with them, the Bank admitted that they were incorrect, but the harm had already been done. What they should have said is that exchange rate policy can facilitate a movement of the real exchange rate, which of course, has nothing to do with the terms of trade.

The final issue I need to comment on is factor mobility. Someone asked me about the importance of factor mobility after the lecture last night. Specifically, he asked if it would be a good idea for Mexico to have a fixed exchange rate with the United States, even though there's little labor mobility between the United States and Mexico. My answer to that question is that factor mobility between Mexico and the United States would facilitate adjustment. But that is only one factor in determining an optimum currency area. Even if there is no labor mobility at all between the two countries, a monetary union or a fixed exchange rate might be beneficial. Back in 1792 when the United States created its monetary union, there was relatively little labor mobility between the 13 colonies. But that did not prevent the United States from capturing the gains from a common currency. The same argument holds for the fixed exchange rate system based around the worldwide bimetallic or gold standards.

As far as North American efficiency is concerned, a strong case can be made for unimpeded labor mobility between Mexico and the United States, but that argument holds equally whether Mexico has a fixed exchange rate with the United States, as it did from 1954 to 1976, as it has when Mexico has a flexible exchange rate, as in the chaotic period since 1976.

ROBERT SOLOMON: Bob Mundell, in talking about asymmetric shocks, implied that they come from exchange rate changes. In Europe, you can have asymmetric shocks not only because the intra-euro-zone exchange rate can't be changed, but also because there is a single monetary policy, and Bob did not mention that. Different countries are subject to different influences, what we call shocks. Euro-zone countries cannot change their monetary policy apart from the exchange rate. And there have been examples of asymmetric shocks quite apart from the oil shock, Bob. German unification was an asymmetric shock in Europe. At the moment, Ireland is growing two or three times faster than the rest of the euro zone countries, but it's subject to the same interest rates as all of the other countries in Europe, and it may be, therefore, subject to some inflationary pressures. One can easily imagine many asymmetric shocks under the European Monetary System.

FAUSTO ALZATI: Using the exchange rate to avoid adjustment is a crucial issue. I would like to get more comments on it, because I think it's critical to economic growth in Mexico and in other developing countries. For example, in the debate right now going on Argentina, it's important to realize to what extent the problems of Argentina are derived from the situation in Brazil. Argentina decided to fix the exchange rate and, of course, the Argentine politicians didn't continue with the needed adjustments and structural changes. But then they suffered, because they have Brazil next door which is willing to use devaluation for the sake of making exports more competitive. This may work very well in the short run, but continuing to avoid adjustments forgoes the increases in productivity that will make countries competitive in the long run.

This has a bearing also on the issue that Bob Mundell raised in his Robbins Lecture regarding the dollar–euro exchange rate. In the current division of labor in the world economy, the U.S. has become the big producer of innovation. Nothing compares to the U.S. higher education system for new knowledge, and much of the productivity gains taking place in the world economy come from the U.S. On the other hand, Europe has fallen behind in many ways and hasn't been able to be as innovative as the U.S. If that difference persists and if Europe does not adjust to become a more flexible economy, I think in the long run the dollar will continue being the preferred currency, simply because it's the currency of a country which has a more productive economy.

PAUL ZAK: I want to follow up on Fausto's and Bob Solomon's points. I can imagine a situation in which if there are large asymmetric shocks, the European Central Bank could be blackmailed. Suppose Ireland experiences a big shock and threatens to leave the union unless the ECB institutes, say, a more expansive monetary policy that would decrease interest rates. Ireland may need to grow faster to satisfy domestic political constituencies. This is a situation in which individuals at the European Central Bank are subject to a kind of blackmail. The euro-zone countries want stability, want to stay together, but also have domestic concerns. How does the ECB do that? Well, it might have to transfer resources to weaker or lower income countries, for example Ireland, or France. That's a fundamental political problem that we have to address if this is going to be a workable system. Hopefully there are institutions in place to do that, but it's a possibility that Bob Mundell didn't address.

DAVID ANDREWS: I want to return to this issue of sustainability. Jeff Frankel already mentioned that the various factors identified by optimum currency area theory appear to be largely endogenous. Countries that join a single currency union become more fit candidates for a single currency after participating in it. The other important point, raised by Michael Connolly, has to do with the physical introduction of the currency in Europe. After 2002, the cost–benefit analysis for staying or leaving changes dramatically. The better time for an asymmetric shock is right now so that a country can leave before there is a physical euro on the ground. The costs of opting out are considerably less today than they will be in 2004 or 2005 when it would involve the reintroduction of a national currency.

One final point: I thought Professor Mundell's comments about his own early writings were tremendously interesting. I'd just like to offer a friendly amendment. Isn't the biggest problem to optimum currency area theory its name? That is, it doesn't identify an optimum currency area. It identifies regions or states as being more or less fit for participating in a single currency. And I think the name itself, although well-intentioned, has led people to imagine that there is some kind of magic formula, and the countries of the euro zone are or are not an optimum currency area, when in fact, in order to make that determination, you'd have to make some assumptions about social welfare functions and the preferences of societies and governments with respect to the trade-off between macro flexibility and micro efficiency.

ROBERT MUNDELL: The problem is not in the name, the problem is the use to which the name is put.

JEFFREY FRANKEL: I actually like the name and I've always interpreted it as the optimum size on the map of a region that merits its own independent currency, because there are many different ways one could carve up the map. Even though Bob invented the term and concept, there have been other contributors, and I think notions that trade integration is important and that asymmetric shocks are important came from later contributors to this area.

I reacted with a bit of surprise to Bob's statement that a flexible exchange rate is not of any use in adjusting to terms of trade shocks. Let's focus on commodity shocks to sharpen the discussion a bit. It is true that a flexible exchange rate cannot completely neutralize the effect of a terms of trade shock. If you produce copper and the price of copper goes down, you're worse off. That's true. But if you don't have exchange rate flexibility and you have stickiness or frictions in wages and prices, you can be worse off than just a terms of trade shock. You can suffer unemployment and serious recession. In these circumstances, changing the exchange rate, as we learned from Milton Friedman, can be easier than changing a lot of local wages and prices, and can allow the economy to adjust to its new equilibrium. Two examples come to mind. In the case of the oil shocks in the 1970s and 1980s, there were some asymmetries. The UK and Norway had oil reserves, and as a result, their currencies appreciated and I think that made sense at the time. An example from last year is the worldwide fall in agricultural and mineral prices. Countries that export these items generally saw their currencies devalue.

CHRISTOPHER JOHNSON: I'd like to pick up one or two points in the discussion. The focus has been on three related issues: exchange rates, shocks, and optimum currency areas. What people don't seem to have noticed is that countries no longer do control their exchange rates, or they can't control them in the way they could under Bretton Woods, where they could select a new parity. Britain in 1967 devalued by 15 percent and that was the new rate of the pound. Now, in a floating exchange rate regime, when countries try to use the exchange rate for policy purposes, it either moves too far in the right direction, which is what happened to Mexico, and you get overshooting, or as it may actually move in the wrong direction and the country has no control over what the markets do to its exchange rate. So it's an almost useless policy tool, even if at one time it looked like a useful one.

Next, a few words on shocks. Shocks which are asymmetric, in the sense that they affect some countries in the opposite way they affect other countries, are atypical. Examples include oil prices and German reunification. There's a lot of talk about shocks being asymmetric when they apply with the same sign to all countries, but with a different magnitude of effect. Germany is more affected by an oil price increase than France, but they're both affected by it. Italy is more affected by the demise of the Russian market for exports, because Italy exports more to Russia, but all European countries export something to Russia. I don't call that asymmetric, that's just a market fact. There isn't uniformity in economic relations, and I think calling this an asymmetric shock confuses the discussion.

Finally, on the question of optimum currency areas, I'm very glad Bob reminded us of what his article really said. There is a useful concept here and

I would like to quote something that I wrote because Bob Solomon quoted it in his book, so I'm going to promote Bob Solomon's book, *Money on the Move*, and not mine. It has a very good reference, if I may say so, to the argument that what the European Union is trying to be is an optimum currency area. Long before we thought about monetary union, the rationale for creating a European economic community was to take down the barriers to the movement in labor and capital, and that is what they have been doing. So if your objective is to create an optimum currency area, it's inconsistent to say that we haven't got there yet, because part of the European Monetary Union program is economic integration, and that produces an optimum currency area. So let's end these discussions asking if we are there yet. Removing trade barriers is part of a long-term process, and creating a single currency is another part.

ABEL BELTRAN: After the discussion this morning, wouldn't it make sense to add to the currency area requirements, brilliantly explained by Bob Mundell, the political sympathies and cultural conditions of a country? I think that the Germans would like very much to have less inflation that we Mexicans. This may reflect a difference in the political atmosphere and the traditions and cultures of these countries.

MICHAEL CONNOLLY: The 1994 peso devaluation put a lot of financial stress on the banking system in Mexico, because it was basically short dollars and long peso assets. A major devaluation tends to reduce the value of the assets of the banking system and raise the value of the liabilities. This puts tremendous financial pressure on the banking system. That's one of the aspects of adjustments in Mexico and other countries in Latin America following a shock. For example, if a fall in the price of oil causes the currency to depreciate tremendously, then pressure is shifted onto the financial system, which then has further negative consequences.

FAUSTO ALZATI: Just a comment on what Abel said. I don't see any reason why Mexicans would like to have a higher inflation rate than the Germans. Mexican politicians may want this, but that's only because they have no accountability. They know very well that we want to have low inflation like the United States and Germany. I don't see any reason why we would want high inflation.

SVEN ARNDT: I think that's a good note on which to end. Thank you to everybody for a great morning session.

4. Monetary policy and economic growth in Latin America

Introduced by

Robert L. Bartley

I'm going to run through the history of Latin America over the last few years. This risks telling you all a lot of things you already know, but nonetheless, I think just setting the scene and outlining some of the issues that need to be discussed will be a valuable contribution. The current problem in Latin America starts with the Mexican devaluation at the end of 1994. Albeit, that was the latest in a series of Mexican peso crises, but I think it changed the outlook for Latin America more generally. Since then, the region has been buffeted by a series of international financial developments and exchange rate developments that are outlined graphically in a chart that came from a Senate banking testimony by [Director for International Economics of Bear, Stearns & Co.] David Malpass.

Argentina, of course, is on a currency board so that all of the financial pressures get reflected directly in the interest rate, so you have a barometer of international pressures, and you see rates peaking at almost 30 percent in 1995 following the Mexican devaluation. When the Asian crisis developed in 1997, which can be seen as an attack on the Hong Kong currency board, there was another peak of 12 percent. Again with the Russian default and again, somewhat less, with the Brazilian devaluation. All of these things have been buffeting the financial systems of Argentina and all of the other Latin American countries, and for that matter, the underdeveloped countries around the world. The Mexican devaluation in 1994 and the currency board in Argentina have been test cases of how well different currency regimes weather external financial shocks. I think it's quite clear that the first conclusion has to be that neither devaluations, nor floating rates, nor a currency board solves any structural problems. All of the Latin American economies are currently in recession, while there is a big boom in the United States. The one exception in Latin America is Mexico, which is not in recession and is doing very well at the moment. This has occurred because Mexico's economy is now so

closely linked with that of the United States and it seems to be following the
U.S. pattern rather than the Latin American pattern. Undoubtedly, this is due
to NAFTA, and unfortunately for the rest of the hemisphere, the momentum
for the expansion of NAFTA seems to have petered out in the United States,
so that other countries are left to their own devices. Brazil reacted to these
pressures by abandoning the *real* program at the beginning of this year
[1999] as they moved to floating exchange rates. The results in Brazil have
not been nearly as dramatic as I and others might have expected; there hasn't
been a big inflationary spike. This may be due to the appointment of [Gover-
nor of the Central Bank] Armínio Fraga Neto as a reassuring figure in of
Brazil.

Brazil may not be out of the woods yet, because they have suffered a
substantial loss of foreign currency reserves, which has upset their relations
with Argentina. Further, there is a question of whether or not a free trade area
such as Mercosur can be maintained without exchange rate stability. Just
before coming down here, I was on a program at the Dow Jones Americas
Conference in New York with private economists from Brazil and Argentina.
A Brazilian got up and said that Brazilians are usually optimistic, but he was
very pessimistic about Brazil's outlook, because of an inability to maintain
macroeconomic stability. The Argentine got up and said that Argentines are
usually very pessimistic, but he was optimistic because the way things are
developing, the governments will have no room to maneuver.

As I look back over these financial crises, I think there are important issues
to be discussed, namely whether the IMF is the cure or the cause of crises.
Indeed, whether the IMF is pursuing the appropriate programs. What was
different about the 1994 peso crisis was the enormous program mounted by
the United States – some 40 billion dollars – that went to bail out the
tesobonos [dollar denominated Mexican government bonds] that had been
paying 15 percent interest with risk written all over them. The question is, did
this introduce an element of moral hazard into the calculations of the rest of
the world? The Asian crisis, I think at least in part, reflected the IMF bias
toward devaluation. We know that [former IMF managing director] Michel
Camdessus was in Thailand four or five times arguing that they needed
external balance, that they should abandon their dangerous link to the dollar.
Certainly there were imbalances that needed to be corrected, but he was not
telling them that if they maintain a link to the dollar, it will exacerbate their
structural problems. Instead, he was telling them that they wouldn't have to
solve their structural problems if they cut loose from the dollar.

The devaluations went much further than anyone expected, causing an
enormous crisis throughout Asia. Various bailouts were then mounted. This
was followed by the Soviet default. All of the markets figured, well if they are
going to ball out the *tesobonos*, they cannot not bail out a country that has so

many intercontinental ballistic missiles. Russia proved to be a black hole to bail out and there was a default. This had a very big impact not only through Latin America and the developed world, but also in the United States. Those of us whose livelihood depends on selling financial advertising faced a downturn in the fourth quarter of 1998.

In the last week, we've had a quite amazing development, which is the default on Ecuadorian Brady bonds [Brady bonds are restructured bank debt collateralized by U.S. zero-coupon bonds, named for former Treasury Secretary Nicholas Brady who invented them in the 1980s]. The interesting thing about this is that this default was backed by the IMF. They had previously tried to get Pakistan to default. In other words, the same organization that mounted 40 billion dollars to prevent the default on the *tesobonos* is now urging default on Brady bonds in Ecuador. The agenda here is that the IMF wants to insert bankruptcy clauses in all of these debt contracts that ensure that countries cannot default on their official debt without defaulting on Brady bonds and their private debt as well. Private lenders are all very upset about this at the moment and don't want to see these kind of clauses inserted. I have kind of a mixed attitude toward it myself, because it certainly is a solution to the moral hazard problem, i.e. the private sector ought to know that it can lose money in these kinds of deals which might make investors more prudent.

The final observation is that there are elections going on all over Latin America, including Argentina and Chile, and there is still political uncertainty in Brazil, and a presidential campaign underway here in Mexico. From a Public Choice standpoint, the availability of IMF aid or bailouts may make it harder to discipline politicians. This is especially true regarding foreign exchange regimes. Politicians seem to have the idea that they can get something for themselves out of devaluation and currency instability. The record before 1994 is pessimistic on that. It's hard to see the benefits, but the notion seems to persist in a great many places.

DISCUSSION

SVEN ARNDT: Thank you very much, Bob. Let's focus in this session on the basic topic of monetary stability. We should recall what Bob Mundell said to us in his Robbins Lecture [Chapter 1]: countries have to figure out how to achieve monetary stability, especially the choice of stabilization instruments. The other point Bob Mundell made was whether national stability should be pursued by nations, or in some kind of group effort.

AL HARBERGER: I thought I would mention a couple of important facts. With respect to the Mexican bailout, the rate on *tesobonos*, up to very shortly before the crisis, was around 7 percent. That is, the market in New York was not predicting any disaster in Mexico. Those who bought *tesobonos* did not believe they faced a high risk. *Tesobonos* went to 15 percent after the crisis when the Mexican economy was in turmoil. Just prior to the crisis, that wasn't the case.

I want to throw in another anecdote from Argentina, because it is vital to issues surrounding currency boards and dollarization. Argentina did indeed surmount what they call the tequila crisis. The tequila crisis was the reverberation in Argentina of the December 1994, Mexican crisis. In the tequila crisis, Argentina lost half of its net reserves in a period of less than three months. If Argentina had been operating under the rules of a currency board, it would have had to cut its M2 money supply by about half. It lost a third of its gross reserves. Either of these would have been like the U.S. depression in terms of the monetary squeeze. It would have forced an enormous squeeze of private sector credit in order to match that monetary squeeze. So, what happened in Argentina? They survived by the skin of their teeth by violating two key currency board features.

There was a moment before these interventions when the heads of the four largest banks in Argentina met with [then Finance Minister] Domingo Cavallo and Roque Fernandez, who was then president of the Central Bank, and they said, "Look, if things go on like this, we won't last two weeks. So you not only have to move, you've got to move with incredible speed in order that the banks will survive." What did they do? Cavallo changed the reserve requirements of commercial banks, so that with a reduced monetary base, they could keep the money supply at over 90 percent of what it had been. So money supply hardly declined while the monetary base had a huge cut.

The second thing was something that I keep referring to as a sly provision that Cavallo stuck in the original currency board law. This condition required that a certain fraction of these so-called solid green dollars, that backed the high powered money of Argentina, could be Argentine Government Bonds denominated in dollars. They weren't real dollars at all. In this crisis, they used that facility to its maximum. In fact, they extended that facility, so they used it to more than the maximum that had been written into the original law. I believe that these two super violations of currency board principles were vital to Argentina's survival of the tequila crisis. It is important to have these facts on the table as this discussion goes on.

ROBERT MUNDELL: The correction in Argentina which Al Harberger discussed was of an enormous proportion. The change in reserves vastly exceeded the losses in Mexico. What was the ratio between the amount of funds needed to bail out Mexico and the amount of funds needed from the IMF to maintain the stability in Argentina?

AL HARBERGER: The amount of IMF intervention in Argentina was not important. The thing that was important in Argentina was the change of its internal monetary machinery. I believe that the Argentine crisis would have been intensely worse had it not been for the Mexican bailout. And while I don't truly believe in bailing out U.S. investors or U.S. banks or any other people in these circumstances, I do believe that if you have two friends who are running tailor shops and they're each in equally bad financial shape, but one of them is able to secure a loan to avoid bankruptcy, it has an impact on the other tailor.

I don't think we should be judgmental about this. It's perfectly within the right of Mexico to request a loan and then pay it back. Since Mexico did pay their loan back, people shouldn't be complaining so much *ex post*. That's my rough take on the Mexican bailout. When people worry about the Mexican bailout, they never seem to be worrying about it in its own terms and for its own sake. They say it gave signals to other countries that they could do irresponsible things and expect international bailouts. Personally, I am agnostic about bailouts, because I don't know enough about the individual cases. I've been to Indonesia a few times and the situation there is a complicated mess. I don't think Indonesia would have avoided their economic problems if Mexico and Argentina had never been bailed out.

ROBERT MUNDELL: The bottom line is that the bailout of Mexico, which by your analysis was due to a smaller shock than the Argentine crisis, was about 50 billion dollars, whereas the bailout of Argentina was a two- or three-billion dollar standby loan from the IMF. This is a tiny amount. My point is that the mechanism in Argentina permitted them to weather the crisis more effectively than Mexico.

Al Harberger said that one of the reasons Argentina survived the crisis is that they temporarily relaxed some of the requirements of the currency board. But, the fact that they kept in place a mechanism of adjustment was vital to their ability to deal with the crisis with a vastly smaller bailout than was required in Mexico. What's more, although we're not talking about Asia, the recent crisis in Indonesia and East Asia also indicates that when a country has a mechanism of adjustment for the balance of payments and people understand the mechanism, then dealing with crises is vastly cheaper for the international community and better for the country than if they don't have such a mechanism. The big difference between the Mexican crisis and Argentina's shock was that Argentina had a mechanism of adjustment that people knew about. Granted, this necessitated a temporary relaxation of the currency board rules, but it was much cheaper to correct, because people understood the mechanism of adjustment.

FAUSTO ALZATI: I think we have a profound problem with the language here. When you talk about the Mexican bailout, you talk about bailing out Mexico. In fact, what was bailed out was not Mexico. What was bailed out was a regime that does not necessarily benefit the Mexican people. The cost of the bailout was not just 50 billion dollars. To that, you have to add the 90 billion dollars of new government debt, and the banking system bailout in Mexico, which is a burden on the next three or four generations of Mexicans. We have to pay those debts as well, and we don't even get a stable financial system as a result.

The moral hazard problem that Bob Bartley raised is a very important issue. A stable world economy is unlikely if international financial institutions and rules of behavior are focused on short-term bailouts and encourage fiscal irresponsibility. Bailouts permit the postponement of structural reforms. Bailouts are nice for the bankers, but in the end the people pay. We have had insufficient growth in Mexico and I'm really surprised when somebody says that the Mexican economy is doing well. It's doing well on whose terms? It's doing well for those who are benefiting from government policies. But it's not doing well for the millions of Mexicans who are not able to find a well-paid job because economic growth rates have been unable to match the growth rate of the labor force for the last 20 years. In fact, growth in Mexico has seldom kept pace with labor growth in the last hundred years. Moving from a low growth and low employment creation economy to a high growth economy requires profound structural reforms. Structural reforms, in turn, require strong rules in the international economy to keep governments from pursuing irresponsible fiscal policies and inflationary monetary policies. Bailing out politicians is not the solution.

ROBERT BARTLEY: The big difference between the Argentine response to the crisis and the Mexican response in 1994 and 1995 was that the Argentines maintained the exchange rate. The way I look at the world, the only thing worth focusing on is dollar GNP, dollar wage levels and so on. In Argentina they came through the crisis without cutting wages. In fact, they had their business classes pony up to bail themselves out by the bond issue Al Harberger mentioned. This is a very healthy thing. In the Mexican case, as is always the case with devaluations, the immediate effect was to cut wage levels in half in Mexico in world purchasing power terms. This is not an advantage to Mexico, although it is an advantage to the export industries, because devaluations every few years keep domestic wages down. Though this reduces the cost of exporting to the world market, providing a temporary advantage, eventually inflation starts to equilibrate prices. Then the advantage is lost and Mexico has to devalue again in order to cut wages again. A country is better off defending the exchange rate if possible, rather than devaluing. Even in nominal terms, the Argentine interest rate spike was much less than the Mexican one. The Argentine recession was much shallower, even in domestic terms, so it seems to me that the Argentine response was much better for the people of Argentina than the Mexican response was for the people of Mexico.

ROBERT SOLOMON: It seems to me that what Bob Mundell and Bob Bartley are ignoring is the fact that Mexico had a serious domestic crisis, a balance of payments problem and an overvalued currency. It had to deal with that while Argentina only suffered from the tequila effect. This is an enormous difference.

ROBERT BARTLEY: Everyone tells me the Argentine peso was enormously overvalued for years, along with the Hong Kong dollar.

ROBERTO SALINAS: Bob Bartley's last remark that the justification following the exchange rate adjustment, at least from some quarters of the Mexican government, in 1995 and in 1996, is that this would enhance the competitiveness of the external sector. That strategy served a useful purpose at one time, although it backfired during 1996 and 1997, as recovery and economic reactivation occurred very quickly. This was due in good part to the structural reforms that were undertaken because of NAFTA. This included trade liberalization and a serious effort on the part of the administration of President Ernesto Zedillo to stimulate the economy. This was followed by a period of capital inflows which led to the peso appreciation – something very similar to what we're experiencing in Mexico in 1999, following the adjustments in 1998, and yet the great concern is the exchange rate. The debate is that the peso is appreciating too strongly. It's not how to avoid these traumatic devaluations. The history of devaluations is centered on the loss of competitiveness in the external sector due to exchange rate appreciation.

There seems to be a consensus among specialists in emerging markets that there are three things that you can't combine when you talk about monetary and exchange rate regimes: independent monetary policy, capital mobility (freedom from capital controls), and pegged exchange rates. Those three are dangerous monetary chemistry. We keep hearing that due to high capital mobility worldwide, there are only two alternatives: either a move towards a truly fixed rate – dollarization, a currency board, or monetary union, or a move towards what some specialists are calling flexible targeting or a completely flexible exchange rate regime. The question to the group is whether this polar distinction reflects a change in the way we view exchange rate regimes, either in Latin America or other emerging markets? More importantly, what would be the requirements of a working flexible exchange rate and the requirements of a working totally fixed rate? Al Harberger mentioned that countries should be willing to violate the requirements of a currency board when it is necessary.

JEFFREY FRANKEL: I've just written down ten major emerging markets ranged by order from the exchange rate regime that they had as of early 1997. Maybe there's some subjectivity here, but from most rigid currency board commitment to freest, most flexible. The list is: Hong Kong, Argentina, Brazil, Taiwan, Thailand, Russia, Indonesia, Korea, Singapore and Mexico on the more flexible end. There could be some quibbles, but thinking about how well these countries came through the East Asia crisis may teach us something. The first thing that's striking is that there is no simple pattern. It's not the case that the firm fixers came through better than the others – Hong Kong and Argentina both had severe recessions. It's also not the case as a generalization that the floaters did better than the others. It's not even the case that the ones in the corners did better than the others – this is the new conventional wisdom that says you have to be in the corners [either fixed rates or floating rates]. It's not the case that the ones with the best fundamentals did better. Argentina has better fundamentals than Brazil. Hong Kong has better fundamentals than some of its Asian neighbors. It's not the case that the ones with IMF programs did better or worse.

One generalization that does seem to hold is that an intermediate regime, a commitment to some kind of exchange rate target going into the crisis that was maintained for a long time and then abandoned after reserves ran out did very badly. I think that is the kernel of truth to the corners hypothesis. It's wrong to think that all countries should be in the corners of firm fixing or free floating all the time. I think it is right that when you're under pressure, when there is a crisis, you do have a choice to make between the really firm institutional commitment of a currency board or dollarization on the one side, versus getting out earlier rather than later. An exit strategy.

ROBERT MUNDELL: The issue is not, I keep saying, fixed versus flexible exchange rates, any more than it's fixed versus flexible price levels or fixed versus flexible money supplies. It's a question of how a country is going to achieve monetary stability. To do this, it has to have an anchor of stability. It could be the money supply, it could be the price level, it could be the exchange rate – these are three alternatives – or it could be a weighted average of three of them that somehow kept a combination of those flexible. The countries or regions that weathered the Asian crisis – Singapore, Hong Kong, Argentina, China, Taiwan and Japan – had two characteristics in common: a target for monetary policy and large foreign exchange reserves. Singapore stabilized a currency basket. Hong Kong had a fixed exchange rate through a currency board system. Argentina has a currency board system.

Taiwan stabilized a commodity basket as did Japan. Those countries survived without drastic inflation or exchange rate instability because they all had a target for monetary policy and an instrument for adjustment, as well as large foreign exchange reserves and relatively low debt ratios, which meant they were able to keep their policy independence and not be forced into the IMF [reforms].

For most small countries, which are near a large and stable neighbor, I believe it's much easier to achieve price stability by fixing the exchange rate. The euro and the dollar make obvious candidates as anchors. That is the best way of operating. It's better because you don't need much monetary sophistication. As somebody said, a monkey can run a currency board system. You don't need a PhD from Stanford or Yale or Harvard! All one has to do is to have an automatic rule and then they get the monetary policy and the inflation rate of the country they're fixing to. For example, the inflation rate in Panama [which has used the U.S. dollar as its paper currency since 1904] is essentially the same as the inflation rate in the United States. In general, a small country that fixes its currency to a large anchor currency area will get the inflation rate of the anchor currency area. As long as there is absolute commitment to the system little or no monetary expertise or discretionary judgment is required.

Al Harberger, I believe, has not given sufficient weight to a factor that Bob Bartley has brought out, that the Argentine experiment was imperfect not because they had a currency board system but because they had to relax the requirements of the currency board, fudging, to a certain extent, the discipline. Having said that, however, the fact that Argentina needed at most less than 10 percent of the money needed by Mexico and the Asian countries has to be registered as a strong argument in favor of the Argentinian approach. Moreover, Argentina not only borrowed a fraction of the amount Mexico borrowed, but in the process kept their monetary stability, whereas Mexico got a resumption of its inflation rate. Both countries had low inflation rates up to the 1995 crisis, but in 1995, Argentina's inflation was 3.4 percent, whereas Mexico's was 35 percent. In 1996, Argentina's was 0.2, Mexico's was 34.4; and so on. So despite the tens of billions of dollars that Mexico could draw on, they gave up their monetary stability and have not to this day recovered it. By contrast, Argentina borrowed little and kept their monetary stability.

AL HARBERGER: There is an interesting feature of debt crises. I'll talk about them in the Randall Hinshaw Memorial Lecture [Chapter 6], but the Latin American debt crisis of the 1980s, on the whole, took the countries more than a decade to get back to the levels of real GDP of 1980 or 1981 – a tremendous loss. The Mexican crisis of 1994–95 is a 'V', the economy bounced right back up again. It's unique in the history of such crises to see such a rapid bounce back. That's a big plus for Mexico. Now what about Argentina? Argentina has not had unemployment under 12 percent since the 1980s. It went up to 18 percent in the wake of the tequila crisis, it drifted down to 12, and now with the Russian and Brazilian crises, it's up to 16 again. Now, the Argentine economy is trying to reduce real wages by internal deflation. Devaluation is a way of reducing real wages quickly and making the economy competitive again. That's exactly what happened in Mexico.

In my analysis, I try to think about the measurable cost to the economy. The measurable cost is the best way we can evaluate the impact of crises on standards of living. I am in favor of a fixed exchange rate in Argentina. Do you know why? Because if Argentina were to devalue a small percentage, most Argentine economists agree that their history of crises is such that people would almost totally avoid holding Argentine pesos. They cannot afford to devalue for that reason. They are almost unique among cusp countries in having this sort of domestic tension, like somebody who has been through several nervous breakdowns and has to be in complete calm, because another little shock is going to produce another nervous breakdown. That is the sense that one has in Argentina if there was going to be a change in the parity. That is the reason everybody favors keeping the parity.

Is keeping the parity something you would do if Argentina had the history of Chile? I don't think so. In this case, Argentina could have devalued long ago. They would have been much better off by avoiding most of their current unemployment if they could devalue.

CHRISTOPHER JOHNSON: I'd like to generalize the argument a bit. There was a suggestion, I think, coming from Argentina, I believe from Mr. Cavallo, that a number of Latin American countries should dollarize their currencies. They should become part of a monetary union with the United States. I think [U.S. Treasury Secretary] Larry Summers jumped backwards several feet when he heard the idea, and he poured a great deal of cold water on it for reasons which one can understand. For example, it would mean that the U.S. could be called upon to, in effect, expand the money supply of these countries without having any political control over them. In addition, the countries concerned would have found that they had no voice in Washington. Even if they'd been represented on a kind of a monetary union board with the Federal Reserve, on almost any set of criteria the Fed would have had an overwhelming majority of votes. So on both those counts, it didn't seem like an idea that was going to get off the ground. But, it's obviously one way of cutting the Gordian knot, just like Panama. I'd like to know what the group thinks of dollarization in Latin America. Is it a serious contender now or in the future?

ABEL BELTRAN: I believe that we should make a distinction between the desirability of stability – monetary stability, price stability, and exchange rate stability – and the implementation and pace to reach that goal. I see only two ways of doing it: the accelerated program (or the cold turkey, as it is called sometimes), or the stepwise program. Besides economic considerations, we should also add the facts on the political and the social systems. Some of these stability problems, when implemented very quickly, can cause severe economic disruptions. But, if it is done in six months, disruptions are reduced. I have the sense that in some cases, the patient has to take the program in small steps, especially if his political and social systems are weak.

MICHAEL CONNOLLY: Al Harberger pointed out the reduction in reserve requirements and the inclusion of the bomex dollar denominated bonds as exceptions to the currency board rules in Argentina following the tequila crisis. But there was one measure that was maintained in the convertibility law of 1991, and this is that the central bank ties its hands and cannot extend credit to the private banks. This is an anti-bailout provision. In other words, under a currency board, the central bank cannot play the role of lender of last resort. Indeed, they did not do this during that crisis. Instead, as Bob Mundell alluded to, they arranged for a private line of credit of 12 billion dollars to the commercial banks in Argentina that were suffering a liquidity crisis. Once this line of credit was opened, it was never drawn upon and it sustained the commercial banking system, knowing that reserves were there and could be drawn upon. The preservation of this limitation on the central bank was crucial during the tequila crisis.

If my recollection is correct, when reserves fell around 50 percent, high-powered base money fell approximately 33 percent, and M1 contracted 16 percent. They were following the rules of the game of the currency board and they didn't relax reserve requirements sufficiently to avoid the decline in the money supply. This contrasts with the Mexican crisis where there was a full sterilization. If Argentina had reduced the reserve requirements sufficiently, or had engaged in open market operations and bailouts, they would have been able to prevent the money supply from falling. But this is not permitted in a currency board. By and large the Argentines obeyed the rules of the currency board system with these kinds of accounting changes that they used in order to smooth out the effects of the shock.

ROBERT BARTLEY: I'd like to argue with Bob Mundell on one narrow, but I think very important point, which is whether or not a zero inflation rate is appropriate for a developing country, or even the same inflation rate as the United States. This question was brought rather forcefully to my attention ten years ago by the observation that the peak inflation in Hong Kong was about twice as great as the inflation in the United States, even though the Hong Kong dollar was linked to the United States and indeed over this period had actually appreciated slightly. This suggests that a country can have some additional inflation even with currency stability. I asked John Greenwood to write an article about it for me and he did. He reminded me that Hong Kong does not allow immigration. This means that they have a fixed pool of labor, and act as the primary financial center for China. As a result, wage rates in Hong Kong are being arbitraged to wage rates of other international financial centers, and in Hong Kong this raises the inflation rate as measured by the consumer price index. This situation represents the population of the country in question getting rich. If a country never has greater inflation than in the United States, it almost certainly means that the living standards of citizens are not gaining on the United States. Probably 15 percent in Mexico is too much; they're not getting rich that fast. But on the other hand, I think Mexico might have made a mistake in 1993 in pressing inflation down too far.

ROBERTO SALINAS: I think it's useful to think of countries in Latin America that are going the route of flexible exchange rate targeting, like Brazil and Mexico, and those that are sticking to a fixed exchange rate. I think it is true that any change in the regime of Argentina right now would be disastrous. Equivalently, it's a great challenge to come up with a successful exit strategy from a currency board. Should flexible targeting schemes, such as Mexico and Brazil, include rules to achieve a certain inflation rate by a certain period of time? If not on an annual basis, perhaps a three- to five-year period? We're beginning to see signals of this in Mexico, and there's a more aggressive move in Brazil to shift to a specific target. I think that for the purposes of this discussion, it would be interesting also to address the requirements of a successful floating regime. Herb Grubel brought up the interesting idea that if we use flexibility as a shock absorber, that that may act as a disincentive to undertake structural adjustments in the economy that are required to achieve high rates of output growth that places like Mexico so desperately need.

I've long questioned whether a floating regime is consistent with an aggressive policy of accumulation of reserves, and if interventions are not taking place in order to maintain the exchange rate, but actually to acquire reserves. An interesting consideration is a recent structural reform that was proposed by [Mexico President Ernesto] Zedillo to shift full control of exchange rate policy over to the Bank of Mexico. I remember a conversation about a year and a half ago with Bob Bartley, who noted that this is just a cosmetic change under a floating exchange rate since, by definition, the exchange rate is a function of monetary policy. However, I've always thought that this was a very significant move, because it went beyond the mechanics; it tried to incorporate psychology. The message of exchange rate autonomy was a signal that Mexico is divorcing exchange rate policy from political considerations. For Mexico, that seemed to be one of the institutional requirements of a successful float. I give that as an example of the ancillary issues arising when considering monetary stability.

ROBERT MUNDELL: I have three comments to make. The first regards Al Harberger's take on the Argentine case. Argentine unemployment has increased and is quite high, as high as 18 percent at one point, but more like 15 percent now. This is certainly a problem. But, it would be a mistake to think that unemployment is solvable by changes in the exchange rate or by changes in monetary policy. Inflation does not necessarily affect unemployment. I'm not saying that there are not cases where it does, just that it isn't always clear. This morning, Al said that since 1994, Argentina has had an overvalued real exchange rate. He might be right. But I would like some evidence. One indication of an overvalued real exchange rate is completely stagnating export markets. Argentina's exports have doubled from 1992 to 1998. The United States, which had a booming economy, increased exports at most 40 percent during the same period. This suggests to me that Argentina does not have an overvalued real exchange rate. Even if Argentina has, by Al's criterion, an overvalued exchange rate, it doesn't mean that devaluation would be the solution. Indeed, he himself pointed out that devaluation, or changing the peg, would be disastrous in Argentina.

What is the problem in Argentina? The first obvious problem is that the country has been mismanaged economically for 80 years. For a good part of that time Argentina was also mismanaged politically. Remember that in 1914, Argentina had per capita income equal to Canada's. Through economic and political mismanagement, it's become a country that's poorer than Portugal, poorer than Greece, with a per capita income in the neighborhood of $8,000, which is a third of the European level in a country with a European population. A specific problem in Argentina is its tax system. This is a tax system with a 30 percent tax on income, and social security taxes that are another 30 percent. This is a European level of taxation. Some European countries have a problem with marginal tax rates of 90 percent on labor, and as a result they have high unemployment rates, some over 12 percent. Argentina's got that problem in spades, because Argentina has imported the European type of social democracy and tax system, but has a per capita income that's a third of the European level. As a result, Argentina's tax system has a substantial impact on the economy. Argentina also has huge wealth taxes in order to pander to leftist sentiments in the electorate. They seem to think that if you put 90 percent taxes on capital, you will collect a lot of money from the rich. But that is not the case. The rich stay across the river in Montevideo [Uruguay] where there are no income or wealth taxes and then make investments from there in Argentina. Argentina needs a complete supply-side tax revolution, including a reform of the regulatory systems. I believe that some part of the Argentine problem is cyclical, and part may be due to overshooting from the successful stabilization of the 1990s. Another aspect might be an overvalued real exchange rate. But a substantial part of Argentina's problems stem from a very bad tax and regulatory system. This is a political problem and it won't be easy to solve.

Bob Bartley mentioned the issue of inflation in Hong Kong. The Hong Kong exchange rate is very interesting for economists trying to understand the relationship between monetary stability and economic growth. Hong Kong fixed the dollar exchange rate under the direction of John Greenwood in 1983. Since that time, the exchange rate's been held fixed. The average inflation rate in Hong Kong for several years was several percentage points higher than the average inflation rate in the United States, so it's tempting for people who look at these things to conclude that Hong Kong has an overvalued real exchange rate. Yet this is superficial reasoning. Over the long-run, one has to look at other factors that affect the real exchange rate. If you compare Japan and Hong Kong in 1993, you see great similarities between these two remarkable economies, one of which is 20 times bigger than the other. Both economies experienced real appreciation of their currencies, and for the same reason. In both countries the causal factor was rapid productivity growth in the traded-(export and import) goods industries. As theory tells us, re-establishment of equilibrium requires an exchange rate appreciation. In the case of Japan, with a floating exchange rate and tight monetary policy, the real appreciation was manifested in nominal appreciation of the yen. Remember the days when the imputed value of the Emperor's palace grounds was larger than all the land in Canada, and the value of all the land in Japan was higher than all the land in the United States?

A similar phenomenon was at work in Hong Kong. In the 1980s Hong Kong was becoming the entrepôt economy, the intermediary for trade between China and Taiwan, and the staging point and headquarters for foreign investment in China, all of which meant soaring productivity in the traded goods industries and a required real appreciation. Given the fixed nominal exchange rate, real appreciation could only be realized with a rising price level and therefore a higher inflation rate. The higher inflation rate in Hong Kong than in the United States was the only means of achieving an equilibrium.

It would be a mistake, however, to conclude from Hong Kong's experience that developing countries should have higher inflation rates than in the United States – or even *positive* inflation rates. If productivity growth is concentrated in the domestic goods industries, the inflation rate in the fixing country would have to be lower than that in the United States in order to achieve the needed real depreciation. Nor should productivity growth in the United States be neglected. In recent years U.S. productivity growth has soared and because this is "new-economy" related, with a concentration in the traded-goods sectors, the real dollar rate may have to appreciate against countries with slower productivity growth in those industries, imposing in effect deflation on those countries.

My third remark addresses Roberto Salinas's comments. He said that monetary policy should be removed from political considerations. I applaud that enormously. It's one of my main reasons for strongly supporting the euro in Europe; it takes monetary policy completely out of the hands of the Bank of Italy, the Bank of Spain and the Bank of Greece and other central banks with weak records that manipulate monetary policy for political reasons. The same political manipulations have occurred in Latin America. The only way to avoid this is through some type of an automatic system. The only policies independent of political considerations are a currency board system or a monetary union. Experience has shown that inflation targeting and monetary targeting are "soft" commitments that are easily bent with the political wind. So I fully applaud Roberto's plea to take monetary policy out of politics.

ROBERT SOLOMON: Bob Mundell claims that a central bank can only maintain monetary stability through some automatic mechanism. Yet, the Federal Reserve has maintained price stability in the United States without political interference and without some automatic mechanism. The Bundesbank has done the same in Germany. The Bank of France has done that in France in recent years. You do not need an automatic system for monetary stability.

ROBERT MUNDELL: I think you could only make those statements in the context of a very short historical horizon. To say that the Federal Reserve has maintained price stability flies in the face of monetary history. Since the Fed's creation in 1913 the U.S. price level rose more than 1500 percent. Since 1969 it went up more than 400 percent. The 1970s was a disastrous decade from the standpoint of U.S. monetary stability. It is only since the 1980s that the Fed has made a successful commitment to price stability and that is partly by imitating the Bundesbank.

JUDY SHELTON: Roberto Salinas raised an interesting question when he asked if there has been an institutional change when choosing the appropriate exchange rate regime for a country. I would like to take us back to one of the last speeches that Robert Rubin made as U.S. Treasury Secretary, where he outlined his approach to changing the global financial architecture. In that speech, exchange rate regimes played a critical role in global financial stability. He made two noteworthy points. The first was a warning. He said that countries that seek to defend an unsustainable fixed exchange rate should not come looking for bailout money to beef up their reserves. The recent evidence suggests that this is a losing game. I think most people agree with that.

Secretary Rubin also said something I found disturbing. He stated that it's up to each country to decide the type of monetary policy that is in their own best interests, whether it's floating, or fixed, or some kind of union. This "do your own thing" approach, sidesteps responsibility for any U.S. leadership in terms of developing a coherent international monetary system. A free-for-all is not a system. Larry Summers followed the same theme in his dollarization testimony last April. He said that before any country considers dollarization, they should consider what they're sacrificing – independent monetary policy. He further suggested that an independent monetary policy is a great boon to an economy, something a country should not give up. But in fact, what does an independent monetary policy deliver for a country? Certainly not lower interest rates. Countries with floating exchange rates have generally had to pay higher interest rates, especially in times of stress in the global financial situation, because they have to reassure foreign investors that they won't lose money in the event the currency depreciates. There is a fundamental problem where one country chooses a system, like a currency board in Argentina, and its most important neighbor and chief trading partner [Brazil] floats its exchange rate. You cannot have an exchange rate regime in isolation in a global economy. The goal is to integrate economies to capture comparative advantage. I believe we need to develop an approach where all countries in a global economy play by the same rules. I do not think it's liberating to tell countries to do whatever they think makes sense in isolation.

FAUSTO ALZATI: I want to follow up on Judy Shelton's comment. Argentina's GDP per capita was 75 percent of the U.S. in 1895, and it fell to less than 30 percent of the U.S. by 1994. Mexico went from 20 percent to less than 7 percent in the same period. Conversely, Japan went from 19 percent to nearly 100 percent over the same period, so there is a lesson to be learned.

The point I want to make, though, concerns what Abel Beltran said regarding a stepwise exchange rate liberalization or going cold turkey and achieving immediate stability. I have some experience with this in Mexico, and the stepwise approach doesn't work. It's like quitting smoking – you quit smoking cold turkey or don't quit at all. Advocates of gradualism signal that they don't want to change, because when a country gradually approaches stability, inevitably something happens to interrupt the process, and you are again back in an unstable environment. Latin American countries, and Mexico in particular, have experience with stabilization policies. In Mexico, we have been trying to stabilize with IMF advice at least since 1976 and we haven't achieved stability yet. So, we need less stabilization and more stability. I would suggest we learn the New Zealand lesson, do it at once, do it well, and stop stabilizing, just get stability. Otherwise, you get what's happening now in Argentina. They failed to dollarize, and now the populist candidate is likely to win the presidential election, and he may shut down the currency board. If that happens, it may take another 40 years to get another Menem elected as president with another Cavallo as finance minister and try the experiment again.

JEFF FRANKEL: A few comments on dollarization. I agree with some aspects of what Judy Shelton said, but in some ways disagree. The theoretical benefit of having your own currency, namely the ability to pursue an independent monetary policy has proven not that useful for many, perhaps most, emerging market countries. Alternatively, for countries that have dollarized, the argument is supposed to be that their interest rates are dictated by the United States, and this may not be appropriate to local circumstances. But most countries in Latin America are in a worse situation than that. When there's a contagious crisis in the world, their interest rates shoot up. When the Fed raises interest rates, and I've actually done a formal test of this, it's true that interest rates in the currency board countries go up one for one, for example in Hong Kong and Argentina. They go up a little bit less than one for one in Panama. But they go up much more in other countries in Latin America that are weakly linked to the dollar. Indeed, when the U.S. Federal Reserve raises the Fed funds rate by one basis point [0.01 of a percent], interest rates in Argentina tend to go up one basis point. But in Mexico and Brazil, on average, interest rates rise by several basis points. So that suggests that by dollarizing there's nothing to lose, and a substantial gain with lower and less volatile interest rates.

A couple more points. We live in a world where each country gets to choose its own monetary regime. I disagree with the suggestion that the United States should be the planner for the world monetary system. These things are decided at the national level, and if Brazil is not ready for further links to the dollar, and I think they're not, that's a fact that Argentina and other countries have to accept.

The conditions under which countries should dollarize depend on the circumstances of the country in question. The same exchange rate regime is not right for all countries. We've discussed some of the traditional criteria coming out of the optimum currency area literature, for example being a small, open economy with sufficient labor mobility, is relevant for dollarization. I was at a conference in Panama two months ago sponsored by the Inter-American Development Bank, and several Central American countries were pretty good candidates for dollarization by such criteria as integration with the U.S. economy and labor mobility. Among Central American countries, El

Salvador seemed to be the leading candidate for dollarization. I saw an article in the *Financial Times* a week ago that reported that the dollar is now legal tender in El Salvador alongside the local currency. Besides the traditional optimum currency area criteria, which have a lot to do with trade and growth, we've learned that we need new criteria in a world of high capital mobility and very skeptical investors. These criteria have to do with policy credibility. Other criteria have to do with initial conditions, for example, the level of foreign currency reserves. A country cannot institute a currency board or dollarize if they don't have sufficient reserves.

When an economy is already highly dollarized, as in Argentina, devaluation doesn't make sense, and they might as well go the rest of the way towards full dollarization. I do think the rule of law is important in these countries. A currency board is a policy to peg the local currency to the dollar. This peg is not just a matter of policy, but it's written into law, and it also says that there's full monetary backing to maintain the peg. This allows the monetary approach to the balance of payments to work. But that first criterion, writing the peg into the law, is not worth much in a country where the head of state can change the law anytime he wants to, or doesn't pay much attention to the law. I have in mind Suharto's Indonesia.

By the way, Bob Mundell said last night that when Bill Clinton and [German Chancellor Helmut] Kohl and others were putting pressure on Suharto not to put in a currency board, he wasn't sure if these leaders even knew what a currency board is. But in fact, I had explained a currency board to President Clinton in the context of Argentina, and I said that it seemed to be working well in Argentina. But, we thought that because Indonesia did not have the rule of law and was looking for a quick fix, a currency board was not appropriate. Indeed, a currency board requires monetary and fiscal discipline that Indonesia did not appear to have. At best, a currency board would have been a way that the elites could have taken more of their money out of the country. The administration's view was that the Indonesian government was not willing to give up their monetary sovereignty. They think of it like the flag. But increasingly, Latin American countries are looking to the dollar for monetary stability. Why do countries acquire such a desperate need to import monetary stability? Usually it's due either to a history of past hyperinflation, which describes Argentina, or an absence of credible, stable institutions, which describes, for example, the countries of the former Soviet Union, or an unusually high exposure to finicky investors who require an extreme measure of reassurance.

EDUARDO SOJO: Just a brief comment following Fausto's mention of the perils of gradualism. The alternative to gradualism is to undertake all reforms at once. Mexico did not do this. It opened the trade sector, but forgot about fiscal reform. Mexico also did not undertake reform in the labor market, nor in the financial sector, or the public sector, or in education. This explains some of the differences between Argentina, Chile and Mexico. Mexico is behind the others in these structural reforms. Any exchange rate will not be sustainable in Mexico unless structural reforms occur, because stability without growth in Mexico will not be socially sustainable. So for any exchange rate regime, structural reforms must be undertaken.

AUDIENCE QUESTION (Aldo Flores, Professor of Political Science at Claremont Graduate University):   As a political scientist, I would like to point out that when Professor Mundell says that a monkey can run a currency board, we should remember that it takes a political act to put in a monkey to run a currency board. An analysis of the political process should be considered in order to determine which type of monetary regime is feasible. For example, not only did Argentina have a currency board, it had Menem as president. He gave credibility to the sustainability of the board. It took [President François] Mitterrand to bring the Socialists in France closer to this way of thinking. It took a pact in Spain to solidify democracy there, so I think that we need to think about the political prerequisites for these economic proposals.

ARMANDO BAQUIERO: A few remarks about Mexico. If we're going to make comparisons, we better make them on the basis of the same numbers. It was mentioned that Mexico's bailout cost 50 billion dollars. That's what the press said, but it was far lower than that. There were a lot of resources that were never used. If we're going to compare that to costs in Argentina, then we have to consider all the costs that Argentina had. In addition to International Monetary Fund money, they had direct money from lines of credit from commercial banks. There is also the cost of wiping out half of its banking system. So if we're going to put the costs together, let's make a list.

Secondly, we must look at the last three or four years and compare Mexico's inflation and Argentina's inflation, and Mexico's growth and Argentina's growth. If you eliminate the first two years in which Argentine growth was very high and look at the last three or four years, real growth has been about the same, even though inflation is much higher in Mexico than it is in Argentina. One would expect that to bring inflation down to zero, growth would have been higher. Nevertheless, Argentina is in a better position now as we look into the future. The growth of exports in Mexico, ignoring oil exports, has been far greater than in Argentina. It's difficult to determine if Mexican exports grew more because we have a floating exchange rate, or because we're more open and there was a boom in the U.S. economy.

5. Monetary policy in the NAFTA area and the possibility of monetary union

Introduced by

Herbert Grubel

I'm going to start by talking about Canada, but in most of my discussion, substituting "Mexico" for "Canada" does not invalidate my analysis. Let me suggest that we should have a North American monetary area equivalent to that of Europe. Mechanically we should go about it on January 1, 2004. On that date, the American currency would be changed very simply into the "amero." The only difference will be that on one side it would have the White House or the Lincoln Memorial, but on the other side would be an abstract symbol identifying it as one amero. On that same day in Canada, one would get, for example, for two Canadian dollars, one amero. Canada would have the House of Commons and various other national symbols on one side, but the amero symbols on the other. At the same time, there would be a conversion of all the accounts in the banks to ameros. It would all be very simple in the United States, with the least cost, although in Canada and Mexico the primary changes are simply book entries.

Let me now discuss the advantages which it would accrue to Canada from using the amero. The history of differences in the interest rates between Canada and the United States on long-term Treasury bonds averages 1.17 percentage points. The real interest rate difference is somewhat lower, around one percentage point. The simplest monetary theory predicts that if the currency is the same, interest rates can't differ because currency risk is eliminated. There may still be a liquidity risk, and perhaps some sovereign risk, just like bonds issued by the state of California carry a slightly higher interest rate than U.S. government bonds. Nevertheless, there would be a very close relationship to U.S. rates. That would mean that overnight in Canada, all interest rates would fall by one percentage point. The Canadian federal government debt alone is 600 billion dollars. That would mean, after the maturity structure has worked itself through, that interest payments on the debt would fall by six billion dollars. That's a substantial

savings that can be used to reduce taxation or implement government policies. Add to that all the benefits accruing to the provincial governments
which have their own debts, and all corporate debt service, which is reduced by 1 percent. Of course, this would immediately be capitalized in the
stock market, which would jump as the cost of capital falls. In the long run,
this would produce a deepening of the capital stock, higher productivity,
and tremendous gains in living standards. This would also eliminate somewhere between half and three-quarters of transactions costs now burdening
Canadian currency exchange markets. Plus, we would eliminate all those
economists and students of Bob and mine, who are out there trying to deal
with foreign exchange risk – they wouldn't have to issue forecasts anymore
on the expected Canadian–U.S. dollar exchange rate, and they could actually go and do some productive work!

The Delors Commission surveyed banks and corporations to determine
their attitudes regarding substituting the euro for all other currencies in Europe, and there was strong support for the euro. Remember that one can't get
rid of the foreign exchange departments of banks and corporations altogether,
because you still have exchange dealings with the rest of the world. But since
two-thirds of international trade for Canada is with the United States, a single
currency would produce a significant cost reduction. I call attention to the
fact that new growth theory indicates that the increased specialization from
lower transactions costs is equivalent to a reduction in tariffs, and will therefore increase trade and productivity by a multiple of the savings in transactions
costs. Over the long run this is likely to be very significant.

The big objection raised by almost all economists trained on the post war
macroeconomic textbooks dominated by Paul Samuelson is the issue of monetary sovereignty. I can assure you, having written textbooks on the subject,
that I know the theory and it is not incorrect as far as it goes – the logic is
impeccable. But the other side of the coin is ignored. It is the other side of the
coin that underlies Bob Mundell's original article on optimum currency areas. That is, there are also costs to having national monetary sovereignty and
flexible exchange rates. These are not only a variety of transactions costs, but
may also reflect a lack of confidence in the currency.

Let me give you an example. When I went to Canada in 1972, I received an
income, converted to U.S. dollars, which I discussed with Albert Rees, a
former colleague at the University of Chicago, who was then the provost of
Princeton University. Rees said that at Princeton, only three professors had
higher salaries, and all three had Nobel prizes in the natural sciences. One
month ago, I retired from Simon Fraser University at a full professor's salary
which, in U.S. dollars is less than what a freshly graduating PhD in economics receives in an American university. That's what happened to Canada,
though I can't blame all of it on the exchange rate regime. But let me tell you

how and why it works, and why, absent the amero, the next generation of Canadians will be worse off.

Jeff Frankel summarized the conventional wisdom on the subject by noting that the real prices of natural resources have dropped dramatically in the past eight years. Canada, with its flexible exchange rate, can escape the need to adjust dramatically to this factor causing the exchange rate to depreciate. Now here's the other side of the coin. Once the exchange rate has gone down, it continues on a distinct downward trend relative to the dollar. In 1972 when I went to Canada, one Canadian dollar equaled one U.S. dollar, but now it's worth only 66 cents. Here is the mechanism as I see it: the recent drop in world prices and the depreciation of the Canadian dollar cause all of the industries that deal in U.S. dollars – exportables and import competing industries – to have a sudden increase in profits.

[1974 Nobel Laureate in economics, Friedrich] Hayek wrote in the 1930s that if an industrial sector is in trouble, you don't fix it by depreciating the currency, because you disequilibrate the other industries. How does that manifest itself? In the last five or six years in Canada, the real per capita after-tax income dropped. There was no increase in wages, on average. Do you know what the automobile workers' union just negotiated with Ford Motor Company of Canada? An increase in wages of 5 percent per year for the next three years. And there is no inflation in Canada. Why did Ford give in? Because they have huge profits. Indeed, prices are written in U.S. dollars, and the depreciation of the exchange rate will allow them now to pay these higher wages. But these wages are not justified by increases in real productivity.

The consequence of this will be an increase in the prices of natural resources, and upward pressure on the exchange rate. But I can tell you, having been a Member of Parliament in the Canadian Finance Committee, an increase in the exchange rate will mobilize pressure groups because their profits are falling – profits they already gave away. Therefore, the only solution is to hold constant the exchange rate to the U.S. dollar. This political process explains the downward trend in the exchange rate in my model. Also note that the adjustment of the economy in response to the falling long-run trend in the world prices of commodities has been retarded because of the exchange rate depreciation. The adjustments that would have been needed if the exchange rate had not depreciated don't have to be undertaken. So the pressure on an economy which is suffering from a fall in natural resource prices is reduced.

What about cultural sovereignty? Canada is very strong on that. We heard it all during the debate over NAFTA. The "sucking sound" of jobs going to Mexico had dozens of advocates. Of course, it hasn't happened. The amero doesn't stop the Canadian Foreign Minister, Lloyd Axworthy, who has a PhD in political science from Princeton, from spitting in America's eye by going to Cuba and having a cigar with Castro. The Canadian Minister of Culture can still call all the ministers of culture in the Western Hemisphere to organize a fight against American imperialism. This is not stopped by a common currency.

What is the benefit to the United States? That is the most difficult question. The U.S. would have to allow representatives from Canada and Mexico to have seats on the Board of Governors of the Federal Reserve. Why should the U.S. do this? The chair of the Federal Reserve has said that they are not going to pay any attention to what is happening in Canada when adjusting the interest rate. On the other hand, Bob Mundell has already mentioned to you last night his studies on what will happen to the dollar if the euro takes off and expands to be a world reserve rapidly. There is a lot to be said with respect to that. But let me remind people that a few years ago, who would have ever predicted that the American government would give up some national sovereignty to the United Nations, to UNESCO, to the IMF, to the World Bank, and to NAFTA. I don't know whether the same conditions which made this acceptable to American society still exist, but I wouldn't rule it out. Studying the way in which NAFTA was adopted in Canada, a big push for it came from one aspirant for leadership of the Conservative Party, and then the Fraser Institute, and Mexican institutes, and then American. There was a massive educational effort that produced supporters in the United States.

Let me run through the alternatives to a North American currency area. When it comes to currency boards, Hong Kong has cheated and Argentina has cheated. As long as there is an easy way of cheating, there will be a premium on the Argentine peso. Of course, one can also get out of a monetary agreement, but an international agreement is more difficult to abrogate. Dollarization may have the disadvantage that the public would be unhappy. There is some value to the nation-state to have the symbolism of its own national currency. I think we can compromise on that by having bills with national symbols on one side.

A couple of final points on the problems of transition. A substantial complication is the exchange rate to convert the peso and the Canadian dollar into the amero. These issues are the famous devil in the details. But I don't believe that they're insuperable. Where there's good will, it can be done. Lastly, there is the issue of political support. Let me tell you that in Canada, the reaction when I give talks on this publicly is surprising. I never have more than half of the people saying no, while the other half doesn't understand why Canada hasn't done this years ago. The Canadian Senate has had hearings on the subject, but it is not empowered to introduce legislation on this topic. Nonetheless, there is increasing interest and we will have to see what comes out of it. I hope that ultimately, with the public opinion leaning towards a currency union, politicians will do what the public wants – the right thing as far as I'm concerned.

DISCUSSION

FAUSTO ALZATI: I really think Herb Grubel has something here. I wish we had heard this before. I like the idea as much as anything else that has been said so far, though I may disagree a little bit with the name. I have another name in mind, NACU, which is North American Currency Unit. My first comment is that if Mexico chooses to teach some American history to its children, and we understand who Franklin, Jefferson, and Hamilton were, I don't think Mexico would have a problem with having these three Americans on our currency. The problem is with the other side of the bill. I don't know if Americans would enjoy having Pancho Villa on the other side, or the child heroes killed in the 1847 American invasion of Mexico. We have to think very carefully about that. What Mexico needs is a stable currency. I think in the long run, our heroes will be more pleased if we have a prosperous country with less poverty, even though not all of them appear on the currency.

PAUL ZAK: I have a question for Herb. You didn't address one of the big issues, which is seigniorage [earnings by the U.S. Treasury from inflation]. There seems to be two ways to handle this. One is to actually make a transfer from the U.S. to Canada every year based on the degree of seigniorage. The second is to hold Canadian currency hostage and do a swap.

HERBERT GRUBEL: I have this all worked out. The idea is to please Canadian nationalists by keeping our mints and printing presses for money. We print our own, you see? Through tourism, Canadian-printed money will migrate to the United States, get turned into commercial banks, and then will be shipped back to Canada. Canada will also ship U.S. ameros back to the U.S. So we would have on average, circulation only of our national currencies, and we would get that part of the seigniorage without any difficulty, including any employment and income effects.

CHRISTOPHER JOHNSON: I'd like to acknowledge that the idea of currency union is spreading. I hope that the example of Europe played some part in this excellent proposal by Herbert Grubel. I would make one or two superficial adjustments to it, because the U.S. currency and the Canadian currency are both called the dollar. For goodness sake, why not just call it the dollar, but strike out the words U.S. for the American dollar and Canada for the Canadian dollar.

HERBERT GRUBEL: That was a slip on my part. It is the amero dollar. But, there is still the problem of changing the popular use of "peso" in Mexico, but I'm sure there is a solution to this.

CHRISTOPHER JOHNSON: I was just coming to that. Anybody coming to Mexico for the first time might think that the currency is the dollar but everything costs ten times as much as in America. It's quite a relief to find that the dollar sign [$] actually means pesos. So why not call it the dollar and divide by ten, which is about the current exchange rate. I don't foresee any political objection to calling it the dollar and I don't see why it needs a prefix. There are no competing dollars elsewhere in the world. There are a few silver dollars which still circulate in the Arabian Gulf, but by changing the word from talo, which is an old German coin, to dollar I think we have given it a new world look. Herb's analysis confirms what I have always believed, that the Canadian economy has been disadvantaged by having a permanently higher interest rate than the United States. This is a [devaluation] risk premium on Canadian dollars, which probably does not adequately compensate people for risk. What I would like to know, however, is if we replay history, how much better off Canada would be today if its interest rates had been the same as in the United States? Looking to the future, I can only say that this looks like a good deal for Canada, to lock into the quite low U.S. interest rates. It's an even better deal for Mexico.

ROBERT BARTLEY: I suggest that the Mexican version of the amero should have [Mexican revolutionary hero Emilio] Zapata on it.

ARMANDO BAQUIERO: Herb, what kind of consideration do you assign to differences in institutional frameworks? Canada and the U.S. have similar institutions and legal practices, but this is not the case between Mexico and the two other countries. For example, collateral requirements for loans is one of the problems in the Mexican banking system. Perhaps if you could say something about the need for convergence – the U.S. and Canada are close enough, whereas Mexico is far from them.

ABEL BELTRAN: Three comments. First, do you anticipate a time frame for a North American monetary union? Second, are there some preparatory stages for a country like Mexico, as my friend Mr. Baquiero asked? In particular, as Bob Mundell mentioned yesterday, factor mobility is typically one of the preconditions for monetary union. Finally, please don't use "amero." "Mero" is a fish in Spanish that one doesn't order in fine restaurants in Mexico. Use "ameri," please.

ROBERTO SALINAS: Armando Baquiero's important comment suggests that we need to address the differences in institutional frameworks in our discussion. Three items come to mind: (1) The Mexican property rights regime needs a complete overhaul, starting from articles in the constitution regulating everything from telecommunications, electricity, and other service sectors which are very important to society; (2) corporate governance, which is the way that private sector companies behave as they try to integrate into the international marketplace – the corporate culture in Canada and the U.S. is very similar, but Mexico's is barely beginning to get off the ground; (3) the banking system is riddled with moral hazards – there's a proposal before Congress to change that, but Mexico would need to work very hard on this. Jeff Frankel mentioned the rule of law earlier. Legal harmonization seems to be a very important step in undertaking a currency union. This suggests another point: let's not use these differences as excuses for not undertaking the required reforms. If these changes are needed in order to achieve a common currency, then by all means let's work hard to implement them.

SVEN ARNDT: I've got a comment from the audience, then Bob Mundell and then a final word to our advocate here.

AUDIENCE QUESTION (Lane David from Universidad Ibero Americana):   Dr. Grubel proposed skipping several stages in North America that the European Union took to get to monetary union, and I wonder if it makes any difference to the outcome? I also have a general question to the entire panel: there's been no discussion of any other form of dollarization. I'm not in favor of dollarization personally, but does your silence mean that none of you supports any of the other forms of dollarization?

ROBERT MUNDELL: I have eight questions – sorry about that! – for Herb Grubel, so let me just state them without argument and let him react:

1.   Would the amero, or any of the other propositions such as dollarization in Canada, make it inevitable that Quebec would separate from Canada?
2.   Would a constitutional amendment in the U.S. be required in order to scrap the dollar?
3.   Would the Mexican and Canadian representatives on the Board of Governors just be another inflation lobby?
4.   Would the amero dollar be tarnished in its international usage?
5.   Would the currency union be open to all the countries in the Western Hemisphere, and/or the rest of the world, such as Australia?
6.   Would changes in labor mobility or the degree of tax harmonization require integration in other political or economic systems?

7. Would this proposal increase American power in the world?
8. Which political party in the United States do you think would find currency union acceptable?

HERBERT GRUBEL: First of all, the interest rate difference right now on long-term Treasury bonds in Canada is about a half a point lower than it is in the United States. But then the inflation rate is one and a half percent lower than the U.S. inflation rate. So, if you take the current inflation rate as a proxy for expected inflation, then we still have a difference in the real rate. *Ex post* calculations show that the real interest rate difference is also 1 percent. The political pundits who don't like my proposal, like the Governor of the Bank of Canada, will pooh-pooh my argument for lower interest rates by pointing out that next year Canada will have to have higher interest rates because of this system. I think that argument does not hold. The question on institutions is legitimate. But I look at the other side of the coin. A currency union is a way of accelerating the necessary changes towards a more efficient and freer society. So often politicians have been able in Canada and in Mexico to mess up the world, which puts the economy in trouble. The safety valve is letting the exchange rate depreciate. But if they can't devalue anymore, pressures will be on them to institute reforms. I don't know how fast they will learn that they can't have free rein with policies, and still the unions will insist that they need to have an advantage and the rest of the world can go to hell. Well, eventually it will be Canada that is going to hell when the opportunity to be bailed out by the exchange rate finally disappears. How long that will take, I don't know.

I agree that Europe had difficulty converging federal budget deficits and national inflation rates. In Canada and the U.S. there is no problem. There is some problem in Mexico, so some time is needed to get this convergence, but we can agree on when this is. But I don't believe that these are crucial issues because of the annually compounded changes in productivity that will follow the currency union. Stimulation of the economy will make differences in institutions effectively disappear as a problem. There are problems that re-quire that my proposal be implemented in stages. I have a couple of colleagues in Canada that I should give credit to, [C.D. Howe Institute research fellow] Rick Harris and [John Deutsch Institute Director] Tom Courchene, who have come out with the same idea, but are more concerned about politics than I am. Their proposal is more gradual because political support is presently weak.

Now the questions that Bob raised about Quebec. Quebec, when they had a political campaign for independence, were confronted with the federalists arguing that they would lose the use of the Canadian dollar. The Quebecois were stumped, because this is a very powerful symbol. If Quebec were an independent country, it would have to have a Quebec dollar, but this has less prestige and standing in the world than the Canadian dollar. It turns out that the separatists in Quebec loved my idea, and the idea of Harris and Courchene, because it gets them out of that dilemma. That should not be an argument against doing what's right for Canada as a whole for the next hundred or thousand years. Now whether or not the United States needs a constitutional amendment to form a currency union, I defer to experts like Bob, but I don't think so.

Next, will the Canadian and Mexican representatives to the U.S. Federal Reserve be lobbyists for inflation? I don't think so – certainly not the Canadians. The only benefit I think Canada will have for their couple of votes, is that alliances could possibly be formed between representatives, for example, between Federal Reserve districts in the prairies and Canadian prairie interests. These interests might also coincide with those in the south of the United States. Nevertheless, Americans will always dominate the Federal Reserve Board. And that brings up the most important issue as far as I'm concerned. One must also take into account the monetary history of the United States. During some periods, U.S. monetary policy was worse than other countries. And that's why the central bank for the amero needs a very strong constitution. I know that constitutions are only worth what they're written on and must be backed by the political system. But the prevailing world approach of a conservative monetary policy and price stability is correct. This relieves the central banks of the pressure to maintain full employment and to accommodate the political wishes of parliamentarians.

How about dollar prestige? Well, if the central bank has the kind of constitution that I suggest, then I don't see any reduction in the currency's prestige. In fact, it might rise because of the number of people that hold it, and the aggregate GDP of North America. This would rival the GDP of the eventual euro-zone in Europe. What about adding other countries? That's a delicate question. I think that Central America and the Caribbean might very well want to join if it is a success. I really have not given great thought to other countries. I see the world in currency blocks, and the big currency blocks would be the dollar in North America, the euro and something in Asia. I'm not sure that it would be the Japanese yen. It could be the Chinese yuan. India is also very big. So, the primary currency in Asia is up in the air, but the defining trade regions are likely to form.

Next, the story on labor mobility. I mentioned this morning that without labor mobility, there will be a greater degree of capital mobility. Consider, for example, what would happen if California was an independent country with its own currency and was hit by a large shock. What happens? The rate of labor migration slows and the interest rate rises. Capital flows into California will be high which helps industries adjust to the shock. There is a degree of substitution between labor mobility and capital, so labor mobility is not essential. Currency union is happening in Europe, so we should have a good look at it in North America.

6. Randall Hinshaw Memorial Lecture: Exchange rate policy in Latin America

By

Arnold Harberger

It's a great honor for me to be the first Randall Hinshaw lecturer. Though I didn't know him well, I certainly knew his professional reputation and standing. He was an exemplary professional economist who brought great wisdom and distinction to our profession. In all of his professional work and in all of his dealings with others he really did us proud. And I hope [his wife] Pearl, [son] Robert, and [daughter] Elizabeth find solace and comfort in the fact that he left behind such an outstanding reputation.

I have very little time and a great deal of territory to cover. What I've decided to do is to start with an elementary introduction to real exchange rate economics, and move from there to a series of Latin American experiences which illustrate the breadth, depth and complexity of this subject.

The first thing to note is that it's really a demand and supply story. I'm going to just introduce a little notation here. Let E be the exchange rate, that is, the nominal price of a dollar. If I divide that nominal price of a dollar by some general index like the consumer price index or the GDP deflator, call it P, I'll have a real [inflation adjusted] price of the nominal dollar, E/P. For many purposes, this is not only the simplest real exchange rate, it is the best real exchange rate. The issues that divide people a lot on the real exchange rate is when you say, the nominal dollar is changing in value over a period you're observing. So you need now a different index to turn that nominal dollar into a real dollar. And we could talk for half a course on that subject, but it certainly is not within the confines of this lecture. Note that what I'm calling the real exchange rate here *is* the real exchange rate if all world prices are given.

Now we have a simple demand and supply story as shown in Figure 6.1. The real exchange rate is on the vertical axis and we have two pictures. One is the demand for imports and supply of exports expressed as a function of this real exchange rate. Next, we have the total demand for tradables juxtaposed to the

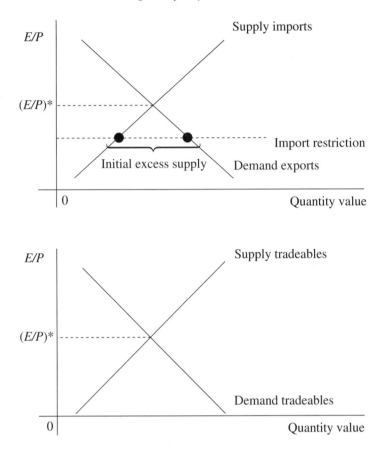

Figure 6.1   Exports, imports, and tradables

total supply of tradables as a function of the real exchange rate. Those of you who are specialists in this area realize that the equilibrium $(E/P)^*$ in those two cases is exactly the same. And not only that, but at every real exchange rate the difference between those two is going to be exactly the same. They are very closely related. We're adding to the imports and exports exactly the same thing on both the supply side and the demand side. You get from that curve to the one below. Another little point that is not well realized by a lot of people – that on the horizontal axis, we are not aggregating tradables in units of quantity. We must aggregate them in units of dollar value. When world prices are known at a point in time, consider the unit of every good to be one dollar's worth of it and then add them up. What I'm doing is taking you through a few classroom exercises in real exchange rate economics.

Now suppose that an import restriction is imposed. This shifts the import demand curve to the left. So, the intersection point is going to be at a lower real exchange rate [the dashed line] and this initially creates excess supply. To close that gap, the equilibrating variable is the real exchange rate. Following this import restriction is an export price boom. When we're measuring quantity in dollars-worth, the supply curve of exports as a function of real exchange rate shifts outward. This is the Dutch disease [a self-fulfilling bubble]. And with that, an excess supply is again created. To equilibrate that excess supply the natural equilibrating variable is the real exchange rate, and so on. The equilibration occurs through capital inflows, which play such a big role here in Latin America. Nevertheless, a capital inflow does not have a quantitatively predictable effect on the real exchange rate. This occurs because when people borrow money, they don't always spend it in a predictable way. Sometimes they're borrowing money to finance construction. Sometimes they're buying generators from Germany, the U.S., or Japan. The borrowed money adds to the supply of foreign exchange, but the use of it to buy the generators adds to the demand – it's as if nothing happened. All that happens is a bunch of generators change hands. If the money is borrowed to dig irrigation ditches, labor is hired. In the process, dollars are converted into pesos or some other local currency, and dollars are dumped on the market. When dollars are dumped on the market, they create an excess supply and the real price of the dollar has to fall. That's the end of the introductory lesson in real exchange rate economics, and I think you'll see the relevance of it as we go along.

My first trip to Latin America took place in 1955. July 1st, 1955 I arrived in Santiago, Chile. I've been observing Latin America steadily since then. In the 1950s, 1960s and early 1970s, the international monetary system was still in the Bretton Woods phase [fixed exchange rates] and people were unhappy and thinking of fixes, which need not necessarily be permanent. The typical story in Latin America was a long period with a fixed exchange rate, but with inflation going on internally, and the exchange rate becoming more and more out of equilibrium to the fixed value. Finally a moment would come when policymakers couldn't maintain the fixed rate anymore and a new start had to be made and so there would be a big devaluation. The nominal exchange rate would be flat, then sharply up, then flat again. The domestic price level would go more or less steadily up, so the real exchange rate was making a sawtooth downward. This happened in Argentina. There were two jumps in the nominal exchange rate, and corresponding big jumps in the real exchange rate. The two big devaluations were about the same size. This was a common occurrence in Argentina, in Chile, in Uruguay and Brazil during that whole period.

One of the things that we learned later was that we were naïve in our way of interpreting exchange rate movements. We thought that countries were generating inflation [by printing money] and that was making prices go up steadily, while the exchange rate stayed flat. But when we learned, with considerable stimulus from Bob Mundell and a few others, about the monetary approach to the balance of payments, we realized that printing all that money shouldn't have made all that inflation, because it should have caused tremendous losses of [foreign currency] reserves. The inflations taking place between the big devaluations would cause reserves to disappear and then the government would implement some restriction. For example, they'd put a surcharge on imports. Chile at one time had people put down 10 000 percent of the value of an imported good, and then held that amount in the central bank without interest while the good was waiting to come to port – terrible restrictions. These were the policies that we're seeking to get rid of at the moment of these big devaluations.

Let's turn to the next lesson. What we learned at that time was that these tremendous sawtooths in the real exchange rate give terrible signals to actual and potential exporters and potential import substitutes. The real exchange rate isn't performing a role in allocating resources, so if a country has inflation, then it should keep the exchange rate moving more or less with inflation so as to avoid the huge ups and downs of the real exchange rate that do not reflect any underlying market conditions. A few countries were pioneers in a type of policy, which in the early days was known as a mini-devaluation policy. The idea was that as inflation continued, there'd be mini-devaluations to try to keep up with it. It wasn't aimed at the real exchange rate, per se, but simply tried to keep the exchange rate moving in something like the same pace as inflation. In the case of Colombia, there are a couple of flat periods in the real exchange rate from 1973 to about 1975 and then again, starting about 1977 and going into the 1980s. This was a fairly successful policy, not only in Colombia, but also in Chile and Brazil, which started it about the same time.

I make a distinction between a mini-devaluation policy, which copes with inflation, and a policy in which the real exchange rate is itself a primary target of economic policy. There were two episodes of that, both of them, interestingly, very successful. One, the Brazilian miracle and the other, the Chilean, I call it mini-miracle, coming out of the debt crisis from 1985 to about 1995. In each case, the authorities said, we're in trouble. We want our economy to grow, move, modernize, liberalize, do all kinds of things, but we need a driving force for this economy, and we want this driving force to be exports. We need to send a signal to our exporters that the market is going to reward them for their effort, and that signal has to be in real terms because they're too used to inflation. The signal is going to be a commitment by the government to try to maintain a high real exchange rate. That is, the price of the dollar is high, so that Latin American exporters will be receiving a good reward for their efforts.

In Brazil, the real exchange rate was just about flat and exports are going up like mad, pulling up real GDP. Note that a country trying to keep the real exchange rate at a certain level can't do it with a nominal instrument. You can't have a real target and think you're going to achieve it by just playing with nominal values. Policymakers need a real instrument to do that. What the Brazilians used was trade liberalization. They started with a heavily restricted economy. The real exchange rate was too low for them – they wanted it to go up, i.e. increase the demand for dollars. They did that by liberalizing imports – making import demand go up. Whenever they accumulated too many [foreign currency] reserves in the process of trying to hold up the exchange rate, they liberalized import controls and they removed the unwanted reserves. They did this in progressive moves and all of us in the profession were applauding. Then the 1973–74 oil price boom hit and suddenly, instead of facing a situation of too many dollars coming in, Brazil faced one of too many dollars going out. At the time many of us thought they ought to change their real exchange rate target to accommodate this oil price shock. Unfortunately, they decided to re-institute some import restrictions in order to bring demand down. So they initially were liberalizing, which was good, and then they de-liberalized, which was bad. But you have to realize that the economy was growing about 9 or 10 percent per annum in real terms, so even in the bad part of this period, the economy was vibrant.

The next country we will examine is Chile. The real exchange rate in Chile, starting around 1986, drifts downward. That's an interesting story that many of you have been talking about today. The world is complicated, and the one assumption that I really don't like is that any small country can borrow as much as they want internationally. This ignores country risk factors. Any finance minister or central bank president from a country with a debt crisis knows this. Indeed, the supply of funds to a developing country is upward sloping with the amount of funds that are coming in. In any case, I really have seen times when that supply curve of funds hardly existed. If a country wants to borrow – think of the Central African Republic trying to borrow a lot of money in the world market – they'll pay LIBOR [London Interbank Offered Rate] plus 6 percent and get a credit limit equal to 20 percent of exports, or something like that. They face a supply curve that starts high and just goes to the roof. On the other hand, you look at a country like Argentina today, it has pretty good access to the world market and interest rates are not too far above international credit market interest rates. If Argentina wants to borrow, the interest rate doesn't go up by much. The supply curve depends on how much the world financial market loves a country. When it loves a country more, the intercept is lower and the slope is flatter. When it loves a country less, the intercept is higher and the slope is steeper. What happened in Chile was that in the beginning of this episode, the intercept was pretty high and the slope was pretty steep, but as the episode moved on the world capital market loved Chile more and the slope got flatter. This is important because it plays into the way that Chile managed to hold up its real exchange rate. Basically, it was what we call "sterilized intervention." But it had a few interesting twists to it.

In the beginning, Chile had been through the debt crisis and there was a lot of Chilean debt floating around in the secondary market in New York selling at a big discount, in a neighborhood of 60 percent of par. The private banks that issued this debt were legally precluded from buying it back in New York. What happened was Chilean entrepreneurs bought the debt and then made deals where the banks retired the debt and split the difference on the 40 percent discount. When the central bank people discovered this lucrative operation, they were scared figuring people are going to want to do this in the billions of dollars worth per month, which would drain their foreign reserves. Chile had capital controls in place all of this time, but they were not very much used; that is, the Chilean government had the power to issue the controls, but in practice they were not very much used. So what they did, and I think this was wonderful, was to auction off the right to bank debt every two weeks. They decided how many reserves they wanted to sell, for example, if they sold 17.5 billion dollars worth of debt they created demand for 17.5 billion dollars by the auction. In the process, the central bank made a huge profit by the auctioning of the right itself, receiving more than half of the 40 percent discount on the debt.

If that could have gone on forever, it would have been paradise. But eventually they repatriated just about all of the debt, and moreover, the discount in New York was reduced as time went on. So when the [President Eduardo] Frei government in Chile came in, much as they would have liked to have followed this same policy, they really couldn't, so they tried to emulate it. They did this by building up assets instead of reducing liability. That's about the same thing. What the central bank did was a sterilized intervention: they issued purchasing-power [inflation-adjusted] bonds in the local market so they had a substantial disincentive to produce inflation. They took the proceeds of those bonds and bought dollars, putting the dollars in New York. Though this worked in a sense, there were two problems that arose. As the Chilean capital market improved when they issued those bonds, the interest rates went up in Chile and so money was attracted back to Chile. For every thousand dollars in New York, maybe 300 would come back to Chile – I call that a reflux. Chile wanted to limit the reflux, which they did by introducing a tax which ultimately amounted to a 3 percent tax on short-term capital flows paid instantaneously, or 30 percent of the interest on deposits in the central bank for a period of a year. The 3 percent is the interest on 30 percent, so it's the rate.

In spite of these policies, the Chileans were unable to maintain the real exchange rate at its original level. Furthermore, in pursuing this operation the central bank incurred significant losses. They were paying more interest on those purchasing-power bonds in Chile than they were getting on the eighteen billion dollars that they ended up accumulating in New York. So you get an interest differential of 3 or 4 percent on 18 billion dollars, that's a lot of money to be losing every year. But in any case, they had a successful economy during this period. They had good growth – export-led growth.

Now we come to some unsuccessful fixed exchange rate countries. Argentina fixed the nominal exchange rate, and the real exchange rate started to deteriorate dramatically because of internal inflation. This happened because policymakers had not gotten control of the fundamentals. They had significant budget deficits, they were printing money like mad and inflation ensued. A more dramatic case was the cruzado plan in Brazil. The nominal exchange rate was held constant, but the real exchange rate plummeted, leading to a huge devaluation. Similarly, Argentina devalued severely three or four times. These are examples where fixing the exchange rate didn't work because they did not understand that it is the real rate that must be fixed.

Next, consider Guatemala, El Salvador and Honduras during 1960 to 1978. The years 1960 to 1978 was paradise in Central America. Just about every Central American country grew at 6 percent per year over that period. It ended with a substantial coffee boom. Very happy time for those economies. They had fixed exchange rates during the entire period, and all three countries were very successful. However, the real exchange rate displayed significant variations no matter which price index one uses. All three countries have patterns that aren't exactly images of each other, but certainly all of them show very significant movements over this period. This is part of lesson number one: things like world price changes in coffee happen, and when they do, the equilibrium real exchange rate will change. If the exchange rate is variable, some of the adjustment will take place through changes in the exchange rate. The other adjustment will be an increase in the internal price level. In my experience, rising prices occur without much of a problem; it's price declines that are difficult.

Next consider Panama. Panama is a wonderful case, because it is the most dollarized economy. Nevertheless, there are movements in the real exchange rate in Panama over a period of about 20 some years, though the range of the real exchange rate is less if you use the U.S. as the world price index. I may just make a small pitch here. I started by using the U.S. wholesale price index as the world price index in my work on real exchange rates, and during the great devaluation of the dollar in real terms under [U.S. President Jimmy] Carter, and the great revaluation of the dollar in real terms [under President Ronald Reagan], the movement of the dollar relative to the other currencies led some of my critics to say, the story you're telling isn't really a Chile story or a Brazil story or a Mexico story, it's really a dollar story. I want to get off the hook on that question. I didn't want to be subject to criticism that my story was just a dollar story, and using the Special Drawing Rights World Price Index [from the International Monetary Fund] is a successful way to deal with relative movements among the major currencies, but it has a lot of idiosyncratic movements of its own. I therefore recommend using the U.S. price index.

The next case is Argentina from 1970 until 1995. During this period there was a tendency for overshooting in the real exchange rate relative to its equilibrium. There are reasons for overshooting in commodity markets, in the stock market, or in anything in which people's passions get involved. I want to make a point here that in terms of the real exchange rate, if the price of the dollar in Mexico needs to rise, there is a gap to fill. In the short-run, there is not going to be a big expansion in the supply of exports. It has never worked that way even in the depths of the debt crisis for all the affected countries in Latin America or in Asia. This doesn't happen because short-run supply elasticities are low. An exporter needs time to get out there and make deals. Overshooting, apart from its psychological explanations, has a fundamental element coming from the supply and demand side of exportables. The exchange rate in Mexico during the same period also overshot its equilibrium, so you can see that Argentina was not alone.

Jamaica and Uruguay have terribly clear exchange rate patterns. In periods of capital inflows, the net resource transfer into the country was going up. That is, a trade deficit means that capital is flowing into a country. When capital flowed into Jamaica and Uruguay, in both cases dollars were abundant so the relative price of the dollar – the exchange rate – fell. But there was a difference between the two cases. The Uruguayan case was what I would call a successful case. The capital coming into the country was capital that wanted to come in. Uruguay was a country that was liberalizing its economic policy and people abroad were interested in bringing money in. Uruguayans who had put their money abroad were interested in bringing it back, and all of this was voluntary movement.

In the case of Jamaica, it was a little bit different. What happened in Jamaica was that [Edward] Seaga had become Prime Minister for the second time. The first time was successful economically due to a boom in bauxite prices and a boom in tourism. So he was awash with dollars and he followed policies I won't even try to describe. [Michael] Manley succeeded him, and during Manley's government two bad things happened. First, prices of bauxite went through the floor, and second, there were riots which scared away the tourists. Because of that, Manley got thrown out of office and Seaga came in and he blithely just wanted to go on. When we asked him how he was going to cope, he said he was going to do exactly like he did the last time. But the conditions of his previous administration were not there. He held the feet of the U.S. and others to the fire by saying that Jamaica is the last bastion against communism in the Caribbean, and so he got foreign aid through blackmail. Unwilling lenders brought in money and then he ignored what the IMF and the U.S. Agency for International Development people recommended to straighten out his economy. Finally they stopped giving him the money and communism didn't take over in the Caribbean, and his economy went to hell. The difference is that in Uruguay, net foreign assets kept going up. What happened in Jamaica is that assets eventually plummeted. When the aid stopped, the Jamaicans had to use up their reserves in order to survive even for a short period of time.

The final topic I will cover is the debt crises in Latin America. The debt crisis of the 1980s is something that I have studied a great deal, and I've looked at it from a lot of different angles in each country. There's no way that within this session I can summarize the whole story for you. What I want to do is discuss how the real exchange rate and the net resource transfer that goes into a country as a fraction of GDP have opposite movements during a crisis. When money comes into a country, the dollar gets cheap. When money goes out of the country, the dollar gets expensive. This happened in Argentina, Chile, Mexico and Peru. The inverse movement occurred in the Asian crisis. Argentina had pressure on the real exchange rate during their debt crisis. The pressure for the real exchange rate to go up is a pressure for the internal price level to go down. This often increases levels of unemployment, which is what happened in Argentina. So with that, I think I will stop and open the floor for discussion.

DISCUSSION

ROBERT MUNDELL: Al, I enjoyed your lecture very much. I wonder if you could tell me if you find a correlation between capital inflows and the real exchange rate in countries that had fixed exchange rates for a long period of time. I would be very interested in what you found for Panama.

AL HARBERGER: That's an interesting question. For countries with fixed exchange rates it's a very complicated story, because the real exchange rate is never a bilateral story, so we can't say between countries – it's one country vis-à-vis the rest of the world. If, for example, one country has a fixed exchange rate and the rest have floating rates, it's a tricky case. I did look into Panama, where there was a very sharp upward movement of the real exchange rate, that is, a sharp devaluation. Within that period, there was one year with a 13 percent decline in GDP. Over a four-year period, GDP fell by 3 or 4 percent. Generally, the real exchange rate tends to devalue when a country is in trouble and tends to appreciate when a country is enjoying prosperity. Certainly, this is Panama's experience. The story in Argentina is that the real exchange rate wants to depreciate. It has wanted to depreciate for some time and the signals to me are extremely clear. We talked a little about exports that had risen during this period. The overwhelming force for devaluation comes from exports – I would hesitate to say all of it, but it might be all of it. Much of this is trade with Brazil. This was within the context of the evolving Mercosur trade area, and it's exactly that set of exports which were the boom element that put Argentina's fixed rate in peril. I have been talking to Argentine economists for the last five years on this subject and they were all worried. If only the exports outside of Mercosur would boom, they would be a lot happier. But that has not happened. Reading the tea leaves, I think the Argentine peso has been trying to undergo a real devaluation.

AUDIENCE QUESTION:　Along the same line, Mexico last year experienced a nominal depreciation of the peso following capital flight as a result of financial turbulence. This year, despite considerable worries at the beginning of the year, curiously enough the dollar exchange rate appreciated somewhat. I don't know if you've done the same exercise for Mexico in 1999, but the results are probably identical. Many analysts believe that the authorities should tinker with the real exchange rate, because they feel that it has appreciated too rapidly. I wonder what your impressions are about that. Can that be done, and if so, how can it be done?

AL HARBERGER:　It is easier for Chile or Indonesia to do such a thing than for Mexico. The reason is that the Mexican economy is so financially porous vis-à-vis the United States. For example, the Chileans had a 3 percent tax on short-term capital inflows, which worked halfway successfully and certainly didn't hurt the economy. It enabled them to put money abroad and have a modest effect increasing the real exchange rate. I am more skeptical about such operations in the Mexican case, because of the difficulty with capital controls on U.S. money. Let me say that I am not a purist in these matters. I don't think policy-oriented economists dare to be purists, because we have so much junk in our policy systems that we can't do anything about. We have to live with what we inherit from the past and we can change it only very slowly, and even then, not exactly the way we want. Individuals respond to a lot of forces in the process of bringing about any change that we implement.

When talking about capital controls, what we really want are concrete measures. To me, at the top of the list of bad capital controls is the compulsory surrender of export proceeds. I think the World Trade Organization ought to prohibit governments from insisting on compulsory surrender of export proceeds. I think it's a terrible device.

Second, I think one has to be very careful about controls which seek to stop capital from leaving a country. I lived in India at a time when everything was under control and all prices were out of whack. I asked a businessman about the rate of interest he earns for money put in London. He responded, the interest rate in London, what else? I asked if he didn't have problems getting his money out. No. He takes it out through the black market and it returns through the black market. So they get their money where they want it to and they don't lose anything in this process except if the black market premium has changed. If they take money out and put money in with the same black market premium, there's no loss. But a black market doesn't effectuate a real transfer. It's just money flows. A real transfer comes from exports and imports. Over-invoicing of imports and under-invoicing of exports is how money goes through the black market. My firm opinion is that no authority can detect over-invoicing or under-invoicing in the 10 or 15 percent range. So if imports are 20 percent of GDP and exports are 20 percent of GDP and they both lie to the tune of 15 percent, that means you have to get 6 percent of GDP out of the country in one year by false-invoicing. Of course, over the years this accumulates. There is no way that this is good or bad for the economy. When we're thinking about capital flows, we've got to ignore black market flows.

I talked a little about the Chilean case of the sterilized intervention and the tax on short-term capital flows, which I did not find noxious and may have been slightly positive about. I strongly support the auction of the rights to repatriate the debt in Chile. Another thing the Chileans did, starting around 1976, was to prohibit banks from going into debt abroad by more than 25 percent of its capital in surplus. Somewhere along the line, people complained about this and it was changed to 50 percent of capital in surplus. And then people complained and it became something like 75 percent. These figures aren't exact but the picture is correct. And then it became 1.0, and then maybe 1.25 and then all of the sudden it became 2000 percent. Now it didn't really become 2000 percent, they simply eliminated any discrimination between foreign liabilities and any other kind of liabilities, so foreign liabilities co-mingled with other liabilities. That one policy move is what gave rise to these vast inflows of capital into Chile that were around 6 percent of GDP in 1979, then about 9 percent of GDP in 1980, and 15 percent of GDP in 1981. It was the collapse of that capital inflow that caused the huge debt crisis. If only they had been slower in permitting the banks to increase indebtedness, Chile wouldn't have had a crisis.

FAUSTO ALZATI: I have a comment. As I've been listening to this lecture, I was increasingly disturbed by the fact that the key character in each case is policy. Behind policy are policymakers. And policymakers tend to have preferences that do not coincide with the preferences of the majority of the people. In the Latin American case, if you look at the historical record, they seldom tend to coincide with the interests of the majority of the people. In the long run, policymakers have sacrificed growth and have tended to have higher inflation than desirable. My point is, if we as economists believe that the market mechanism allocates resources efficiently, why should we prefer policy and government intervention, even if well intentioned, even if done by very well-trained people, over market mechanisms of a more automatic nature?

AL HARBERGER: Wow! This is a course in the philosophy of life and government and in a way, of our profession. I try to live in this world and I have seen good economists get some degree of influence on policy in countries, and I have seen them make huge differences for the benefit of their people. I think that it's my job as a teacher of policy economics to try to teach students, so that if they ever get that opportunity they'll know enough not to lose their chance. Many people are very good and never get the chance. They're frustrated by circumstances. But, to just let the market system work for any monetary policy is something that [1974 Nobel laureate Friedrich] Hayek would have said. He'd say a country doesn't need to have its own currency at all. But you still have to enforce contracts. You still have to have laws when effecting transactions. The convenience of a national currency is present in every text on money and banking.

There is also something I call the Reagan problem. I'm a considerable admirer of [former President Ronald] Reagan. I think he and the Pope are the people who won the Cold War, and the history books give him great marks for that. But he had spent all his life going around the lecture circuit saying how terrible government is, that all they do is waste our money and none of the bureaucrats is worth a damn. Then one day in January 1981, there he is, he is in charge of it. What is he supposed to do? How is he supposed to deal with his problems? Should he fire all bureaucrats as fast as possible? I think not. I think his problem is to try to make a lean, clean government that will really work – a small government that performs its functions well, that regulates the private sector's actions well, that provides rules of the game within which the private sector can function. I think that's the way it has to be. And those rules of the game include the monetary and exchange rate system.

ROBERT BARTLEY: I hope this is a question. It follows from what Al Harberger just said. Under Mr. Reagan's administration in the first half of the 1980s, exchange rate policy was consistent with Fausto Alzati's point of view – no government discretion whatsoever. Mr. Barry Sprinkle, who was then

Undersecretary of the U.S. Treasury, put out a policy that stated that it's not the business of governments to interfere with exchange rates. Let the market take care of them. And the market did take care of the dollar and it gave us the largest appreciation, in real terms, in the history of this country. I wonder if you'd like to comment on that.

AL HARBERGER: That's a fine last question, because it gives me a trampoline to tell a story that I like. There are a lot of people who still talk today about the Carter inflation and the Reagan disinflation. The thought is that Carter's government was totally profligate and the Federal Reserve was printing money hand over fist and goodness knows what all that was happening, while the Reagan government came and put on all kinds of breaks and squeezed things down. None of the above is true. If you get the Federal Reserve chart book and look at M1, it's a straight line, M2, it's a straight line, M3, it's a straight line, bank credit, they are all straight lines in semilogs [increasing at a constant rate]. From before Carter to after Reagan, you can hardly see blips in this thing. So if the monetary expansion is the same, how did we get the Carter inflation and the Reagan deflation? I have a hunch about that.

Carter is elected and the great gnomes of Zurich are scratching their heads and saying, this peanut farmer is running the country? What are we going to do? Who do we really trust here? Then people decide they kind of like the deutsche mark. So, the dollars that are floating around are unwanted and come back to the United States. Now we have a high-powered money supply with two components: the high-powered money from the Fed, and the redundant high-powered money which is floating around overseas. What happened in my view is that during the Carter administration this redundant money became a part of the active money supply and it fueled the Carter inflation.

When Reagan is elected, the gnomes in Zurich believe this man is for real and we can really believe what he says, so they replace the deutsche mark with the dollar. They take out of the active money supply an amount larger than they send in, and they create a recession. I believe that the Federal Reserve ought to operate to soak up that redundant money. I had a conversation with [Federal Reserve Chairman Alan] Greenspan and I asked him whether the Fed considers it part of their job to see how people's demand for money balances changes. He responded that they do, but doing this detective work is a hell of a lot harder than it appears.

7. Is monetary stability possible in Latin America?

Introduced by

Michael Connolly

The theme of this conference is monetary stability and growth, and I'm going to discuss the issue of monetary stability in the context of rules versus discretion. In particular, I will discuss the idea of targeting – having nominal targets and having real targets. Let me start with a basic principle: if you want monetary stability then you should target nominal variables. For instance, you could have a monetary growth rule that targets the price level, or on the other hand, you could have a fixed exchange rate anchor that gives you monetary stability. Now, the real exchange rate, the price of tradables over non-tradables, is a real variable and as Professor Harberger correctly pointed out in his Randall Hinshaw Memorial Lecture, the real exchange rate is endogenous. Therefore if you're going to change the real exchange rate, it has to be targeted by a real instrument such as a tariff or a tax on capital.

I like to look at the real exchange rate issue in terms of the labor market. One of the main issues that came up after Al Harberger's talk was the effect of the Brazilian devaluation on Argentina's real exchange rate. As you know, Brazil in January 1999, had a 50 percent devaluation of the *real* in the dollar price, and hence the Argentine peso price. This caused a tremendous real appreciation between two major trading partners – Brazil and Argentina – and there was no corresponding real instrument to offset the consequences of the real appreciation of the Argentine peso with respect to the Brazilian *real*. The reason there's no corresponding real instrument is that within a customs union such as Mercosur, the Argentine authorities don't have the possibility of raising tariffs against Brazilian goods – the rule of a customs union is that there can be no tariffs. Now, the government of [Argentine President Carlos] Menem has on occasion resisted that and has imposed what are called statistical taxes of 6 percent. That's been a source of tremendous dispute within Mercosur, but the Argentine government has been trying, from time to time, to impose a tariff, essentially, on Brazilian imports, either calling it a consu-

lar duty or a statistical tax. These have been rejected by the Brazilian government. A real instrument in this case cannot be used on a bilateral basis.

Let me discuss the issue of unemployment. The real appreciation of the
Argentine peso caused a rise in real wages and possibly the higher unemployment that Al Harberger alluded to in his lecture. Consider labor supply and
demand, in the diagram of Figure 7.1. Let me put the nominal wage, W, and
then we'll put one plus t, where t will represent taxes on hiring labor, payroll
taxes, for example. In the denominator is the price level, P, for example, the
Argentine price level, so that $W(1 + t)/P$ is the net-of-tax real wage. Now the
price level is a weighted average of traded and non-traded goods. So we'll put
the exchange rate, E, that's pesos per *real*, for example, times the price of
traded goods, P_t, and then we'll add the tariff, one plus *tau* (τ) with P_{nt} the
price of non-traded goods. So the peso price of *real*, the price of traded goods
times one plus the tariff and then we'll multiply that by a weight *alpha* (α),
that is the weight of traded goods in the Argentine price index. Then we
multiply $1 - \alpha$ times the price of non-traded goods. The price level is therefore $P = \alpha E(1 + \tau)P_t + (1 - \alpha)P_{nt}$.

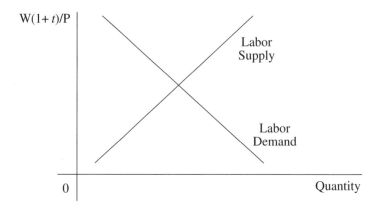

Figure 7.1   Unemployment and prices

What happened in the Argentine case with a fixed exchange rate, so E is
fixed to the dollar, with a real devaluation, the peso price of the *real* falls in
half, so P falls and the real wage rises. The question for policymakers is the
availability of instruments to offset the rise in the real wage, which is in part
the cause of high unemployment. At one point, Argentina's unemployment
rate exceeded 18 percent. Argentina can't devalue because E is fixed by the
currency board. It can't raise tariffs bilaterally, which would be a real instrument adjusting the real exchange rate. That's not a policy instrument, because
they're in Mercosur. So there are two ways of reducing the real wage and

reducing unemployment, either reduce the numerator or raise the denominator. If nominal wages are fixed, then the only way to reduce the net wage is by reducing payroll taxes – a real instrument to reduce the real wage. Alternatively, increasing the denominator causes unemployment to fall. For example, a devaluation will cut the real wage. For most of the real devaluations that have taken place, especially where there's overshooting in the exchange rate, the real wage tends to plummet.

This I think is the basic difficulty in choosing policy to clear the labor market. Either one lowers the real wage with a real instrument, like lowering payroll taxes, or through the nominal exchange rate. My inclination is that it's better to do this through fundamental real reform rather than using a nominal instrument in order to adjust a real variable. So that's a major point. One of the problems with using a nominal instrument to adjust the real wage is that it has other, perhaps unintended consequences. The financial distress that's imposed on the banking system as a result of an unanticipated devaluation may be quite large.

Consider the case of a bank that has borrowed abroad, so it has dollar liabilities. If there's no deviation in the exchange rate from the expected rate, then there are no unanticipated profits or unanticipated losses. However, if there's a large unanticipated devaluation, then the short position is translated into a large loss. The banking system, to the extent that it has liabilities in dollars, is vulnerable to an unanticipated exchange rate depreciation. If they hedge by going long on dollars, a devaluation means banks will make large gains on their dollar loans. However, when there's an unanticipated devaluation, dollar debt and debt service rises in terms of pesos. If for example, a loan is made in dollars to a Mexican trucking company or transport company that has used the dollars to buy imported transport equipment and has its revenues in pesos, if there is a devaluation, the company may default on this loan.

The point here is that even if the banking system attempts to hedge by making loans, unless the borrower from the bank has revenues in dollars, they are exposed and the borrowers from the bank will have a tendency to default on these loans. So one of the unintended side-effects of adjusting the real exchange rate by a large devaluation that adjusts the nominal exchange rate is that this puts a tremendous amount of stress on the financial system. In essence, the financial system is short dollars and long pesos. This is an often unintended and very distressful side consequence of using a nominal variable aggressively to target the real exchange rate. My inclination is that one should use nominal targets for monetary stabilization. I tend to agree with those that have argued that there really is a bipolar choice, either free-floating with fiscal balance and a monetary rule, or on the other hand, a rigid fix in the exchange rate, for example through a currency board or through dollarization, also with fiscal balance, but that these nominal rules should be used to achieve monetary stabilization.

DISCUSSION

PAUL J. ZAK: I'm skeptical of the use of taxes as an instrument to raise employment after a devaluation for a couple of reasons. I think your analysis suffers from partial equilibrium bias. There's a government budget constraint involved here and presumably during a devaluation revenues are falling. A tax cut further puts pressure on revenues, so taxes are a fairly blunt instrument. There are also several deeper questions to be addressed: what's the source of the shock? Is there overshooting? How much uncertainty is there regarding its impact on the economy? These are all relevant questions when choosing a policy response to an economic shock.

CHRISTOPHER JOHNSON: I'd like to raise another question, because I was waiting for a word to come up in Mike's presentation which I didn't hear, and that word is "productivity." There have been countless examples one could refer to – Japan, the UK, Italy – where countries have for different reasons had an overvalued exchange rate and where the immediate reaction on the part of the tradable goods industry has been a dramatic increase in productivity. Indeed in some cases, overvalued exchange rates have been viewed as a beneficial incentive to countries who improve their economic efficiency. In the case Mike presented, Argentina, I wonder if the Argentine tradable goods industries were forced to increase productivity. The other side of that story is the layoffs of less productive workers and consequently higher unemployment. In the long-run unemployment corrects itself, because the productivity of unemployed workers rises as much as that of the workers who remain in employment, because development creates employment. A negative shock encourages domestic and foreign firms to invest, given that labor is more productive. I would be interested to know whether this is part of the Latin American experience.

ROBERT MUNDELL: In my view, real exchange rate economics is one of the softest areas in economic theory. I'll illustrate that by the use made of it by people, not necessarily in international trade, but outside the profession, in finance for instance. I went to a finance seminar just last week of a young man who did a beautiful job with the theory, calculating investment rates through all the latest financial techniques. He had in the model rates of return in one country, say Japan, compared to the United States and one of the elements in it was the real exchange rate. He emphasized his calculations of the real exchange rate and how it entered into the model, but then he said that he didn't find any empirical relationship between the real exchange rate and rates of return. That is, the real exchange rate didn't give any insight into rates of return. I told him that he shouldn't be disappointed. He should be happy with that result, because I'd have regarded his work as highly suspect if he had gotten a clear-cut result.

Both Mike Connolly, and Al Harberger in his Randall Hinshaw Lecture [Chapter 6], identified the reason that the real exchange rate and interest rates are unrelated. There's a huge difference whether real exchange rate changes occur because of a change in supply or a change in demand. A big increase in productivity or a big increase in demand for, let's say, Japanese goods causes the real exchange rate to rise because earnings rise. Conversely, a rise in wage costs would cause the real exchange rate to fall. Economists can't avoid the hard work of placing the analysis into a model and drawing out your implications regarding the mechanism that is causing the real exchange rate to change. Changes in the exchange rates can be caused by a vast number of things. Most importantly, of course, are changes in productivity. Productivity differentials in international goods relative to domestic goods is a very important cause of real exchange rate fluctuations. They can also be caused by erratic temporary changes in the nominal exchange rate, because we know the nominal exchange rate and the real exchange rate are, at least in the short run, quite correlated. They can also be affected by the fact that in one country real wages rise because of strong labor unions that price a country out of the market. But this is the only case where one could make an argument that a nominal exchange rate change should be used to offset that change in the real wage rate. That would be the Keynesian argument if one believes that devaluation is a correct policy to stimulate output expansion.

I've come to believe, to a large extent, that exchange rate changes are the problem, not the solution. Very often one observes enormous sudden changes in the real exchange rate. We know that that's not optimal, because from the law of one price, the real exchange rate, like the terms of trade, reflects long-run productivity changes. Large swings in the real exchange rate result in false pricing that sets into motion a whole range of forces that lead to inflation. Christopher Johnson mentioned Hong Kong, where the real exchange rate has appreciated since they went onto a currency board in 1983. People who only look at that and don't understand that it reflects a productivity phenomenon and not some wage problem would say that Hong Kong has to devalue. Hong Kong's currency board got into difficulties after 1997 when Governor Patton knew that Hong Kong was going to revert back to China, and so whereas three commercial banks had established and maintained the currency board up to then, the government now established the Hong Kong Monetary Authority, which immediately became a political agency. With the embarrassments of the Asian crisis, this agency started talking about altering the rules of the currency board system, and in particular, supporting the stock market with newly printed money. The end result of this process would be devaluation. The main point I want to make is that real exchange rate fluctuations in Latin America are due primarily to instability of economic policy in Latin America and, frequently, simply unstable nominal exchange rates.

This should be contrasted with the lack of real exchange rate economics discussions within the ERM area, as it existed before. One does not hear in Austria or the Netherlands, whose currencies were tied to the deutsche mark, that their real exchange rate has gone up relative to Germany's and hence they need to change it. One never hears that in a framework of monetary stability. Real exchange rate fluctuations are a big problem, and they are caused mainly by monetary instability which breeds nominal exchange rate instability.

CHRISTOPHER JOHNSON: In Europe we don't talk about exchange rates, we talk about competitiveness. It's just another word for the same thing.

AL HARBERGER: Let me try to respond to what Bob Mundell just said and then get back to a couple of points in Mike's presentation. I am both troubled and applaud Bob's statement that real exchange rate theory is one of the softest areas of economics. I applaud it, because real exchange rate economics basically did not exist when I was a student, and it has only come into being in recent decades. What I applaud also is that in this literature people use 20 definitions of the real exchange rate. In other words, they ask the real exchange rate to be many different things as a concept, and there is total confusion. The *International Finance Statistics* publication from the International Monetary Fund gives six different definitions of the real exchange rate, none of which in my view is the correct one. What then is the correct one? The one I discussed in my lecture. The real exchange rate must be viewed as the fundamental equilibrating variable of international trade. One cannot use a definition of the real exchange rate that doesn't do that, because that is what this price must do.

We have a not too subtle battle of wills going around in this room in terms of exchange rate systems and I want it to be known that I am not opposed to the European Monetary Union, and I would not be opposed to Canada and the United States getting together in a monetary union. I have seen so many cases of different exchange rate regimes being successful over long periods in different countries, that I don't think we should disparage different systems, but should recognize that the move towards something like dollarization requires a lot of preparation. A country with zero reserves has no option but a floating exchange rate. A country with very little reserves can do maybe a dirty float, but not very dirty. By the time you move up a sequence of different exchange rate systems, you get to fixed rates, which require a lot of reserves. A currency board requires even more reserves, and full dollarization requires still more.

I think of a country where it is. If a country wants to dollarize, most poor countries in the world will have to work for a generation to build the reserves that are needed. As I said, there are many good systems that will allow their economies to function very well and we shouldn't be putting an idol on a pedestal and say there is only one way to go. For example, in a completely dollarized world, what happens when negative shocks occur? There is no home currency to deal with. I'll tell you what happens, because we saw it in Argentina within the last ten years. That is, the provinces of Argentina issued their own money. I have thousands of australs that I bought for less than a penny each that were issued by the province of Tucumán to cover its debts. They circulated in Tucumán, basically at par, because they could be used to pay taxes. But outside of Tucumán, they sold at varying discounts. We in the United States in the Great Depression had script issued by American states and cities. This is a way in which you can still get devaluations when you don't have a fixed exchange rate.

On to Mike's couple of points. On the issue of banking legislation or regulatory rules for banks with dollar debts, one requirement is that if you borrow in dollars you have to lend in dollars, as Mike pointed out. The trouble arose when the banks lent in dollars to people whose income was in pesos or rupiahs. If I were writing the banking regulations, I would certainly put a penalty on any such lending, and I would have significant supervision to make sure that dollar lending was done to entities that had income in dollars with which to repay their loans. It seems to me that this kind of legislation would have immunized the countries that suffered from this problem.

On the issue of instruments to influence the real exchange rate, Mike neglected to mention a sterilized intervention. I want to point out that a sterilized intervention is a real instrument. The dollar is a real asset and so a sterilized intervention can be effective, semi-effective, or ineffective depending on what I discussed in my Hinshaw lecture [Chapter 6], how much the world financial community believes in the monetary authority's credibility. If the financial community is uninterested in a country, sterilized intervention is easy and effective. If the financial community loves you, you put money abroad and it comes right back through the back door and that's where you get into trouble. So the ability to execute a sterilized intervention depends on the degree of interest that the financial community has in a country.

ROBERT MUNDELL: The phenomenon that Al talked about in Tucumán exists in the United States, and not just in the 1930s, as Al mentioned. It exists now in the United States. I read an article last summer about a large number of communities in New England that are each issuing their own chits. This is the temptation to garner seigniorage. If a local community can issue chits that the mayor stamps and that people locally will accept as payment, then they can economize on the use of "outside" currencies, including the U.S. dollar. It's a process that goes on in every monetary area and I think this is a process that will trouble Europe once the euro is circulated. The Italians, for example will try to find ways of economizing on euros, because from their standpoint, it's an external currency. I thought when Al started to talk about Tucumán, he was going to take the real exchange rate argument further and say that Tucumán should have a separate currency from the rest of Argentina. Then they could devalue it! But you didn't follow that line, so I assume that you wouldn't extend the arguments that you apply to Argentina to the different regions within Argentina.

ROBERT BARTLEY: Sometime in the late 1970s, I was sitting with a hard-bitten banker who was later head of one of the most famous banks in the world, and we got to talking about these subjects and he said that he thought the "real" interest rate is the nominal rate. After that, I stopped using the word "real," because it can mean actual or it can mean inflation-adjusted. I have trouble with the real exchange rate argument because it is the exchange rate adjusted for inflation, but *changes* in the exchange rate affect inflation. Devaluations are inflationary, and it seems to me kind of a numerator and denominator issue – they're mutually interdependent. What really bothers me is I see this abused in practice in a rather simplistic kind of way. If one starts from some base year, and if a country has 20 percent more inflation than its trading partner, it is entitled to devaluate 20 percent. That is typically how this concept is applied by policymakers. That's not what our discussion was of, but this behavior by policymakers is troublesome. I would like to ask Al about his definition of the real exchange rate as the fundamental equilibrating variable in international trade – what's the difference between the real exchange rate and the terms of trade?

AL HARBERGER: The textbook definition of the real exchange rate is approximate for a country with a stable price level and a flexible exchange rate. In this case, the real exchange rate adapts to disturbances in either supply or demand. With a tariff on imports, or an export subsidy, or capital coming in and being spent on tradables or on non-tradables, or a productivity advance in the production of exportables or importables, for each of these disturbances one can figure out how each shifts supply or demand and how the exchange rate moves to reach equilibrium. The way I stated these problems keeps the internal price level constant, so all the adjustment takes place through the exchange rate. The mirror image analysis supposes that the exchange rate is fixed and that these same disturbances occur. The way the same equilibrium will be reached in real terms will be by the inverse movement of the internal price level. That's why the ratio $E' = E/P$ is the real equilibrating variable in international trade. With a fixed exchange rate, the economy still adjusts to these disturbances, but it is through a change in the denominator [the price level, P] and not of the numerator (E, the nominal exchange rate) of this ratio. That's the basic story of the equilibrating variable.

The terms of trade is another disturbance so that if your export price goes up in the international markets, then you're flooded with dollars, increasing the supply of foreign currency and causing the real price of the dollar to fall. In the case of a fixed exchange rate, that same adjustment occurs by the internal price level rising. If a fixed exchange rate country – Brazil or Colombia – has a coffee boom, dollars come in, monetary expansion takes place, and dollars keep coming in, so when is the new equilibrium reached? When there is enough demand for more imports or lower supply of other exports that this inflow of dollars from the raised price of coffee doesn't add to the reserves of the central bank and there is no further monetary expansion. This produces a new equilibrium price level corresponding to the change in the terms of trade.

ROBERTO SALINAS: Following Al Harberger's comments, I'd like to go back to the requirements for a change in a currency regime. On the controversial topic of currency reforms such as dollarization, I don't see this as the panacea that is going to fix all. In the same way, the serious efforts marketing the North American Free Trade Agreement never announced NAFTA as the solution to all economic problems. These are important reforms, but if they are going to be implemented, a set of conditions must be fulfilled. I wonder if we could develop a list.

Al, you mentioned that a country must have a sufficient amount of reserves. Others that were mentioned yesterday include the health of the banking system, property rights enforcement, and fiscal responsibility. The Dallas Federal Reserve recently presented a set of guidelines for effective dollarization that included disciplined fiscal policy, a long maturity structure for public debt, a sound banking system, financial supervision that instills public confidence, effectively defined and enforced property rights, generally accepted accounting principles, a credible public pension program, a market-based economy, free trade, privatization, moderate regulation, constitutional democracy, and I thought it would be interesting to add here "no rain and a lot of sunshine."

The point of this list is that in Mexico and in Latin America many have questioned whether once we fulfill these conditions, the dollarization debate will actually lose steam. Is it still relevant to talk about the viability of a shift in currency regime? My personal opinion is that the debate remains alive, especially in countries with a poor economic track record; Argentina comes to mind, but the same case could be made about Mexico. In any case, this leads me to another point. Recent studies by [University of California at Berkeley economist] Barry Eichengreen and [Chief Economist of the Inter-Development Bank] Ricardo Hausmann have argued that under dollarization, countries lose an anchor to absorb external shocks. Whether this loss outweighs the benefit of removing the tremendous internal monetary mismanagement of the type that Bob Mundell mentioned has occurred throughout Latin America is not clear. According to Hausmann and Eichengreen, countries with floating exchange rate regimes in Latin America have averaged in the 1990s 9 percent real interest rates versus countries with fixed exchange rate regimes in Latin America that averaged 5 percent real interest rates in the 1990s. I think that reveals a problem of currency credibility.

MICHAEL CONNOLLY: I agree with Paul Zak's point that tax reform and reducing social security taxes may indeed reduce tax collections and so there's a fiscal implication when using taxes as a real policy instrument. I think that's an important point. I was talking about cutting the real wage paid by the employer, but the after-tax, or after-social security-payment-tax wage received by the employee actually rises. The idea of fundamental reform in the labor market is to cut the tax wedge paid by the employer. This actually raises the after-tax real wage of employees and therefore increases employment. As a result, this policy reduces unemployment compensation reducing government expenditures. My analysis banks on a supply-side effect, a Laffer-curve, because Argentina, for example, is one of the most heavily taxed economies in South America. As Bob Mundell pointed out yesterday, they have a European level of social programs and taxes to support them and so the point is well taken. I think a reduction in social security and payroll taxes would have a strong supply-side effect so the tax base would rise. As Christopher Johnson stated, productivity is the key to growth, and it has risen under the currency board system and due to the general reforms in Argentina.

MICHAEL CONNOLLY: I have an article that lists about a hundred reforms enacted by the government of Argentina, including deregulations of the port and traded goods sector, elimination of quotas on trade, and licensing reforms. So there were fundamental reforms in the tradable goods sector supported by deregulation, and this in part supported the strong real appreciation in the exchange rate between 1991 and 1995 that Al Harberger pointed out. One could argue that because of these fundamental reforms and increasing productivity in the traded goods sector, real appreciation doesn't necessarily mean that the exchange rate did not need to be devalued as Al mentioned; it may just be an equilibrium appreciation in the real exchange rate. There was tremendous growth between 1991 and 1996. Real GDP in Argentina was growing at an 8 percent real rate immediately following the convertibility plan. The productivity in the traded goods sector is especially important.

To answer Bob Bartley's query, the terms of trade is the price of exportables divided by the price of importables, and the real exchange rate is the price of tradables divided by the price of non-tradables. These are different things, and I thought it would be useful to give the definition. Bob Mundell's point was that the state of Texas underwent quite an adjustment to falling oil prices in the mid-1980s, and thereafter from time to time. It has been a boom–bust resource-based economy. The adjustment takes place by labor and capital mobility without an issue of script or a devaluation. With a currency union for countries in Latin America, the adjustment to shocks would be similar to the adjustment in Texas without the possibility of an exchange rate depreciation.

JEFF FRANKEL: I have a question for the audience. Everybody probably had some notion of what the real exchange rate is when they came in here. How many people are more confused now than when they came in? Everybody agrees that in the numerator you have the nominal exchange rate, which given world prices is going to be the price you pay for imports. The controversy is what you deflate by. There are two different views. One is that you should only deflate by the price of non-traded goods, goods that are not internationally traded. The other is that you should deflate by a measure of the entire price level. There is too much fuss being made out of this disagreement for two reasons. First, in practice it's hard to tell the difference. Al Harberger has worked on this a lot, and I think he would agree that when you get down to the nitty-gritty, it's actually hard to identify which sectors are not traded internationally and which are, and to measure the prices in each. In practice we use proxies and it doesn't make that much difference. Indeed, every sector is at least a little bit traded and a little bit non-traded, so we're making too much fuss about this. The other thing is that both definitions are widely used, and for somebody to say my definition is right and everybody else's definition is wrong is just being dogmatic. They're so widely used that we have to acknowledge that fact, otherwise we're going to be very confused.

For small, open economies and less developed economies, it's true that domestic tradable prices tend to adjust pretty quickly. The reason there is a sense of ideological conflict here of significance is that there is something significant. There is a hypothesis that when a country devalues, all the prices of internationally traded goods go up instantaneously and proportionately. If that were literally true, there'd be no point talking about the real exchange rate as opposed to the terms of trade, unless you specifically identified it as the price of non-traded goods. It's useful for small, open economies because prices of traded goods do tend to go up, but it's simply not true for any economy that all prices of traded goods go up instantaneously and proportionately, and so therefore a nominal devaluation has no real effects whatsoever. It's just not true. This is very clear when you look at the data. It is a useful simplification, and I teach this to my students that for small, open developing countries, one can use the definition that looks at non-traded goods, but it's an overstatement to say that that's all there is.

FAUSTO ALZATI: I'd like to bring this back into the context of Latin America. Let me give you a couple of facts that are relevant to this discussion. In some research I did recently, with a sample of countries including the U.S., Japan, Indonesia, Spain, Italy, Brazil, Argentina, and Chile, I tried to see if over a hundred-year period, there was convergence in growth rates in terms of GDP per capita. Surprisingly enough, the only sub-sample of countries that did not exhibit long-run convergence towards the U.S. GDP per capita level from 1895 to 1994 are the Latin American countries. I wondered why, so I examined more data. It turns out that the Latin American countries had the highest volatility in real exchange rates over the hundred-year period.

What does this tell us? We don't discuss the real exchange rate in Holland, or in Austria, and it brought to my mind Albert O. Hirschman, who in 1968 published a remarkable paper entitled, "The Political Economy of Import-Substituting Industrialization in Latin America" [*Quarterly Journal of Economics*, February]. In this paper, Hirschman showed that macroeconomic policies are not made in a vacuum. He showed very clearly that macro policy decisions were influenced by specific vested interests. I mention this to return the discussion to which monetary regimes are better in the long-run. If prices act as signals for resource allocation, then I suggest that a regime with less discretion and more rules is better than a regime with more discretion.

SVEN ARNDT: Bob Mundell suggests that people be given two minutes to summarize their view of what we've achieved in terms of relating real exchange rates to monetary stability and economic growth. He'll start off and show us what he means, and then I invite anybody else who wants to participate.

ROBERT MUNDELL: Let me start by saying that I'm having a little running discussion with Al Harberger about how to test the proposition that nominal exchange rate changes have been a *source* of instability rather than a needed adjustment of the real exchange rate that mitigates instability. My view, and I haven't tested this, is that if you took the period in Mexico when it had a fixed exchange rate, between 1954 and 1976, there were fewer fluctuations in

Mexico's real exchange rate than there were after 1976 when Mexico moved toward a wide range of different, eclectic regimes, e.g., floating, adjustable pegs, and so on.

The second point is that it's very important to distinguish the causes of changes in the real exchange rate. If changes in the real exchange rate have been caused by technological developments or productivity changes, they're desirable changes. There's no reasonable argument that I've ever heard that says that for those types of factors, that exchange rate changes are necessarily the best way to effect policy goals. To choose between the monetary systems in Hong Kong and Japan, where Japan let its currency appreciate and Hong Kong fixed and had a real appreciation, the role of technological change must be understood. The argument for real exchange rate changes comes when wages overshoot, for example, after a stabilization plan. The question is, is that a good case for a devaluation? I recognize the argument along the lines of Keynesian short-run theory, that a devaluation is a good solution to offset undesirable changes in the real exchange rate. But there is a cost to this policy in the long run. I take the longer run view that this does more harm than good. I recognize, for instance, that all these countries in South and Central America, when they had difficulties in the late 1970s, there was an argument in each case for devaluation after 50 years of monetary stability. One can always make an argument for a devaluation, but the costs of the devaluation in terms of future instability may exceed the costs of adjustment and sticking to a disciplined policy.

HERBERT GRUBEL: I have a different take on the issue of the exchange rate changes and regimes. With a flexible exchange rate regime, it is possible for the government and for special interest groups in society to fight over the distribution of income which will lead to resource misallocations, including inflation and other problems. The exchange rate in that sense is a safety valve that protects these groups from having to face the consequences of their actions. The dilemma, of course, is that exchange rates also change when there is a boom in coffee prices or in oil prices, or other tradeables. But even in these cases, the systems for adjusting to such exogenous shocks is endogenous to the exchange rate regime. As somebody said, in Texas they have no choice but to adjust in real terms if the oil price falls. If Texas had an exchange rate, they could postpone making the real adjustment by devaluing. I think that's been neglected in our discussion of the real exchange rate. Why is it necessary to have nominal exchange rate changes? To adjust to what? The emphasis is always as if there is some disturbance coming from outside. I think it's the other way around. Let's have the fixed exchange rates and then force the institutions internally to adapt to deal with external disturbances.

ROBERT BARTLEY: We started out discussing the problem of what Argentina does when it's in a free trade area with Brazil, and Brazil stages a large devaluation. We're going to have an empirical test of that, because we're going to see what Argentina does. Basically its options are to devalue and pay all the costs of that, which will be considerable in terms of its trade with the rest of the world and the living standards of its citizens, or to break up Mercosur. I think those are the two options and the question that arises is, can you have a free trade area if you have these kinds of changes in the exchange rate? I suspect the answer is "No."

CHRISTOPHER JOHNSON: I'm very sympathetic to Bob Mundell's preference for fixed exchange rate regimes as against floating regimes. But as has been pointed out, to maintain such a regime, a country needs foreign exchange reserves – and if not its own, then big brother's reserves. That is, some countries will need the U.S. Treasury to provide reserves, and that, of course, is a political decision. I remember the saying about Mexico: so far from God, so near to the United States. The latter is an advantage when trying to support the exchange rate. The answer to this problem is to form a currency union where exchange rates are unnecessary. That's what has been done in the euro zone in Europe.

In a monetary union, countries no longer need reserves in order to support their currencies against each other because they don't have separate currencies. This frees up resources for other uses. Reserves are needed if, for example, the European Central Bank wants to affect the dollar–euro exchange rate. That's not quite as painless as it sounds, because in a currency union if one region of the union gets out of balance with the rest it has, in effect, a balance of trade deficit with the rest of the union. This requires a flow of bank credit or government credit to the region which is not doing so well. So instead of needing foreign exchange reserves, domestic currency reserves are needed to support credit operations within the union. Note that these credit operations carry no exchange rate risk because they can occur without separate currencies.

ROBERT SOLOMON: I would like to state what I think is a majority view in the economics profession in contrast to the minority view that we've heard, with all respect, from Bob Mundell, Herbert Grubel, and Bob Bartley. The majority of economists, certainly in the United States, are *not* in favor of fixed exchange rates. When I get to speak later [Chapter 10] on the future of the International Monetary System, I'll report to you a recent set of recommendations from a very distinguished commission established by the Council on Foreign Relations. Their recommendations are far from fixed exchange rates. Consider Mexico in 1994. The country's policies were not perfect.

Mexico got into serious trouble in 1994 due to a large current account deficit. It was clear that the currency was overvalued. Bob Mundell explained that a devaluation was necessary. The Mexican Finance Minister, Mr. Sera, explained it very poorly to U.S. institutions and did not back the devaluation with an adequate macro stabilization policy. That's what led to the crisis. Bob seemed to assume that the devaluation was necessary. I'm trying to state what I think is more of a majority view than what we're hearing from these respected gentlemen.

AL HARBERGER: I want to call attention to the opinions of two great men who are not present here. One is Jacob Viner and the other is Milton Friedman. Each of them spent a lot of time with their very brilliant minds grappling with these problems, and they came to opposite conclusions. So, it's true that there are significant differences of opinion here. Milton is a free-market person. He is against rules and imposition by an authority. Milton thinks that the fixed exchange rate is a rule and that a floating exchange rate is the one that is the free market price and it should be equilibrating markets all the time. Jacob Viner was a free-market person too, but he distrusted monetary authorities and political authorities. Viner thought that there would be a lot of temptation for governments to pursue inflationary policies with a flexible rate. I believe he was right – that there is more temptation to pursue inflationary policies with a flexible rate. In order to have a good system under either rate, you need discipline. But when a country has discipline, a flexible rate provides a more rapid adjustment to external disturbances. The problem with fixed rates comes with big negative shocks. The fixed rate record is wonderful when there are big positive shocks, when there are small positive shocks, and when there are small negative shocks. With a fixed rate, difficulties arise if, for example, civil disturbances break out and nobody wants to put their money in the country, and everybody wants to take their money out at a fixed rate. This happens when unreliable governments take power and put bad policies in place.

How should a country handle natural disasters that knock out half of its productive capacity? How does a country handle a huge drop in exports if the country is small and has a single big export? What happens when the world price of that product falls to a third of its prior level and the country is driven into poverty? These are the cases for which the adjustment under a fixed exchange rate is far more painful and far more costly than adjustment under a flexible rate. What happens is that countries are paying a price. If they follow a flexible exchange rate system, it's like buying an insurance policy. With an insurance policy, you pay every year for insurance you may not need. So having a flexible rate, to which Bob and others have referred, is, in a well ordered system, the cost of an insurance policy to then have the capacity to really handle the fire, the earthquake, or whatever it is when it occurs.

8. Monetary policy and economic performance in Mexico

Introduced by

Judy Shelton and Abel Beltran Del Rio

JUDY SHELTON: Mexico has a checkered history when it comes to monetary policy and this is reflected in its anemic growth rates in the last 20 years. Even though the economy is doing much better today, the credit markets are not functioning well. Interest rates in Mexico are, for most borrowers, 30 percent annually or higher. This is clearly a hindrance to economic growth. Opening up credit markets is an important part of monetary policy that Mexico needs to address.

Mexico has recently undertaken important reforms in the way it handles monetary policy. For example, it has pursued a policy to insure that it can weather external shocks. This includes setting up in advance access to 24 billion dollars worth of loans and building up 30 billion in reserves. Then, with an election year coming up in 2000, in the event of something comparable to 1994, an uprising in Chiapas, or the horrible murder of [Presidential candidate] Luis Donaldo Colosio, stress like that can be handled by having financing in place. This is critical as Mexico's integration with the U.S., following the passage of NAFTA, results in a greater number of individuals and firms earning income in dollars rather than pesos.

Acquiring reserves is a good first step toward monetary stability, but still lacks credibility given Mexico's history of monetary crises. An additional policy to insure monetary stability and stimulate economic growth would be a currency union with the U.S. Is there some approach to currency union between the United States and Mexico that could be a winning political issue either in the United States or in Mexico? This is a point Bob Mundell brought up. My own sense is in the United States you could find democrats and republicans who could support some kind of monetary union or shared currency with Mexico in the interest of stability and free trade, but I think you can rule out support from the Reform Party. Now in Mexico, would any candidate for president of Mexico dare to make currency reform part of his campaign, or is the fate of the peso too politically sensitive in terms of national sovereignty and delicate feelings about patriotism? Some polls in Mexico indicate that those most worried about national sovereignty are the sovereigns themselves – government officials – and not citizens. The citizens just want money that works, but I think all these issues are open to discussion.

ABEL BELTRAN: The theme of this conference is monetary stability and growth. In Mexico we are currently in the process of searching for stability in order to be able to regain the growth that we need. Indeed, [Presidential candidate Vicente] Fox has argued that 7 percent per capita GDP growth is sustainable, but I am skeptical. Why? Because Mexico had a population explosion that multiplied by five our population, from 20 million people in 1950 to the 100 million that we have today. As a consequence, the labor market has to absorb one million new entrants per year, minimum. My own calculation is more like one and a quarter million per year, but let's put it at one million to be conservative. If productivity, that is GDP divided by the number of workers, is growing at 2.5 percent per year, which is more or less the trend in Mexico, and the growth of the labor force is 3.5 percent per year, output needs to grow at 10 percent per year in order not to create the conditions of social and political instability caused by falling incomes. This is as important as monetary stability.

Keep in mind that Mexico had stability and growth between 1955 and 1975, growing at 5 to 6 percent per year, with inflation equal, and in some years lower than the inflation of the United States. This period is known as *desaroyo estabilizadores* in Mexico.

During this period Mexico was a closed economy and the government was the leading actor running more than 3000 enterprises. Growth depended on government investment and government spending, while monetary policy was set not by the central bank, but in Los Pinos [the presidential residence]. But then after that period, this tradition of an omnipotent government decided to solve the problem of unemployment by growing at 7, 8 percent year after year, monetizing fiscal deficits and causing inflation. Then, every six years at the end of each president's term, we would have a devaluation and inflation would spike. The price of assets fell each time and this decapitalization is still affecting our banks.

Today Mexico is searching for stability after a fundamental and wide-ranging reform started in 1985 under President [Miguel] de la Madrid. This reform is ongoing and has completely overhauled the fiscal system. Instead of an 18 percent government budget deficit, now we have 1 percent. Instead of making monetary policy in Los Pinos, now we do it at the central bank. Instead of having a closed economy, we have NAFTA. Instead of 3000 government enterprises, now we have 200. So there has been an enormous restructuring of the economy. The last element added to Mexico's economic reform was a managed floating exchange rate.

During this transition to stability, we have had no growth. From 1982 to 1989, real GDP is the same number. Of course we did not have growth in employment either. This is the reason that we have such a huge informal economy. Mexico is at the brink of being able to enjoy growth on a steady basis. Since 1992, foreign direct investment has been eight to 12 billion dollars per year in spite of everything, including 1995 [the wake of the 1994 currency crisis].

Now let me make some predictions. I predict that Mexico will not leave the floating exchange rate system during this administration. I also predict in the medium to long term a monetary union. But please, "ameri" instead of "amero," Herbert. And finally, we need your help. What is the best way a country in transition can regain stability without causing the social and political turmoil of unemployment? I know that we can stop inflation by taking some of the measures that we have been discussing. Armando Baquiero was commenting that he can stop central bank inflation, but at what political and social costs? So, why don't you help us, what do we do from now until we've again reached stability with an open economy with private markets? Shall we trust markets with a capital "M" as we used to trust the state with a capital "S" as perfect institutions, as if they were made by angels more than humans? Or shall we recognize that all human institutions have deficiencies and they have their pathologies, deficiencies, they overshoot, they undershoot, and they get stuck.

DISCUSSION

ARMANDO BAQUIERO: The fairest way to begin will be to say that for the policy planning horizon, it is safe to assume that no North American currency union will be born. Perhaps the next Mexican administration will examine this issue and then take it to the other side of the border. So for me as a central banker who has to make decisions about monetary stability and growth, as I look at the medium-term and short-term, well that's a question I can leave aside.

Since we're talking about monetary stability and growth in Mexico, let's see where we are right now. I think Mexico is going to have the highest rate of growth in Latin America, so that takes care of economic growth. Regarding monetary stability, we have one of the highest inflation rates in Latin America, with the exception of Colombia and Ecuador. But inflation is coming down and I want to use this as a point of departure. At the beginning of this year, most private analysts were expecting inflation of 17 percent. The official target was 13 percent and at this point it's pretty safe to say that we're going to have the 13 percent rate or somewhat lower. Now, I don't want to say that this is only a matter of the correct monetary policy, there was a combination of factors that occurred this year that have contributed to lower inflation: an appreciating exchange rate and favorable food prices.

Looking ahead, what do we have to deal with? A difficult issue is the rigidity in expectations, that is, the credibility of policy. The expectations of inflation by the private sector have not adjusted as far as we would have liked. This is due in part to past experience. The only way to gain credibility is to do something to deserve it. The central bank can move toward greater credibility if it can deliver lower inflation this year, right on target, and lower inflation next year, right on target. We have recently announced our targets for next year and the medium-term, and we are aiming for 10 percent inflation next year. This is a little ambitious, but a very safe assumption is, and I'm sorry to disappoint Abel, that our policy is going to be restrictive. That doesn't mean that we're going to stay there, but what it means is that it's a basic assumption that we're not going to ease monetary policy.

The way to lower interest rates in Mexico is not to expand the money supply. Mexico's experience is that as we expand the money supply, perhaps we can get a very short-lived fall in interest rates. But sooner or later, that's going to feed inflationary expectations and up the interest rate goes. I don't know of any case in which interest rates are low, be it nominal or real, without stability, and that's what we want to get to. We have announced not only next year's inflation rate goal, but also a medium-term goal which is to bring inflation down to the level of our main trading partners. Now we're talking about convergence to the inflation rates of the U.S. and Canada so private agents have a very clear picture of where we want to go. This is very important in Mexico. For the first time, individuals have a clear indication of the central bank's goals. Reaching our inflation goal also requires other factors, especially sound public finance. We're also hoping we don't suffer a major earthquake or a major external shock. The important point is that we have said where we want to go.

Now I want to address some of the points that Judy Shelton made. First, is currency a shock absorber? Well it could be, but there are other shock absorbers. Second, is devaluing a winning strategy? In the case of Mexico we have not devalued as a strategy. We have devalued because we had to devalue, because the last dollar just went away, not as a strategy to push exports. Next, is Mexico accumulating reserves? Yes, we are accumulating reserves under an automatic mechanism in which we purchase dollars under certain circumstances and we sell dollars under certain circumstances and the public knows about this. It is very transparent, and this year we are accumulating reserves, maybe three billion dollars, and most of them have come through this mechanism. I don't know if it protects us from every possible major event, but I think that we're better off with the reserves than without them. The question about the polls that citizens want the money that works – you are absolutely right. I think Mexican citizens want a stable currency, be it pesos, dollars, ameros, or whatever, but they want a stable currency. My opinion is that the answer that one gets in the polls depends on what you ask. If you go out on the street and ask people if they would like to earn their salary in dollars, just about everyone is going to say "yes". Would you want to have a mortgage at very low rates? Everyone is going to say "yes". But, this is an oversimplification. In the case of housing, for instance, interest rates are rather low. Now, those that don't have access to credit for housing in pesos won't have access to credit for housing in dollars because of the credit risk. I think that if you word the question properly, then I'm not sure that this supposed majority of people want an economy that is totally dollarized.

ABEL BELTRAN: I would just like to ask Armando Baquiero if he agrees with the fact that the peso has appreciated 20 percent from 1996 to the end of 1998. A 20 percent appreciation of the peso using the nominal 48-hour peso rate divided by the GDP deflator. After the 42 percent real devaluation of 1994–95, we have an appreciating peso, and you see more and more license plates from Jaurez buying in El Paso. Wouldn't it be part of monetary policy, Armando, to try to manage the rate of exchange, which apparently is appreciating because of increased trade due to NAFTA, and other elements that are creating an inflow of foreign direct investment into Mexico? With an appreciating peso we may not be able to continue exporting and creating more jobs in Mexico.

FAUSTO ALZATI: First of all, I want to congratulate Armando Baquiero for being such a professional central banker. I really wish that everybody in the Mexican Government were as apolitical and as professional as he has been in his remarks. Perhaps eventually, when this country is really a democratic one, and we have a professional civil service, we will get more Armando Baquieros. Of course, that will give us a more reliable and less politicized monetary policy.

Now, two remarks. One concerns Abel's question about the market and the state with a capital "M" and a capital "S." I think this is a dangerous intellectual trap, because I reject the idea that "market failure" is always an argument for state intervention. I think if the market has some problems and some defects, what we need to do is try to improve the market first. Correcting the absence of markets or the supposed failures is the first thing to do, and only as a last resort, and hopefully as a temporary one, use state intervention. The problem with state intervention is that it creates its own agenda. It creates its own vested interests. And it's always started on the idea that it's not going to last, it's going to be temporary, and it turns out to be permanent. In Mexico we have had experience with this. Every president had his favorite proposals and we still have many dinosaurs of past administrations that are taking public resources because we haven't found a politically acceptable way of dismantling something that was supposed to be there only for a short time. So I think it's a very dangerous approach and something in which I would recommend a lot of care.

Will the bullet-proofing by accumulating reserves work? I like what Armando said, if it won't work it won't hurt. The only problem I see with it is that if the corruption that we know is taking place in many areas of the government continues, these people will eventually want to put their ill-gained wealth out of the reach of the next government and this will create a huge demand for dollar denominated assets that perhaps the currency reserves will not be able to handle. I hope it will be able to suffice, but I am unsure it will.

If I had a chance to give advice to a presidential candidate, I would strongly urge him to take a firm position on currency reform. It's a matter of political skill, how one communicates this to the population in a way that it is non-threatening and understood that it's for the benefit of the people. If we really believe in democracy in Mexico, we should stop underestimating the population. People are a lot more intelligent, a lot more rational, than we think. If we present them with choices, they will understand what's really at stake. Good policy is also good politics.

Finally, I want to insist that the history of exchange rate and monetary instability in Mexico is such that it's very hard for a Mexican of my generation to look at it in a cool, unemotional way. When I was listening to what Professor Harberger discussed in his Hinshaw lecture [Chapter 6], with exchange rate overshooting and devaluations, I was looking at the history of my life. I was born in 1953 and started with a very small job at 18 years old in the mayor's office in Guanajuato. I was very briefly Secretary of Education of this country, I've been working all my life, and I haven't been able to save a reasonable amount of money for my old age. Every time I save, there's a devaluation and my savings are wiped out. I think every Mexican in my generation shares this feeling, we are really tired of it, and we want it to stop. Whatever we have to do to stop it, we're going to do it.

EDUARDO SOJO: Just a few comments on economics in the state of Guanajuato. I want to report what our local entrepreneurs are telling us about the exchange rate. We Mexicans have learned a lot about economics in the last ten years: our children know about inflation, about devaluations, about things that we didn't know at that age. Our entrepreneurs have their own definition of an overvalued exchange rate, a definition that has to do with cost. They compare, for example, the cost of producing a shoe in Mexico with the cost of producing a shoe elsewhere. What they see right now is that the exchange rate is overvalued. I don't know if it is or isn't, but it's what they perceive. When they see that the exchange rate is overvalued, they start taking the money that could be invested in productive assets and they convert it to dollars. This kind of behavior leads to self-fulfilling prophecies, as money is pulled out of Mexico causing a devaluation. Even with a floating exchange rate, the money that could be invested in productive assets is being invested in financial assets or in dollars. The other dissatisfaction by entrepreneurs with the floating exchange rate is that it floats too much. They cannot make a plan for the future. So entrepreneurs have two current dissatisfactions with the foreign exchange system: one, they believe that the exchange rate is overvalued, and two, they cannot plan for the long-run, because the floating exchange rate is quite variable.

ROBERT MUNDELL: I am tempted to start off with a local issue by asking Eduardo how Guanajuato has been fairing since the increase in the price of silver improved the real exchange rate in Guanajuato. But I want to talk about the general issue of monetary stability, and particularly address the situation in Mexico. The thing to start with is whether there is a consensus in Mexico that monetary stability is necessary, and that people want it. That's the first thing, because of course if there's a lot of dissension, if people think that the ideal rate of inflation is the current one, 15 percent or more, then there's not going to be a political consensus to remedy the situation.

If there is a consensus that "monetary stability" is desirable, then how should we define it? Is it going to mean a rate of inflation of 1, 2 or 3 percent or less than that, or is it going to mean something else, or is it going to be defined in terms of a stable money supply, or a stable exchange rate? These are the three main options. You know my views on this, that the best of those three options is, for Mexico, a fixed exchange rate to the U.S. dollar. Now, don't come away from this meeting with the view that I believe fixed exchange rates are appropriate for every country. A fixed exchange rate is not an option for the United States. There's no currency out there that the United States, which has the largest currency area in the world, could fix to. The issue is less clear for the euro, but I can well understand the arguments of those who believe that the euro should target the inflation rate and let the euro float.

My view is that if a country is near a big neighbor with a stable currency, it will achieve monetary stability easier by fixing its currency to its neighbor's than by going it alone. The Mexican economy is about a half-a-trillion-dollar economy, the U.S. economy is a nine-trillion-dollar economy, it is 18 times larger. The size issue is satisfied. Second, the neighbor has to be stable and has to have a track record of greater stability than the home economy, otherwise fixing wouldn't make any sense.

I spent some time in Uruguay in the 1980s, and reporters were insistent in asking me if I thought Uruguay should fix its currency to Argentina's. I replied that it should not, because even though Argentina is a big neighbor, it was then an unstable neighbor, and Uruguay would simply import the instability. Uruguay would become a monetary province of an unstable area.

Once it is decided to pursue monetary stability we have to choose between inflation, monetary or exchange rate targeting. I argue that stabilizing the peso to the dollar is the best policy in the long run for Mexico. If so, what is the process by which one should get to that position and what is the end result – what kind of fixed exchange rate? In this conference we have discussed three options for fixing: one is a monetary union, as Herb Grubel eloquently argued in his case for a monetary union for North America, including Mexico. I think that's ideal. But it is not at the moment an option for Mexico. Perhaps it will become one in the next decade or so. But unless we are talking about a monetary union based on the U.S. dollar, I don't think it is a political possibility for the United States. Nor do I believe it would be good for the world economy at the present time to scrap the U.S. dollar for an amero.

The second possibility is dollarization. That is a real possibility, but it's also a desperate one. Dollarization means phasing out the Mexican peso. That's a political step that I think would be difficult for Mexico to take politically. I'm not against it, I just think that you're not going to get consensus in Mexico for monetary stability achieved by scrapping the peso for the gringo currency.

The third option is a currency board system. A currency board system restricts the central bank to all but foreign exchange purchases, unless there's some special provision for excess reserves, and it can buy some domestic assets. It would be a system that guarantees that all future issues of pesos are backed by dollars. Argentina did this with its convertibility law. There are different types of currency boards and this isn't the time for me to talk about which is better. The system has to be tailored to the particular economy.

Argentina came close to a currency board system solution. With it the country achieved a high degree of stability and a rapid expansion of exports. But there was a problem. The currency board system was not rigidly adhered to and throughout the 1990s Argentina never did really get complete control over its fiscal situation. External shocks created speculation against the peso. Whenever there was a crisis abroad, doubts arose about the country's commitment to the currency board, and that gave rise to big blips in interest rates.

The innovation that I suggest, and that could work here if Mexico establishes a currency board, is to do everything that Argentina did, but in addition negotiate and buy a guarantee of the exchange rate from the U.S. Treasury. This would avoid the "Menem" problem of Argentina.

Now I can't speak, of course, for the U.S. Treasury. The United States will not do this easily or quickly, nor should they. There is the problem of moral hazard. The worst-case scenario would be that Mexico would start to slacken off on its monetary and fiscal discipline and hold fewer reserves than really necessary, relying on the guarantee rather than fiscal and monetary performance. To guard against this possibility the guarantee should be available for shocks arising *outside* Mexico.

No one should think that a successful stabilization plan will work without meeting the preconditions. These include a balanced budget, a complete commitment of monetary policy to the international equilibration mechanism, and unanimity of support from the entire economic team.

I should mention that a guarantee from the U.S. Treasury would break new ground for the United States, but it would have earlier precedents. The French Treasury has been guaranteeing the CFA (Communauté Financière Africaine) franc area since 1946. I spent the summer of 1970 analysing that system for UNECAFE (United Nations Commission for Asia and the Far East) in Africa and Paris, and came away as a great admirer of it. The 13 central banks in Africa were some of the few central banks that had monetary stability.

But now, how does Mexico get to the point where the currency board can be established? First of all, budgetary stability is necessary. Abel Beltran's figures show Mexico's budget deficit in 1998 was 1.2 percent of GDP. Mexico has a primary economic surplus in this budget, meaning that if you take account of interest payments, which are quite high, if interest rates drop, the budget will be in surplus. That is, you'll get more than 1.2 percent of GDP in revenue because instead of paying 15 percent interest rates, you'll pay 8 or 10 percent.

The next thing Mexico must do is get its inflation rate down. What should be the mechanism? Deceleration of the money supply is one approach. When discussing the former socialist countries in Europe, with inflation rates over 50 percent, I've often argued that the most important first step is to slow the rate of monetary expansion, without worrying over fine-tuning by price-level targeting. But once inflation has been reduced to, say, 15 percent, then it is desirable to shift into inflation targeting. By this means, get the inflation rate below 5 percent and then you're within the ballpark where you can announce that at some future date you're going to fix the exchange rate. For example, you announce you're going to fix the exchange rate in six months' time, while the rate of monetary expansion continues to slow. Monetary growth in Mexico in 1996 was 40 percent, in 1997 it was 29 percent, in 1998 it was 17 percent. Work to get the inflation rate down to 5 per cent, and then prepare the stabilization plan.

In something like two years from now, Mexico will be ready to announce a date in the future that you're going to fix the exchange rate. Then you have the problem of deciding what the rate is going to be, avoiding the inflationary problems of undervaluation, and the deflationary problems of overvaluation. Labor unions need to be part of the discussion, to pre-empt overshooting of the wage rate. Probably it's better to err slightly on the side of undervaluing the rate.

Now I said earlier that a currency board system could be run by a monkey. This is because there is no discretion, it is entirely automatic. But its preparation requires a very intelligent person or group. Leadership is very important. Argentina was lucky when it established its currency board system to have not just [Argentine President Carlos] Menem, but [Argentine Finance Minister Domingo] Cavallo, [Central Bank President] Roque Fernandez, and other economists like Carlos Rodriguez, all of whom had PhDs. They knew what to do and there was solid leadership. Success requires that the minister of finance, and head of the central bank and all the important political leaders support the plan. If possible it would even be desirable to have a consensus that incorporates more than just one political party, so that there will not be speculation during election times.

ROBERTO SALINAS: Judy Shelton suggested that over the next three to five years, we will see major policy decisions regarding exchange rate and monetary policy in North America, and arguably the entire hemisphere. I remind you all of the question that Al Harberger posed at the end of the last session: what happens under a fixed exchange rate when you get a major negative external shock? In Mexico, we're very familiar with this type of scenario, because in 1994 we had a fixed exchange rate; benchmark interest rates were at 9 percent in February of 1994, despite the Chiapas uprising and the corresponding stories in the international media. Nevertheless, there was still great optimism surrounding capital inflows under the North American Free Trade Agreement and expectations were highly positive. March 23, 1994, that's when our big negative external shock came – the assassination of [leading party Presidential candidate] Luis Donaldo Colosio. Retrospectively it would be very interesting to do exercises: what should Mexico have done in April 1994 to avoid the hemorrhage of reserves following the assassination of Colosio? It's that type of question that identifies one difficulty with a fixed exchange rate.

Another question that Judy posed concerned whether we should use devaluation or exchange rate tinkering – Bob Mundell calls this exchange rate "gadgetry" – in order to stimulate export growth. I fully concur with Judy that this is a form of cheating. I beg to differ, though, with Abel Beltran del Rio's opinion about whether we should weaken the exchange rate if there are more Mexican license plates in El Paso than there are American license plates in Juarez. This also has to do with the policy of accumulation of reserves. The explanation of its purpose under a floating exchange rate was not clear to me. The reason I mention this is that on August 1, 1997, there was a press bulletin issued by the Comisión de Cambios, with the logos of the Bank of Mexico and the Ministry of Finance, that stated that the Comisión de Cambios had decided to increase the accumulation of reserves, "in order to avoid an undesirable appreciation of the currency that might undermine the rentability of the tradable sector." In other words, to enhance exports. This disturbed me a great deal because it sent the wrong signal of the purpose of the accumulation of reserves – is it really to avoid appreciation of the currency so that exports will be higher, or is it really to serve some other purpose? Indeed, the whole idea of exchange rate intervention under a floating exchange rate seems to me to make very little sense.

This would be the equivalent of some sort of exchange rate Robin Hoodism, because what it entails is cheapening the salaries of Mexicans in order to improve the cost position of those that are earning in dollars. It's not surprising to me that every time that Mexico has had large exchange rate devaluations, there was subsequently a wonderful trade surplus in Mexico. For instance, after the 1994 devaluation, the World Competitiveness Report dropped Mexico from number seven among 59 countries to number 53 in 1995. So did it really improve our overall competitiveness, or did it actually constitute a wealth transfer, not a wealth creation, a wealth transfer from the poorest sector of society to a richer sector of society? These are the issues that go beyond technical monetary policy and are actually ethical issues. Are we falling into the broken window fallacy of [French economist] Frederic Bastiat? Are we falling into the medieval practice of curing a patient by letting all the blood flow out of the body, in this case out of the economic body? All the red in the trade figures is gone, but has that actually improved the patient? I think if we're going to talk about monetary stability, we have to start with one premise: a country does not get strong by weakening its currency.

DAVID ANDREWS: I want to return to the issue of a currency union in North America. Let me preface my remarks by saying that I agree with Bob Mundell, both in terms of the policy problems and the political problems – a currency union is not a short-run option. Inasmuch as we will in the long run all be dead, I'd like to turn to the medium term, say, ten to 15 years from now. The question has been raised in various guises over the course of the conference: what lessons can be learned from the European experience and applied to North America? Let me begin by saying that the lessons don't appear to be very positive. As Bob Solomon pointed out, the European monetary integration process was a very long one. It's been going on for about 40 years, since

the formal initiation of monetary integration as a project of European governments. Let me point out as well, that the success of the EMU relied to a very
substantial degree on some special circumstances. In Europe, the regional
monetary hegemon, Germany, was committed to the principle of political
partnership and was willing, for the first time in monetary history, to retire a
successful and stable currency as a demonstration of that commitment. I
would submit that those circumstances do not prevail in North America.
Professor Grubel's piece [Chapter 5] concludes with the remark that the
biggest obstacle to a North American monetary union would be indifference
in the United States. I think that's a substantial understatement. I think there
would be hostility in the United States.

But rather than just paint a picture of gloom and doom, I want to suggest
some positive lessons that can be learned in order to alter the constellation of
forces in the medium term for a North American currency union. Let me
suggest three from the European experience: Number one, look upon crises
as opportunities. The monetary unification project began in Europe following
the 1968–69 exchange rate crisis between the French franc and the deutsche
mark. It was shortly after this crisis, at The Hague summit of 1969, that
governments first announced their intention to move towards monetary union. Likewise, it was after a very unsatisfying realignment of European
currencies in 1987, that central bankers came up with the Basle reform,
which introduced technical reforms to the monetary system that led to foundations for what ultimately became the Delors Commission Report. It polled
governments for the political responses to unsatisfying circumstances. How
can we make, in the North American context, exchange rate alignments
unsatisfying, as unsatisfying to Americans as they are to Mexicans? It seems
to me that's the critical point.

Moving to point number two: the development of constituencies in the
United States that rely upon exchange rate stability with the peso. To a
substantial extent, NAFTA will serve that purpose – a growing constituency
with a stake in a single currency. Constituencies could be mobilized by an
inappropriate use of state intervention in exchange rates. The common agricultural policy in Europe developed large, political constituencies in Europe
that had an interest in exchange rate stability. Are similar programs possible
within the North American context that would help develop a U.S. constituency in favor of exchange rate stabilization with the peso?

The final point is the most controversial one, and that is the importance of
linkages to other issues. In Europe, the move to monetary union both in 1969
and in 1987 had to do with linkage between this economic issue and other
issues, in particular having to do with German policy priorities. Germany
offered to sacrifice the deutsche mark in 1969 in the context of its Ostpolitik
policies as a reassurance to the other countries of Western Europe that Ger-

many was not turning eastward. Likewise, [German Chancellor Helmut] Kohl offered essentially the same deal in 1989 to his Western European partners in the context of German unification.

We have to think creatively about what kinds of deals are possible between the U.S. and Mexican governments that would interest the United States government in undertaking a formal currency union arrangement. Let me put one on the table – a controversial one – the United States again has nothing immediately to gain from a supranational monetary institution. It has quite a bit to gain from a supranational anti-narcotics force, for example. Now, could these two issues be linked? Could drug enforcement be handled on a regional basis in exchange for handling monetary relations on a regional basis? Let me conclude my remarks by responding to Sven's invitation to submit new names for the North American currency unit. Let me suggest that Canada, the United States and Mexico form the North American Regional Currency Organization, or NARCO.

AUDIENCE QUESTION: I am Isaac Baila from Anáhuac University and this is my question: There are many conflicting ideas here. But I guess we all agree that inflation reduces Mexican growth. As Mr. Beltran said, the state still holds enterprises, and one strategic enterprise is Pemex [Petróleos de Mexicanos]. Pemex sells gasoline in Mexico and it has a monopoly. Gasoline is used to produce many services and goods in this economy. Why allow the gasoline price to keep on increasing? Why lose all this efficiency through a monopoly?

PAUL J. ZAK: I want to return to the issue of economic growth. For those of you who were at the press conference on the first day, that was the first question a reporter asked: why is Mexico less developed than the United States? This is a fundamental question. We have said so many things here that I thought I would try to distill this down to three or four general rules about growth and see if I can draw a couple of implications from them that most economists would agree with.

Number one: the source of economic growth is individual opportunity. Number two: growth increases when opportunities increase. Number three: growth falls when instability or risk increase. Number four: risk falls when institutions are stable and transparent, particularly monetary institutions. That is the theme of this conference. This is the link between monetary stability and economic growth.

Judy mentioned that the interest rate in Mexico is 30 percent. Why is that? Risk premium. The risk premium in Mexico is very high compared to the U.S. Bankers making loans have to forecast the policy that will be in place during the life of the loan. When policy is uncertain, bankers have to charge a large risk premium to ensure that they don't lose money. As soon as there are institutions that allow this instability and risk to fall, growth will increase.

What are the implications of this? Most prominently, if you look at the Asian tigers, and compare them with Mexico, two things were different in Asia – a more rapid increase in incomes, and a substantial decrease in birth rates. The same thing will happen in Mexico. My own work has shown that policy stability and freedom decrease birth rates, while political instability raises births. The issue is what happens to per capita incomes. Not only can you raise the denominator of income divided by population, you can decrease growth in the denominator, producing a double effect driving up the ratio. When this happens, within a few years a country's numbers look much better. This all comes back to having institutions that will guarantee stability for the medium to long term, including institutions that promote monetary stability such as a currency board, or dollarization, or maybe a floating exchange rate, but it's the institutional level at which the reform has to take place. The linkage between monetary policy and growth is simple. It is the construction of the institutions that is difficult.

AL HARBERGER: I'll take off from where Roberto was in his last two statements. One could easily have understood from the first statement that a fixed rate makes a country vulnerable to huge negative shocks. And then the second statement, which seemed to say countries should go to a fixed rate. This is a dilemma. The way I deal with this problem is to say that the insurance policy of a flexible rate is worthwhile if a country has a big risk of negative shocks. Paying the costs a flexible rate year to year, insures that when a fire or earthquake comes, a country can respond with a devaluation, which will be an equilibrating devaluation. With a negative shock, the real equilibrium price of the dollar has gone up. The purpose of the devaluation is to get to it. Nobody in his right mind is in favor of a devaluation when the real equilibrium rate hasn't changed.

In El Salvador, they have something like a billion dollars a year coming in from expatriates. This has made the dollar abundantly cheap in El Salvador since about a fifth of Salvadorians went to the United States. So, those in the agricultural sector used to complain that the government should devalue the currency because they can't live with the cheap dollar. So twice they tried. They doubled the exchange rate, and within eighteen months the price level had doubled. Then they more than doubled it, and within another couple of years the price level had doubled. Why? Because they were changing the exchange rate just as a gimmick. That's the type of thing that Judy was talking about. But, if we're talking about maintaining an equilibrium real exchange rate and having that move up and down endogenously, I think a floating rate is a useful thing.

One should realize that those who favor monetary stability don't have to favor fixed exchange rates. The United States is not on a fixed exchange rate, and it's a stable monetary country. The European countries have not been on a fixed exchange rate since the early 1970s and they are stable monetary countries. Developing countries can also function with a floating exchange rate and still be considered as stable monetary countries.

ROBERT MUNDELL: I think Al is a hundred percent wrong on this. I'm also picking up on Roberto's questions about how a country handles shocks. Of course, we all hope that countries don't have big negative shocks. Mexico had a great shock in the mid 1970s when it found that it was sitting on one of the great reserves of oil in the world. It reacted to the shock by a policy of excess spending. Then when it became ten times richer than it had ever been, it moved toward a program of monetary instability after 23 years with a fixed exchange rate.

Why the move to monetary instability? There are a lot of American economists who came out very strongly in opposition to the idea of a European currency. They hated the idea of the European currency. And the wish was father to the thought. Many of them predicted at the last Bologna–Claremont conference [see *Currency Crises, Monetary Union, and the Conduct of Monetary Policy: A Debate Among Leading Economists*, Paul J. Zak, Ed.] that it wouldn't come about.

One of the main arguments against a common currency or fixed exchange rates is asymmetric shocks, events that affect countries differently. But I do not believe that asymmetric shocks are best dealt with by exchange rate changes.

Just think about what happened when the United States had an asymmetric shock. Oil prices soared fourfold in 1974. New England became a basket case, in a kind of quasi-depression. Conversely, Texans became oil-rich millionaires and they loved it. Had New Englanders had a separate currency they might have devalued and America would have lost its monetary unity. But no new resources would have been created by devaluation.

In 1985 an oil shock came in the opposite direction: New Englanders were gleeful and Texas was a basket case. If Texas had a separate currency, they'd have devalued. If both of those things had happened, they would have ended up with monetary instability in both areas and the country would have been worse off. Nobody says that real shocks don't hurt a lot. Terms of trade shocks hurt a country. But exchange rate changes do not have any clear-cut effects on the terms of trade.

In 1974, when oil prices went up four times, the Italians said that they had to devalue. Why, when the price of oil goes up four times do you want to devalue and make it go up ten times? Monetary instability isn't the solution.

If a country has an earthquake, no new resources are going to flow in by devaluation and inflation. Now you could argue that a devaluation redistributes the burden differently, so the exchange rate can be used for a redistribution of income. But surely that is using the wrong instrument to redistribute income. If there are bad shocks to the distribution of income, there are also bad shocks that come from excessive devaluation. One can see the effects of this in Abel Beltran's figures. For instance, in 1994 real wages in Mexico fell steeply and they've never recovered. Therefore, the poor people are bearing the burden of this. There's a transfer of the burden away from the financial sector of the economy – very unfairly – because when you've got a permanent inflation, it's the financial sector that gains, because they can hedge against inflation. It's the poor who can't hedge against inflation.

ROBERTO SALINAS: As a point of clarification, I didn't mean to suggest how shocks should be handled, which I think is an extremely important question for any type of exchange rate regime. In addition, I do have a bias towards fixed rates, and I won't hide that, but whether you're under a floating regime or a fixed regime, it still remains a legitimate question – whether exchange rate intervention should be used to subsidize those that earn in dollars and not those that earn in pesos, a point Judy raised. That's completely independent of the very difficult question of how to handle external shocks.

Under the floating rate that Mexico has today, along with the reforms advocated by the Dallas Fed, what would happen if Mexico had a disciplined fiscal policy, a long maturity structure for our public debt, a safe and sound banking system, financial supervision that instills public confidence, enforceable property rights, generally accepted accounting principles, monetary transparency, market based economic reforms, the opening up of Pemex, the opening up of electricity, the rule of law, free trade, low inflation and exchange rate autonomy? My impression is that Mexico would have capital inflows. This is very good, as wealth would go up. But, under Abel Beltran del Rio's formula, there would be a lot more Mexican license plates in El Paso than American license plates in Ciudad Juarez. Should we attempt to tinker with the exchange rate in order to correct any potential imbalance there, or should we continue along this path of what would probably lead to 7 or 8 percent growth per year with stability?

HERBERT GRUBEL: I have two comments. The first is that I ask Al Harberger, if there is an earthquake in Monterrey, but not in Mexico City, why should the exchange rate disequilibrate a finely functioning economy of Mexico City and the rest of Mexico? It makes no sense to me. The second point is that I am not in favor of fixed exchange rates in the traditional sense, whereby we have an independent monetary authority which sooner or later will have to abandon the fixed exchange rate. In my judgment, the fixed exchange rate is the worst of all possible worlds, because it tends to accumulate disequilibria and then there is the big shock when the rate finally has to be adjusted. So in my judgment, what Bob [Mundell] and I are talking about is that we want the benefits of a fixed exchange rate without the negative consequences that are attached to having a fixed exchange rate in the traditional sense. What we therefore want is a permanent commitment that countries cannot abrogate, so that there is no opportunity for devaluation. Under the traditional definition of a fixed exchange rate, there is an opportunity for devaluation.

ROBERT BARTLEY: In 1976 the peso was at 12.5, it had been there for 20 years. In 1993, Mexico lopped off three zeroes from the peso. Today the exchange rate is at 9.5, which is equivalent to 9,500 pesos to the dollar on the old basis. Thus, since 1976, Mexico has devalued from 12.5 to 9,500 for the dollar. This is the magnitude of devaluation we're talking about.

AL HARBERGER: My answer to Herb is that an earthquake in Monterrey is not a major external shock. A major external shock is when the equilibrium real wage of the whole country's labor force, broadly counted, goes down by at least 10 percent and you have to either try to push wages down that far or devalue the currency to avoid that.

AUDIENCE QUESTION: As Dr. Beltran noted at the beginning of the session, we have economic growth in Mexico, but population growth is faster. That implies that per capita GDP is going down. So we can't say that welfare is improving. Now, if we follow up with what Dr. Zak said, that the birth rate should go down, then we can say that per capita income is going up in the country. However, I'd like to include what Dr. Salinas said, which is that this growth in per capita income is not evenly distributed, and the distribution of income in this country is skewed. Studies have shown that inequality in the distribution of income in Mexico is increasing over time. I would argue that monetary stability is a first step towards economic growth, but as long as we have this huge inequality in distribution of income, that's a barrier to economic growth Mexico.

AUDIENCE QUESTION: I'm Cauhtomoc Sanchez and I want to make a brief comment. This is a hard comment to make in front of such an important group of international monetary experts. I believe that monetary policy and money printing does not create value at all. Therefore, the monetary policy question is a secondary question, in my view, that should come as an answer to a first set of considerations. Here I differ a little bit from Mr. Zak, who said that the first step for growth is opportunity. I think it's more what you do with that opportunity. You need entrepreneurship and productivity to create growth. I believe monetary policy should be designed after considerations are made regarding the entrepreneurial capacity and the productivity of a nation. Given a set of productivity and entrepreneurship conditions, monetary policy should be different from one country to another. I've been hearing here advocates of fixed exchange rates and floating exchange rates, and I think that should be a consideration made after understanding the real capacity of the economy to create value, which depends on entrepreneurship and productivity.

PAUL J. ZAK: Both the points raised by audience members are good. I'll take the second one first. Entrepreneurs are not created. They are already there. Policy creates opportunities for them. Entrepreneurs will emerge if you give them the chance – it's happened everywhere.

The first questioner made a very good point about income distribution, an area that I've worked in quite extensively. Income inequality changes not only the amount, but the form of transactions. That's very important, but it is a second order effect. If you can get your economy to grow, you can always compensate those who don't benefit from growth. The first order effect is to get the economy growing.

CHRISTOPHER JOHNSON: I want to answer the gentleman from the floor, because I think he raised an important point. If all other things were equal, which of course they never are in economics or in life, maybe each country should have its own monetary policy because it has different banking traditions and different cultural views of money. But, for example, in the European Monetary Union, countries have abandoned any advantage they might have had by having a separate monetary policy and a separate currency. They've abandoned that in favor of the advantages of a single market and I think this is extremely relevant to Mexico and the United States. If Mexico had the same monetary policy as the U.S. in return for having an enhanced version of NAFTA, trade would grow considerably. Free trade is not at all the same as having a real common market.

FAUSTO ALZATI: I think there is a false dilemma in this discussion that I will try to clarify. Flexible versus fixed exchange rates is really a discussion of whether we should have a discretionary policy on one hand, or a long-run commitment to targets on the other. It's not flexible or fixed, it's discretion or rules. In the ultimate analysis, what's the difference between a "competitive devaluation" and an increase in tariffs? I mean, a competitive devaluation is equivalent in a sense to protectionism. We have known since Adam Smith that protectionism is always a device for preserving the distributional arrangements of a society. It's never a device for enhancing the growth of an economy.

The real choice we have is: do we want a limited economy with flexible policy choices, or do we want rules – commitment to long-run targets that provide the incentives for economic agents to develop a flexible, more diversified, more resilient economy which is not only capable of dealing with short-run shocks, but is capable of innovation and growth in the long run. That's the real choice we're facing here. Historically, the countries that are rich now are the countries that in the past made the commitment to good institutions, to good rules, and to less discretion. The countries that are poor are those who created a very risky environment for entrepreneurship by having too much discretion in the hands of policymakers. That's the real choice. It's not flexible or fixed.

ARMANDO BAQUIERO: In the final analysis, I think that nothing that I said goes against the spirit of the discussion. We want growth and low inflation. This is the practical application of monetary policy, that's what we're aiming for. But some statements disturb me here. One thing that I want to address is the suggestion that the exchange rate is overvalued. We can say that the real exchange rate has appreciated, but that doesn't mean that it's overvalued. If it is, under a flexible exchange rate system, run out and buy dollars. That will take care of the problem. So we're not really worried about that. If the market doesn't like the exchange rate, the market will correct it.

Next, our interventions in the foreign exchange market aren't dictated by the foreign exchange rate because that is the law. Central banks which have control over the exchange rate are the exception rather than the rule. I don't even think that the U.S. Federal Reserve legally has the right to move the exchange rate, nor the Bundesbank [the German central bank]. Mexico in this respect is no exception. It really doesn't make any difference. Once the exchange rate regime is set, then policymakers operate within that, and the government does not interfere. The latest purchase of dollars in the market by the Bank of Mexico was announced just recently (it's announced at the end of each month for the following next month). Sometimes the options are exercised, and sometimes they aren't. To give you an idea, the latest amount was 250 million dollars for the entire month in a market that moves about nine billion dollars every day. So, we're not talking about a big intervention.

JUDY SHELTON: I want to respond to some comments made during this session. First, Mr. Baquiero, thank you very much for being responsive to the questions I posed. I appreciate it and I think your answers were helpful. I do not think the U.S. should impose currency reform on its neighbors. But I do feel strongly that U.S. leadership, in the context of monetary developments, especially in this hemisphere, does require some vision of where we want to go. Both President [George H.W.] Bush and President Clinton have supported a free trade area of the Americas by the year 2005. We're talking about 27 countries that would form a precursor to a common market that would be larger than the European Union, would have higher combined gross domestic products, and would certainly have a much larger population. What we've seen from the European example, to put it simply, is first you establish a common market, and then a common currency. So the U.S. should not be indifferent. Like NAFTA, this is a major policy issue that goes beyond administrations or political parties – it's the future of the international monetary system, which we will address in the closing session. I would just like to end by reminding the group of an infamous U.S. Treasury Secretary, John Connally, under President Nixon. In 1971, when the U.S. ended the Bretton Woods international monetary system, he found himself confronting our trade partners in Europe and Asia, some of whom were rather upset that the anchor for international monetary stability had been removed. Connally said, rather flippantly, "It may be our currency, but it's your problem." I would hope that now, some three decades later, the attitude has changed somewhat, and perhaps we could send the message: "It may be our currency, but it's your opportunity." I hope we can develop a mutual interest in a common monetary system.

9. Economic policy in Japan and East Asia

Introduced by

Jeffrey A. Frankel

There seems to be a trend in the Western Hemisphere to a dollar block – at least some movement in that direction. Europe, with the adoption of the euro, is clearly moving in that direction. It would be nice for the symmetry of the world monetary system if we could talk about a yen block in Asia, but I'm going to argue that that's not really the trend. I'm going to talk about four things: a yen block, Japan and yen–dollar rate developments, whether exchange rate movements caused the East Asia crisis of 1997–98, and lastly, some thoughts about the "corners hypothesis."

Five years ago it was quite the rage to say the yen was taking over Asia, or earlier in this decade that Asia was becoming a yen block. I'd looked at a number of tests and decided, even then, that this was not the case. If you look at trade patterns, they're stronger across the Pacific once you adjust for natural factors. If you look at financial influences, New York interest rates have a bigger effect on interest rates in Asia than do Tokyo interest rates. And if you look at currencies, even in Asia, the dollar has always dominated the yen as a currency. For example, several years ago I estimated that the weight given to the dollar in countries that have basket pegs for their currencies is on the order of 80 to 90 percent, with at most 10 percent weight on the yen. At the time, that seemed sort of a novel finding.

Today I think it's even more clear that we don't have a yen block forming in Asia. The decade-long recession in Japan has undermined any worries that some Americans had that Japan was going to pass the United States as the number one economic or monetary power. More broadly than just the issue of currencies, in the 1980s there was a lot of talk about how Japan Inc. and Asia in its footsteps had found the secret of growth, that Asian values had something to do with it, and that the structure of the financial system there with the emphasis on banks and relationships and long-term horizons had something to do with it. Many assumed that the Asian system was better than the Anglo-

American system with its financial structure emphasis on securities markets and quarterly profit and loss statements and shorter-term horizons. It was said that Japanese capital was more patient, waiting through the temporary downturns. Now everything looks different. The American brand of capitalism is looking a lot better. We now call the Japanese system the Asian system, or even crony capitalism. There is probably a danger of overdoing that swing of the pendulum. People who talk as if Asia can do nothing right today can't be any more correct than ten years ago when they said it could do no wrong. The idea that Asia might be adopting the yen as an anchor currency, which in my view was never very plausible, is even less plausible now. Asia remains more linked to the dollar.

Now a bit about Japan. I won't say much about the real economy. They have had two quarters of positive growth now, and hopefully Japan, after eight years of recession, is beginning to come out of it. Mainly I will talk about the yen–dollar exchange rate since this is a monetary conference. I agree with Bob Mundell that exchange rates are often a source of disturbances. Sometimes exchange rate changes are a response to disturbances and useful, but I agree that often they are a source of disturbances, and maybe even more often the source of disturbances than the means of equilibration to them.

There have been some very big movements in the yen–dollar exchange rate over the last 20 years: a strong appreciation of the yen after 1985, and in my view, up through 1993, it made a lot of sense. In the first place, I, like many people, thought that the yen–dollar rate had overshot, that in 1985 the dollar was unreasonably strong. Initial dollar appreciation in the early 80s was for good reasons, but that it had gone too far, that it had overshot. So coming back from that made sense and we've had ever since then very large U.S. trade deficits. In my view, in 1994 and 1995, it went too far. I think the yen overshot its equilibrium in 1995 analogous to the way the dollar overshot its equilibrium in 1985. One can speculate on why this occurred – it may be that bubbles often follow a pattern that begins based on fundamentals, but then the fundamentals level off or even turn around – but the market gets carried away just by some sense of sheer momentum.

There also was a remarkable misunderstanding of U.S. policy all through late 1993 to 1995, when the U.S. Treasury wanted a strong dollar. This is nothing new. Now [Treasury Secretary] Larry Summers gives a speech and says he wants a strong dollar and the papers report it like he's coming out in favor of a strong dollar. His predecessor [Robert] Rubin had been saying exactly the same thing since 1993, that a strong dollar is good for America. For some reason, the markets didn't believe it and nor did the newspapers. Even though there was intervention in support of the dollar in 1993, 1994, and 1995, for awhile the market didn't believe it and then finally it turned around in mid-1995 following a G7 meeting. From 1995 to 1998 we saw a fairly strong appreciation of the dollar against the yen and other currencies. In my view this again made sense. Part of it was a correction from the overshoot that I mentioned, but also the U.S. economy was remarkably strong.

One of the things that one does on the Council of Economic Advisors is the U.S. forecast that goes into the budget process, and I did a terrible job – for three years in a row I grossly underestimated the growth rate of the U.S. economy. We said 2 percent each year roughly, and it came out 4 percent each year. Meanwhile, the Japanese economy was unexpectedly weak, and the rest of Asia had remarkably divergent economic paths. For these reasons, it made quite a bit of sense that the dollar was strong. Some were concerned about what this did to the U.S. trade balance, these very large trade deficits, but in my view eventually we're going to have to have a correction. At a time when the U.S. economy has been so strong as it has over the last three years and the rest of the world economy has been so weak, it makes a lot of sense to have a strong dollar and a trade deficit. This relieves some of the pressure that would otherwise build up, to have cheap imports to hold down inflation and to have capital inflows that hold down interest rates.

In the last year, we're completing the cycle once again as the yen has appreciated rather sharply against the dollar. I don't presume to explain every fluctuation in exchange rates. It's hard to tell whether the current appreciation of the yen is appropriate or not. It presumably has something to do with the incipient Japanese recovery. But the Japanese are concerned that this will be an overreaction, that the yen will appreciate too much, and that it will choke off the Japanese expansion because exports will lag. As a result, they've been trying to intervene to hold down the strong yen. So far, their interventions in the foreign exchange market have not been very successful. That's true throughout the last 20 years, but it's true in the last year as well.

There are two theories as to why their interventions have not been successful at holding down the yen and supporting the dollar. One is because the interventions are not sterilized. The Bank of Japan claims they can't sterilize, in other words, that they are allowing their dollar purchases to increase the Japanese money supply. The argument of the Bank of Japan is that they can't sterilize because they can't push interest rates down any farther. I don't think that's quite right. There are many who would argue, including most American economists, that sterilized foreign exchange intervention can't have an effect. I don't think that's quite right either. I did a study with [University of Michigan economist] Kathryn Dominguez looking at the pattern of interventions since the Plaza Accord in 1985 and we found that often intervention does have a short-term effect, aside from whether or not it's sterilized. There is a lot of truth to the second explanation, which is that intervention doesn't have much effect unless it's coordinated, and in particular, unless the U.S. authorities join in with the Bank of Japan.

The Japanese have been asking for a coordinated intervention in the G7 meeting in Washington last weekend [September 25–26, 1999] where I went to watch what was going on. There were some who thought they might get a deal, that the U.S. would agree to join in with intervention and the Bank of Japan would be pressured into increasing the money supply and, in other words, not sterilize their interventions. That didn't happen. What did happen was a weaker initiative where the Japanese got some language saying that yen appreciation might be undesirable, and hinting at possible intervention. As language in G7 communiqués goes, it's pretty strong to say that apprecia-tion of the yen is undesirable, but it was only a hint at an intervention. On the Japanese side, it was only a hint of further monetary expansion. The Bank of Japan, I think, was a little misunderstood. Their language was perfectly consistent, they could claim, with what they'd already been doing, by using the phrase "within the context of a zero interest rate policy." The Bank of Japan has not changed their policy at all. My prediction is that the United States would not go along with intervention at current levels. The dollar–yen rate would have to go quite a bit farther, and conditions would have to change before the U.S. would join in and buy dollars and sell yen as we did in the first Clinton administration.

Third topic: Did exchange rate movements cause the East Asia crisis? There are several versions of the proposition that movements in exchange rates were responsible for the East Asia crisis. The first version says that China's devaluation in 1994 was the source of the problem, because Korea and South East Asia had been rapidly increasing their exports of basic labor-intensive manufactures over the preceding decade. Then, many of the products that they were producing moved their manufacture to China. As Chinese exports of consumer electronics, sporting goods, textiles, and shoes increased, exports of the exact same products from the NICs [newly industrialized countries] to the United States fell at the same rate. This perspective claims that trade deficits in the rest of Asia eventually forced the other Asian coun-tries to devalue.

I don't buy this view for three reasons. First, what China did in 1994 was simply to lower the official rate of the yuan, to bring it into equality with the parallel market rate. But it was the parallel market rate at which most trade already had been taking place. So that wasn't that big a change for most Chinese trade. Second, the nominal devaluation was not a real devaluation. It was offsetting inflation. One could argue how much inflation was the result of the devaluation, but a fair amount had happened before. So whatever you think of that, it doesn't seem that it would have caused the others to lose competitiveness, given that it was not a real devaluation. Third, looking at the precise timing of the loss of exports on the part of Korea and the Southeast Asian countries, especially among basic low-skilled manufactured exports, most of the shift took place before the 1994 devaluation and not after. That is pretty convincing.

The second possibility is that the depreciation of the yen against the dollar that I mentioned from 1995 to 1998 was the source of the problem. One hears this a lot – that the Asian countries were tied to the dollar, and so when the dollar strengthened against the yen, they lost competitiveness and that was why the Thais had to devalue, followed by the others. There are two reasons why I don't buy this, though there's probably some truth to it. First, the movement in the yen–dollar rate just reversed the preceding appreciation of the yen, which I think went too far. Even at 130 yen to the dollar, it was just retracing what it had done in the early 1990s. A second and related point is that in the early 1990s and the late 1980s when the yen was so strong, there was some concern about debt problems in South East Asia. The concern was the yen was going to appreciate so much that these South East Asian countries, which had a fair amount of yen debt, would have trouble servicing that debt. The Indonesians and others were quite concerned about this. You can't have it both ways – an appreciation of the yen makes things difficult for East Asian debtors and a depreciation of the yen makes things difficult. It is true that exchange rate volatility in general is a problem, nevertheless I think there is a tendency when the yen was strong to focus on the debt service problems of the East Asian countries, and when the yen was weak, to focus on the export problems of the East Asian countries, and in both cases to ignore the other side of the equation.

Next I'll discuss the Thai devaluation, which was the source of the East Asian crisis. We have learned that devaluations often are not as smooth as reported in textbooks. The Thai devaluation was very costly. We've learned that there are big contractionary effects of a devaluation. My textbook actually lists ten of them, but the one that has turned out to be the most important is firms and corporations that have dollar-denominated debts, but that have earnings in local currency. After the devaluation they can't service their debts and they go bankrupt, and that has a contractionary effect on the economy. We've learned about contagion, that it is transferred to other countries that didn't seem to have problems with their fundamentals. There's a lot to this, but my answer is something that Al Harberger mentioned: when a country is out of reserves, it has no choice but to devalue.

For the Thais in July 1997, there was no alternative. If there is a balance of payments deficit and there are no more reserves, there's nothing else you can do. The same was true with Korea a few months later, and pretty much the same thing was true with Mexico in December of 1994. One could argue that these countries should have done something earlier to protect the exchange rate, like tighten monetary policy, or go on a currency board, but one has to acknowledge that in the end, there really was no choice. A country can't defend a currency if it doesn't have any ammunition to defend it with. The mainstream view of the lesson to be learned is that Thailand should have exited earlier, probably like Mexico in 1994. There is a kernel of truth to the corners solution – when a country comes under attack, it should either adopt a really firm institutional commitment to a fixed exchange rate if it can sustain that, or if not then it should exit early enough while it still has reserves.

There is another story about the way exchange rate arrangements caused the East Asia crisis. A very popular hypothesis is that it's not movements in exchange rates that caused the problem, it was the fixity that caused the problem. We have models of balance of payments crises called speculative attack models – we have what's called the third generation model based on moral hazard. The idea is that firms had unhedged foreign liabilities and they knew that they would get bailed out in a crisis and the banks knew they would get bailed out and so they took large risks. That was the claimed source of the problem. One version of this model indicates that unhedged dollar liabilities are the problem, and may suggest an argument for floating rates. Barry Eichengreen, for example, has argued that the fixed exchange rate created the illusion that there was no such thing as exchange rate risk and so banks and firms were careless. They took on dollar debts because they didn't see the risk. One suggested cure is to have a rule against unhedged dollar liabilities. Another is to have floating rates. Again, there is some truth to this, but I see some problems as well.

First, one should recognize that for most emerging market countries today, telling them not to have unhedged dollar liabilities is the same as saying don't have liabilities period, because the world's investors don't want to lend to these countries in local currency. If Indonesia had tried to borrow rupiah, nobody would have lent to them. Then you might say, okay, they should borrow in dollars but then they should hedge. That doesn't help because hedging means transferring the rupiah risk to foreign investors who generally won't take it. Initially a bank, but then some foreign resident somewhere has to take an unhedged liability. This is not going to work if foreigners don't want to take this risk. A prescription to Indonesians not to borrow in foreign currency is a recommendation not to borrow. The world financial system cannot support the high levels of capital flows that happen in each of these boom phases like the early 1990s because we always seem to have a crisis which ends up discouraging lending. If that's our line of argument, we should be aware that that's what we're arguing.

Those who say that this is an argument for floating rates, that exchange rate volatility forces borrowers and lenders to confront exchange risk, have to

acknowledge (1) people are irrational in these markets, in that without volatility they don't see the risk, (2) it says you're introducing gratuitous volatility,
not just some natural volatility under floating rates, which will reduce people's desire to undertake unhedged foreign liabilities, and (3) this is de facto a
Tobin Tax – a way to reduce the volume of capital flows. Gratuitous volatility
reduces capital flows, reducing foreign indebtedness, and therefore there are
fewer crises. I have never heard any of the proponents of floating rates carry
this argument to its full extreme.

Lastly, I will discuss the corners hypothesis, which states that intermediate
regimes – adjustable pegs, target zones, crawling pegs, basket pegs – don't
work. Thus, countries have to go to the extremes of either firm fixing exchange rates, or on the other hand, free floating. It is true, after all, that the
East Asian countries did not have explicit dollar pegs, with the exception of
Hong Kong. They had various combinations of basket pegs with big weights
on the dollar and narrow bands. It's ironic for me that five years ago I had
some trouble convincing people that the yen was not taking over Asia and
that the dollar played the dominant role in these baskets, and now I have to
remind people that even though the dollar played the dominant role in the
baskets, that's not the same thing as saying that they were literally pegged
100 percent to the dollar. Nevertheless, they were pretty closely tied to the
dollar, particularly Thailand and some of the others.

The question is whether these intermediate regimes should either firmly fix
through institutional arrangements such as a currency board or dollarization,
or go the other way and freely float. As far as I know, this hypothesis is new
in the last six years; I first heard it in the aftermath of the 1992–93 crises in
the European exchange rate mechanism from Barry Eichengreen and a few
other people. The idea then was that we were wrong to think that the path to
European Monetary Union is a continuous one where you go from floating to
wide bands – plus or minus 6 percent the way the Italians and the British
initially had – and then plus or minus 2.25 percent, narrowing the bands, and
then plus or minus 1 percent and then all the way to fixing. That didn't seem
to work in 1992–93, and the alternative is very wide bands, for instance, plus
or minus 15 percent in 1993 that turned out to be right in a sense. The phrase
was, you don't cross a chasm in two jumps. You take a big running start and
you cross it in a single jump and if you try to stop at a halfway point, you end
up at the bottom of the canyon. I was skeptical of that analogy at the time, but
one has to say it worked.

Over the preceding year [1998], the euro-land countries went from very
wide bands to a monetary union. After the 1997–98 crises in emerging
markets, the corners hypothesis, sometimes called the hypothesis of the vanishing intermediate regime, became a general proposition. The reason is that
all the countries on intermediate regimes – Mexico in 1994, Russia in August

of 1998, and Brazil in January 1999 – had crises. In every case, not only was it not a currency board, it wasn't even a simple dollar peg, it always had some crawl or some band. So one can see that if you're involved in running policy in those countries or you're at the U.S. Treasury or the IMF, the temptation is to think that life would be a lot easier if these countries would abandon these intermediate regimes and go to free floating, because a country can't get attacked by speculators if they float. The other possibility is to go to the other extreme of giving up your currency completely, because then again you can't be attacked. There's some plausibility to this, though I have not heard anybody offer a theoretical rationale for it, other than observing that intermediate regimes don't seem to work. Some think it follows from the impossible trinity.

The impossible trinity says that a country cannot have monetary independence, exchange rate stability, and open capital markets all at once. It can have any two of the three, but it can't have all three. It doesn't quite follow from that, because increased capital mobility forces a country to choose between monetary independence and exchange rate stability – not quite true. It's true that the increasing integration of financial markets sharpens the choice between exchange rate stability and monetary independence. Still, there is nothing in the logic of current theory, or the impossible trinity, or modern financial markets that says that you can't have both. Still, it's true that it doesn't seem to have worked very well.

Let me conclude by saying that I do not accept the new conventional wisdom, as Larry Summers calls it in *The Economist* and *Foreign Affairs*, that the corners hypothesis is now U.S. Treasury and IMF policy. I think it's wrong to apply this to all countries everywhere all the time. By far the majority of IMF members have intermediate regimes. Even if you classify the managed floaters with floating, and even if you classify the Francophone countries with fixing, even then, fully half the members of the fund have intermediate regimes, and in many cases I think it's appropriate. What I do think is true, is that when a country is under pressure in the capital markets, when it has a lot of debt and is exposed to international investors, when for some reason confidence is lost in the country, because of an assassination or an increase in U.S. interest rates, or profligate fiscal policy, such a country should move to the safety of one corner or the other.

The principle behind this is – transparency is the buzzword – but I'd rather use the word verifiability. Taking our theories of nominal anchors, there's no reason why you can't get all the benefits of a dollar peg – visibility and credibility – from a basket peg or even a basket peg with a band around it. The trouble is if you have a policy like, for instance, Chile's, which for most of the decade was a basket peg with a band and a crawl, and you announce the anchor but the public doesn't trust you to begin with, they won't trust you after you announce, because they can't tell the difference. Looking at an exchange rate, you can't tell whether it's floating or following a basket peg with a crawl and a band. With a dollar peg, you can look the exchange rate up in the newspaper the next day and see if it's the same as it was the day before and you can verify it right away. You need a year's worth of data or more to verify if a country is doing what it says it's doing when it's following a basket peg with a band and a crawl; you don't get instant verifiability. That's the best I can do at modeling the notion that when you're exposed to finicky international investors, the intermediate regimes don't work. The other possibility is it's just that the grass is greener. All these countries have had trouble with intermediate regimes because most countries have been on intermediate regimes. So now they run for the corners, and then the next time there's a crisis at the corners, they're going to run back for the intermediate regimes. That's a possibility.

DISCUSSION

CHRISTOPHER JOHNSON: I want to make a comment first on Jeff's last point about corner theories as the conventional wisdom that only two things work. The first is not just fixed rates, but actually a currency union, and the other is complete floating. The problem is that countries which adopt one extreme suddenly move to the other. This is known in economics as time inconsistency. It can be quite advantageous to a country to fix its exchange rate apparently for all time if financial markets accept this and then suddenly to loosen the strings and float. Then they may go to a new fixed regime, and if they really can't decide which works best then they end up with a managed float.

I also want to comment on the position of Japan and the yen in what is now a tripartite world currency system, not in terms of currency areas, because I think we've all realized that the yen is not used widely outside Japan as a world currency. There is no yen block the way there is a euro block, and a dollar block of countries pegging to the dollar. Nevertheless, the exchange rate triangle between the three currencies has now become the sort of focus for worry and indeed for volatility. This is partly due to the fact that we now have the euro as a single European currency. Before that, we had different currencies which tended to move differently. There was no kind of focus in Europe for the world triangle with the exception of the deutsch mark. We can now focus on the movements between the dollar, the euro and the yen, which are volatile and bewildering, and in some cases prejudicial to stable economic growth in the countries concerned. We talk about the dollar being strong against the euro, but looked at from America, the dollar is weak against the yen. Maybe the yen is the more important relationship. But this tripartite relationship is going to keep changing. The pecking order will change quite regularly and unpredictably. And I think the high yen is going to postpone any hope of a Japanese recovery unless the yen is brought down. The world economy is only firing on three cylinders out of four, and this must be a worry to all of us.

The world's central bankers and finance ministers cannot practice a policy of benign neglect towards this very important tripartite currency relationship. My ideal would be to have a simple world monetary union, where one hundred yen equals one dollar, equals one euro, equals one Canadian dollar, or one heavy Mexican peso. We need to think very hard about what is really a new situation. We've got a focused, unstable triangular relationship and each apex of the triangle matters a great deal. It's a mistake to concentrate on one edge of the triangle or two without looking at all three simultaneously. So I think the mathematical modelers are going to have quite a time trying to get their minds around this one.

ABEL BELTRAN: Jeff, perhaps can we learn about the financial markets by seeing what other disciplines have found. It struck me that in political science, for example, it's very clear that mixed regimes are the ones recommended in practice. There isn't a pure democracy or a pure aristocracy or a pure oligarchy. We combine the best of each system in practice. Does something like this make sense to you? The other thing that came to mind is a course I took in maritime engineering in which a system is composed of many compartments to maintain stability. A sudden and massive movement of fluid from one part of the system to another keeps it afloat. Don't we have something analogous for what you are studying and presented so well?

ROBERT BARTLEY: I'd like to put the Malaysian case on the table for at least a little discussion, because I had a very interesting lunch last week with [Prime Minister] Mahathir [Mohamad]. The subject of the lunch was to try and get him to keep his courts from throwing our reporters in jail and keep his son from suing us as a source of revenue. But we also talked a little bit about his economic program. In response to the crisis, Malaysia instituted capital controls. Mahathir said the first thing they wanted to do was to fix the exchange rate so that businesses could plan. So they put controls on expatriation of capital. Since that time, one must accumulate profits over the last five years to expatriate them. A year later, he claims to have saved the investors a lot of money compared to selling off their loans. They also banned offshore trading in their currency and stocks, which had been previously traded in Singapore, and they passed rules prohibiting the repatriation of the rupiah. The purpose of that was to keep hedge funds from getting their hands on the currency and stocks and shorting them. That means that the currency is still kind of convertible – you can bring in dollars and change them to rupiah or can take rupiah and change them to dollars just as long as you do that in Kuala Lampur. I don't entirely trust his account of these laws, but it's not clear to me that that is necessarily a worse response to the crisis than letting everything go the way the Indonesians did. I wonder whether there are any thoughts on this?

HERBERT GRUBEL: After the dramatic depreciation of the currencies for Indonesia and Malaysia, textbook descriptions came to mind of a manufacturer that supplies windshield wipers to all the General Motors plants around the world. Now that their costs have fallen so much, why aren't they going to be able to drive out of business everybody else supplying windshield wipers to the world? Of course, it takes a while to renegotiate contracts. But one of the things missing from your description was that even if they had perfect business plans and contracts, nobody would lend them any money. So I wonder to what extent the fragility of the banking system was responsible for the depth and the duration of those crises. You didn't mention that at all.

JEFFREY FRANKEL: Let me respond to Herb's point first. I didn't go into detail, but I think Herb is right. After some of the Mexican devaluations, I heard that exporters couldn't export because they couldn't get intermediate inputs. One often hears about the inability to get credit for production or imports, but one thing that was quite remarkable in the Asian crisis is that firms in Indonesia, Korea and elsewhere couldn't export because they couldn't get credit – working capital – even though they had very competitive prices. That was really quite surprising, and I would attribute this to unhedged foreign liabilities. It's one of a number of reasons why devaluations don't always stimulate exports and output as the textbooks say.

Working backwards, Bob Bartley said, correctly, that the situation in Indonesia was so bad for this reason and a number of other reasons, and anything must be better than what occurred. I tend to agree. This is what led [MIT Economics Professor] Paul Krugman to say, even though we don't like capital controls, many of us see some advantage to Chile-style controls on short-term banking inflows during the boom phase, although almost no economists like controls on outflows. But compared to what? When things get so bad, maybe the part of the impossible trinity that you have to give up is the open capital markets. By the way, the Cambridge Massachusetts version of the impossible trinity is Krugman, [Harvard Economics Professor Jeffrey] Sachs and [MIT Economics Professor Rudiger] Dornbusch, because they're all impossible, no, they all take different positions at any point in time. Recently, Dornbusch's position is that developing countries should give up monetary independence and have a currency board. He's a convert. Sachs's position is that developing countries should give up exchange rate stability and these countries should have devalued. Krugman's position is countries give up financial integration and put on capital controls. Although, I think he was a little appalled when Mahathir took his advice, and he wrote a letter saying, "I didn't mean you," but I think that's just because he doesn't like Mahathir, the way we all don't like Mahathir.

I don't think the outcome proves that the advice was wrong. Certainly Malaysia did not fall apart. It has recovered pretty well. The other viewpoint is that controls came so late in the game that they couldn't screw things up that much, and the recovery was already underway. We don't have a clear verdict, but we can rule out that as soon as a country puts on controls it is doomed because this is anathema to the international financial community. As I understand it, people are rushing to put money back into Malaysia now. I'm not ready to support capital controls on outflows even under those circumstances, but it does definitely give one food for thought. Bob, I never thought I'd hear the editor of the *Wall Street Journal* be willing to give up the free trade area of Mercosur, and willing to give up free capital markets, but maybe monetary stability is sufficiently valuable that it's worth giving up these things.

Let me now respond to the question that Abel raised: isn't there an intellectual presumption for intermediate regimes? He used the analogy of political scientists, but actually, economists almost have a creed when it comes to interior solutions – everything in life is a trade-off. Trade-offs are fundamental to economists' thinking. In this case the trade-off is between the advantages of exchange rate stability which many of the people around the table have spoken eloquently about, and the advantages of monetary independence. Until recently, one would have thought that the proper answer for most countries was in between – an intermediate solution – you get some of one and some of the other. That's less clear now than it used to be. I personally believe in intermediate solutions as opposed to corner solutions, but I think where the corner solution is most applicable is in our good old friend, the optimum currency area. My definition of an optimum currency area is a geographic area where it makes sense to have its own currency. If you draw it over too small a region, just the city of San Miguel de Allende, that doesn't make sense because all the people who come in from out of town have to change pesos every time they go in and out of town. It can't be the case that a very small, open region should have its own currency. On the other hand, I'm not one of those that thinks that the whole world should be on one currency. I think the optimum size for a currency regime is intermediate, it's somewhere in between San Miguel de Allende and the whole world.

ROBERT MUNDELL: I'd like to talk about the yen–dollar rate and a possible solution to the problems that have been raised. As you know, in 1948, Japan, under the American occupation, had like Germany, a ten-for-one currency conversion. This rate lasted until the 1970s, after which it went to 360 yen to the dollar. This was a period that the Japanese call the sudden economic rise in which Japan moved from a country with a per capita income and wage rates of about one-tenth of the United States, to something more than one-half of the United States by the 1970s. This rapid growth continued and by the 1990s, Japan has achieved something close to parity in per capita income as measured at current exchange rates. But since the 1980s, there has been a big problem with the yen–dollar rate, reflected in bickering between Japan and the United States over the rate. This began in earnest with the Plaza Accord in September 1985. The whole idea of the Plaza Accord was to get the G-5 countries – the five countries that were then included in the IMF SDR [Special Drawing Rights] basket – together to talk, so they could put pressure on Japan to appreciate the yen. But it put the whole burden of adjustment onto Japan, which was forced to tighten its monetary policy, leading to a crash in the Japanese bond market. The yen did rise, but slowly at first. It was not until the price of oil plummeted, greatly improving Japan's terms of trade, that the yen soared and, of course, we know that by January 1988 the dollar was falling toward 120 yen.

I remember asking, at a conference in Zurich in 1987, Akio Morita, the founder of Sony, whether Japanese companies could survive at a dollar exchange rate of 120 yen. His reply was that it would be difficult at first but he thought they could do it if they could rely on that rate to continue for several years.

In January 1988, I was asked to write a column for a Japanese paper. In it I suggested that, to stop the appreciation of the yen, which was getting close to 120, the Bank of Japan should intervene in the forward market, putting a floor to the dollar. At this time, as today, there was a lot of skepticism about the effectiveness of intervention because the amount of funds that could be committed by the central bank was only a tiny fraction of daily turnover in the markets. But once a country decides to commit itself firmly to a particular forward rate, it can be very easy. A quick announcement of intervention of untold amounts in the forward market and you get a complete turnaround, because no one is going to fight the central bank in the forward market. To this day I don't know if the Bank of Japan did intervene in the forward market, but the slide of the dollar did stop before 120.

We know that in 1995, in the wake of the Mexico Crisis, the dollar went down as low as 78 yen, its all-time low since World War II. Then in 1998 it shot up to 148 yen and speculators said it might go to 200. Several hedge funds lost huge amounts of money on this bet as the rate came back down near 100. I can't imagine an exchange rate creating more damage to an economic system than the tremendous volatility of this rate, so crucial to the Asian economies. If that doesn't seem to bother countries like Canada or Mexico or Europe too much, you can imagine, though, how disturbing it is to countries that have big markets in both Japan and the United States.

Japan has achieved more or less parity in per capita income with the U.S. and close to technological parity. There's a high degree of capital mobility between the countries. But Japan has almost anorexic consumers – high saving rates leading to huge trade surpluses with the United States. These two economies are in many respects complementary. And they achieved a convergence in inflation rates. Inflation has been virtually eliminated by all practical means in the U.S. and Japan. Nevertheless, with the build-up of all these current account positions, Japan has an enormous surplus of assets abroad. Its net creditor position is close to a trillion dollars. The U.S. net creditor position is about 1.2 trillion dollars – so those two things cancel out.

It seems to me that these two countries are very complementary in the right sense. They're ideal for a monetary union. This may be mind-boggling, but the two are magnificently complementary in the world sphere. The United States' military position is enormous and provides the defense umbrella. Japan is unlikely to be able to solve its political problems in Asia on its own. The problem of the currencies in Asia would be solved if there were a monetary union between the United States and Japan. With a common currency and the trappings of royalty, you'd have a monetary area that represented 14 trillion dollars of GDP, roughly 45 percent of world GDP.

A monetary union between Japan and the United States could be achieved on the same principles as those on which the present European Monetary Union is based. Five conditions are needed: (1) agreement on a common inflation target for the combined area; (2) agreement on a common price index for measuring inflation (like Eurostat's HICP – Harmonized Index of Consumer Prices); (3) locked exchange rates; (4) a common monetary policy – say a Monetary Policy Committee composed of Bank of Japan and Federal Reserve governors; and (5) a procedure for dividing up seigniorage.

Because of the asymmetry in sizes of the two economies, the Bank of Japan could undertake the task of fixing the exchange rate (with a US guarantee!) by means of unsterilized intervention. The system has worked without any important flaw in the European system, where currency speculation has disappeared. With this kind of monetary union between the two countries there would be no need to follow Europe in its advance to the next step, so filled with political implications, of scrapping the national currencies in favor of a single currency.

HERBERT GRUBEL: I attended a conference where I listened to a representative of an investment bank with a branch in Jakarta, but headquartered in Hong Kong. He told the following story: he said there was an entrepreneur in Jakarta who wanted to borrow millions of dollars in order to monopolize and make more efficient the taxi system. The local office looked at the proposal and said, no way, we shouldn't commit money to this. Then suddenly, a wire comes from Hong Kong, from headquarters saying, make the loan anyway. And they made the loan. What was the reason? It turns out that the entrepreneur was a relative of [former President] Suharto and the loan was approved and, of course, it crashed and the investment house had a big loss.

How can we talk about the problems of Southeast Asia without talking about the structural problems of the economy, structural problems which have destroyed the banking system? Can you imagine what kind of a problem they would have had if they actually had gone ahead and built the proposed mile-long building in Malaysia? These are megalomaniacal schemes, not the market working. We are applying our textbook models to an environment in which it is not applicable, because we don't really have market forces working in the way in which we assume they work as we wrote our textbooks.

JEFFREY FRANKEL: I did not give my complete lecture on sources of the East Asia crisis and the lessons to be learned from it – that's a very long lecture. I'm sure all of us could do that, but there's still a lot left unsaid. But to briefly respond to Herb Grubel, I think we've learned that it's not just macroeconomic policies that matter, but also crony capitalism, corruption, and other aspects of the structure of the financial system. I actually defend the IMF for broadening the conditionality of their programs beyond the traditional macroeconomic conditionality and going into some of these other aspects which I think are relevant, for example, the rule of law. There are limits to what the IMF can do far afield from the financial system, but I think we have learned a lot. Because after all, there was an Asian miracle. It was based on a lot of good things – high saving rates, good basic education, export orientation, and even an equal distribution of income that many people think helped – those fundamentals were there. None of that has changed, but we see that there are other things that matter as well.

Next, I want to respond to Bob Mundell. It's true that it seems that Japan and the United States in many ways are natural complements, and there's been suggestions made of a marriage. The Japanese save a lot, invest, and build a lot of factories that produce a lot of goods. Then they use some of the saving to lend Americans the money to buy the goods and the cycle is complete. In 1983–84, I had a previous stint at the Council of Economic Advisors working for Martin Feldstein. At the time, U.S. fiscal policy seemed to us much too loose and Japanese fiscal policy too tight. The idea was we could solve the whole problem by sending Ronald Reagan to be Prime Minister of Japan and importing [Yasuhiro] Nakasone to be President of the United States. Then we'd each have the right fiscal policies.

I agree with Bob that Japan could bring the yen down if they really wanted to. He emphasized the forward market – he said that any central bank if it intervenes massively enough in the forward market can work its will on its exchange rate. I have to mention that this is how Thailand got into trouble – they intervened very heavily to protect the baht. They bought baht and sold dollars on the forward exchange market. Then suddenly on July 2, 1997, they had no foreign exchange reserves. Needless to say, at that point they had to devalue. But Japan could bring the yen down if they're really determined to do it. The standard way to do this would be expansionary monetary policy. They need to stop sterilizing yen intervention. Short-term interest rates have been close to zero for some time in Japan, and the Bank of Japan claims they are already doing everything they can – they can't possibly further stimulate the economy because short-term interest rates are zero. That's not quite right.

First, they could buy Japanese government bonds, because long-term interest rates are not zero. Second, there might be a credit channel or a wealth channel, where just by creating money through the banking system or otherwise, you stimulate the economy. Third, there's the expectation effect – if the Japanese Central Bank creates a lot of money and raises expectations of inflation, that will push real interest rates down, even if the nominal interest rate can't be pushed down. This is Paul Krugman's point. Fourth, the Japanese can push the exchange rate down similarly. If they create a lot of money that creates the expectation of future inflation, then the future price level will be higher, creating the expectation that the exchange rate will be higher, that the yen will be weaker in the future, and then arbitrage passes that to the present. So I agree that if the Japanese really were determined, they could get past the newfound independence of the Bank of Japan and push the yen down.

10. The future of the international monetary system

Introduced by

Robert Solomon

In the 1990s, the developing world grew much more rapidly than the so-called industrial world. The developing countries were a locomotive for the world economy in the 1990s. This is quite different from the era of *dependencia* [claimed exploitation of developing countries by developed countries], which existed in many people's minds in earlier decades – quite a change. The increase in capital flows to developing countries also brought with it a certain amount of volatility in capital movements and crises as we all know. I'll get back to that later. That's one big change international monetary system.

Trade has also increased, increasing faster than output in the world as a whole, so that trade connections among countries have become closer. This increases interdependence, just as the increase in capital mobility increases interdependence. These two major changes have led, in part, to crises that we've talked about here. These crises have led to discussions about how to change the international monetary system.

What I shall do to discuss the future of the international monetary system is to summarize a new report published by the Council on Foreign Relations in the United States. A commission was established at the suggestion of President Clinton by the Council on Foreign Relations with a number of very eminent people on it. I won't name them all, but they include [former Federal Reserve Chairman] Paul Volcker; [senior advisor at Lehman Brothers and Counselor to the Center for Strategic and International Studies] Jim Schlesinger; [Harvard Economics Professor] Martin Feldstein; [Director of the Institute for International Economics] Fred Bergsten; [University of Chicago Law Professor] Ken Dam; [University of California Berkeley Economics Professor] Barry Eichengreen – who has been a member of the Bologna–Claremont group; [Dennis Weatherstone Senior Fellow at the Institute for International Economics] Morris Goldstein, who wrote the report; [Chairman of the Financial Stability Institute at the Bank for International

Settlements] John Heimann; [former U.S. Trade Representative] Carla Hills; [Princeton University Economics Professor] Peter Kenen; [MIT Economics Professor] Paul Krugman; Nicholas Lardy from the Brookings Institution; [Chairman of the Council on Foreign Relations] Pete Peterson; [Vice Chairman of Citibank] Bill Rhodes; [Financier] George Soros and a few others. These people met over a period of time and put out a report. I will highlight their recommendations.

Let me start with the IMF. There continues to be an important role for the International Monetary Fund in reducing the vulnerability of its members to crises and its concern with two elements of crises. The first is the fact that crises can occur; and the second is contagion – when a crisis occurs in one country or one area, it has effects elsewhere. The purpose of the various proposals are to try to, if not eliminate, at least reduce both the number of crises and the contagion. They make a number of suggestions for what the IMF should do in its relations with its members, and in the loan conditions it applies to its members. These include what are called "good housekeeping" measures: sound macroeconomic policies, compliance with international financial standards, including the dissemination of information, adhering to the Basle principles, and efforts to put into place non-IMF sources of liquidity for support in case of need.

The commission also recommends that the IMF should narrow the focus of its operations to macro policies and exchange rates – the usual variables that we talk about. I should add that they also put in a plug for another proposal that's been widely made, namely that when a country does get into crisis, private sector lenders have to be somehow brought into the solution – "collective action" is the term that's used. The private sector should share in the solution to the problem.

Another proposal of this group put forward without qualification is that they propose a Chilean-type of tax on capital inflows. This 1 percent tax is not to be imposed continuously, and constitutes a non-interest bearing reserve requirement equivalent to a tax on the first year in which capital comes into a country. Its purpose is to discourage short-term, in and out, capital movements. This is quite different from the Tobin Tax, incidentally, which Jeff mentioned a little while ago, which was a proposed tax on foreign exchange transactions. This is simply a tax on capital inflows primarily for developing countries.

With respect to exchange rates – this will not please everybody in the room – their recommendation for developing countries is to avoid pegged exchange rates. They go on to say that the IMF should not lend to support pegged exchange rates, recommending managed floating for emerging markets. I happen to have a certain sympathy for this proposal. They do not rule out currency boards in cases where currency boards look to be appropriate, as in the case of Argentina. And they do not rule out currency boards in what they call "unusual circumstances."

The commission also recommends that the International Monetary Fund should stick to its normal lending limits, but should be able to lend in larger amounts to deal with contagion. They recommend that a new contagion facility be set up in the IMF to replace both the supplementary financing facility and the new Contingent Credit Line facility. They recommend that a new larger facility be set up to deal with contagion problems.

I've summarized the commission's major proposals because this is a way the system may move in the future. I think that this is a reasonable set of proposals for the future of the international monetary system. In particular, since we spent so much time on exchange rates, I think it's interesting that this group of distinguished people, with some disagreements among them, recommended managed floating for most developing countries. Of course, Fred Bergsten was not in favor of that proposal. He wants target zones, and some of the commission members joined him, but hardly a majority.

Finally, let me say that as we look to the future, I don't know whether or not we'll get a currency union between Japan and the United States, but we do have a currency union in Europe, as of January of this year [1999], and this certainly is going to change the nature of the international financial system. It remains to be seen, as we've already discussed to some extent, what effect the euro will have on the international monetary system. Some people have predicted, such as my friend Fred Bergsten in a *Foreign Affairs* article, that there would be a rush out of dollars into euros. We haven't seen that yet.

My own judgment, and I guess I've written this more than once, is that the euro's role as a reserve currency will grow only gradually over time. That seems like a reasonable forecast. This is not, though, a development that Americans should worry about. It's not going to hurt the United States at all for the euro area to become a reserve center. I don't think the reserve currency function of the United States is an exorbitant privilege as General de Gaulle referred to it back in the 1960s. The United States does pay interest on funds that foreign central banks deposit in the United States. We may get a slight interest advantage in it, but it's not an enormous benefit, and it's not something we should worry about losing. That's the way I see the future – it's an incomplete picture, but it's sufficient to start a discussion.

DISCUSSION

SVEN ARNDT: Thanks, Bob. I would like to hear from members around the table whether the international financial architecture needs changes. If so, how should it be changed? If not, why is the system perfectly adequate? Bob suggested that recent changes might require that the architecture needs some adjusting. The CFR report proposed changes that are fairly cosmetic, fairly minor. The IMF stays in place, but its purview is narrowed somewhat.

ROBERT SOLOMON: The word "architecture" is an exaggeration. Some people have said all we're really talking about is changing the plumbing. Maybe a little bit of interior decorating. These are not enormous changes that are being discussed, but that word architecture somehow became popular. I did mention two or three proposals that are not insignificant.

AL HARBERGER: My first proposition is that, from my own sense after floating around the developing world for 40-odd years, is that the benefits of the [International Monetary] Fund in particular, and to a lesser degree the [World] Bank, substantially exceed their costs. I think we have to not think of them as lending institutions. I was once asked to write a set of guidelines for a World Bank president. I said, the worst thing you can do is think of this bank as a lending institution. Think of the following: the previous year, the gross lending of the World Bank was seven billion dollars. Consider the following thought experiment: suppose they had not lent that seven billion dollars, but given it to India. And suppose that India had done the impossible, investing that seven billion dollars at a 20 percent real rate of return. That would have produced 1.4 billion dollars of income which is precisely 1 percent of India's GDP; that is to say, it would have produced a one-time addition of one percentage point to the growth rate of one country. If they were to add one percentage point to India's growth rate for a decade, they'd have to do that ten times over. So, that's not the mission of the World Bank.

ROBERT SOLOMON: May I say, I didn't mention the World Bank even once?

AL HARBERGER: I understand. I'm using that example because the Fund fits in the same category. If the product of the Fund's lending is 10 percent or 15 or 20 percent real return, multiplied by the amount of lending that is being done, consider that product as the increment to GDP of the recipient countries. Compare that to the GDP itself, and it's a tiny fraction.

ROBERT SOLOMON: Why don't you compare it with the balance of payments need of the country that's borrowing?

AL HARBERGER: In any case, I think that where the Fund and Bank have had a positive effect is in the fact that they have provided better economic advice than the average recipient country has had. They've dramatically improved economic policy. In 75 percent of the cases, the good technocrats within the countries have been on the side of the Fund in their advice, and this has promoted better policies. We have to think in those terms.

I think that the Mexican bailout was a great thing, particularly because if Mexico had not been bailed out, Argentina would have gone under. That is a very interesting twist. However, I think that it's very hard to justify the Fund's bailouts in Eastern Europe, particularly Russia, except on very broad political terms. They are probably considering that Russia possesses a huge nuclear arsenal. But, if you set aside the nuclear story, if the Fund were to do similar things in other countries, I think we should all be against that. The type of facility that is being suggested by the CFR commission is probably a good thing. But one really has to worry about the use of Fund assets for purposes that go significantly beyond economic stabilization. I think when you get into politics, it ought to be political money that implements such policies.

ROBERT SOLOMON: That's consistent with this report.

FAUSTO ALZATI: When we bring up the issue of architecture, we also need to think about the engineering underlying the architecture. The question of what changes we expect to occur in the international financial system is closely linked to what changes we expect to occur in the global economy. In the last decade and a half, we have a clear movement towards freer trade and freer capital mobility. We don't have the tendency towards freer movement of labor, as in the Victorian era of pax Britannica. This is a major issue. Are we expecting trade and capital mobility to make all the adjustments, leaving labor as a fixed factor?

The second issue I would like to raise is whether the "new economy" is real. Is there really a new industrial revolution taking place, moving us toward a knowledge-based, information economy? If that's the case, what kind of international monetary system do we need for this kind of economy, which is radically different from an economy based on the movement of manufactured products and primary inputs going from one place to the other? The speed of mobility is very different. In the new economy, it takes the shape of a network, rather than a bilateral, or trilateral relationship. So it's a more complex kind of animal. How does this affect monetary relationships? The conventional wisdom of the Washington consensus type, with very nice covers and very nice sponsoring institutions doesn't do any good, and may actually do a lot of harm, because it precludes an open discussion of what's really taking place.

I have two final comments. First, the collective action problem is very important. In the discipline of international relations, it's perhaps one of the classical problems. If you don't have a hegemonic power taking care of stability, there is no way to ensure that stability in case of major systemic crises. So if that's the case, are we going to witness a world with two hegemons – Europe and the U.S. – or three, as was suggested, or only one, and who is going to take the responsibility for that hegemonic role, if anybody, in the global economy?

Second, a brief aside on the Chilean tax. I think the problem with the Chilean tax, given the Mexican experience, is that if a country wants to prevent short-term capital inflows and outflows, capital is not attracted to such a country in the first case. We had this situation in Mexico. We had short-term capital because we intentionally attracted it by having very high short-term interest rates, and then we complain when the relationship between Mexican and U.S. interest rates changes and the capital leaves. It was attracted artificially by discretionary policy decisions which are not sustainable in the long run, so we shouldn't complain if they go away when the situation changes.

JEFFREY FRANKEL: I'm going to try to put a little structure on the architecture. It's a word that is in need of definition even more than the real exchange rate or an optimum currency area, because there are many definitions floating around. I think [U.S. Treasury] Secretary Robert Rubin popularized it during the Asian crisis when we were examining what we could do to reduce the frequency and severity of future crises. Reform proposals typically focus on one of three attributes of the architecture: the exchange rate regime; the degree of capital mobility; and whether there is a global lender of last resort, and the nature of that lender. It's also important to make the distinction regarding the level of reforms we are talking about. The most fundamental reforms, which have to do with changing the foundation of the building, are politically unlikely. That doesn't mean we shouldn't talk about them, but we want to talk about them in a different way or maybe even in a different venue than the more practical tinkering.

The most fundamental reform in the area of an exchange rate regime would be if the whole world went on a common currency. In the area of capital mobility, it would be serious capital controls to reduce the degree of capital mobility generally. Alternatively, it could be complete liberalization, the way that a few years ago the IMF was going to do – modifying the articles of agreement so that capital account convertibility was something that every country had to do. In the area of a global lender of last resort, the truly fundamental level of reform would be, on the one hand, abolish the IMF, for which there are some proponents, or on the other hand, create a true lender of last resort that could print money at a global level, which is also an extreme proposal.

The less extreme proposals would be like the ones in the Council on Foreign Relations report, which I would describe as remodeling – moving some walls around in the house. The even more moderate proposals are like the ones that the G7 [Group of Seven Industrial Countries] and G22 [Group of 22 Industrial and Newly Industrialized Countries] prepared and presented at the IMF annual meetings in October 1998, which are more like interior decorating because they were tinkering so much at the margins, and had little to say about exchange rate regimes. In the area of capital mobility, they didn't go as far as the Chilean tax, and the U.S. Treasury was really not enthusiastic about that sort of thing, but they did say that there is something to this notion.

We haven't talked much about the composition of capital flows, but this appears to be as important a determinant of which countries are going to get into trouble relative to total capital flows. If you look at statistical studies of warning indicators, such as total indebtedness, or a current account deficit, or the debt to GDP ratio, these are not very good predictors of the countries that get into trouble. The proportion of capital inflows that are short-term, dollar denominated, intermediated through banks, and particularly if you express this value relative to the level of reserves, is a pretty good predictor of which countries will get into trouble.

The G7 and G22 said to forget about putting a tax on short-term flows to discourage it, we have the opposite problem. Korea actually liberalized short-term capital inflows without liberalizing long-term flows and direct investment, and Thailand went out of its way to establish an international banking facility to increase short-term borrowing. On the lender side, the Basle rules of behavior for banks discourages banks from lending short-term securities to emerging market governments. These have a low risk rating because the money is lent to a government, and leads to more lending, which can be a problem.

Regarding the lender of last resort, the most they said was the private sector needs to be more involved in rescue operations to reduce moral hazard. There is also a tinkering provision that seems to be on everybody's reform list that permits bond and loans contracts to be amended so that in the event that country gets into trouble, with a majority of the creditors voting, the debt can be restructured, rather than having a minority of creditors who can hold out against restructuring.

Let me finish up by talking about the intermediate level, the things that were in the Council on Foreign Relations report that Bob mentioned. This was inspired, by the way, by a speech President Clinton gave to the Council on Foreign Relations at the Bank/Fund meetings last year [1998]. In my view, this was a turning point. After the Russian default, lenders seemed very risk averse and it looked like we were going to have a general contagion. A number of measures were taken, some of which were in the President's speeches and some of which were in these G7 reports, and maybe the most important one was [Federal Reserve Chairman] Alan Greenspan reducing interest rates and the rest of the world's central banks following suit. I think that the entire set of measures did help. Here are the three most important things in the CFR report that Bob mentioned. On exchange rate regimes, it's the corners hypothesis – they suggest avoiding intermediate regimes. On the capital flows, they support Chile-style taxes. And on the lender of last resort, they come out against the large-scale bailouts that we've had. They want to go back to IMF programs that stay within the original quotas, and not have these super-large bailouts like in Mexico, Korea, and Thailand.

My own view is that it depends on the circumstances. Chile-style taxes, yes, when a country is at the stage in the cycle when there appear to be excessive capital inflows in the form of short-term bank dollar-denominated lending, and when you don't know if the money is going for a good use or not. It's a good way to play for time. This may only buy you a few years, but it can help. On the corners hypothesis, same thing. Yes, under certain circumstances in a crisis, head for the corners for security. But that doesn't mean everybody should be at the corners all the time.

JUDY SHELTON: The expression we keep hearing – the need to rebuild the global financial architecture – it's not that the rhetoric is too strong, but in my opinion the actions have been too weak. Just over a year ago [1998], President Clinton and Secretary Rubin, as Jeff said, were talking about the most serious global economic crisis since World War II. Exactly a year ago, the IMF was looking for 18 billion dollars in new funds from the U.S. Congress and it really came down to the wire. I recall being at a lunch at the time sitting next to [Mexican Central Bank head] Guillermo Ortiz, and everyone was very glum. [House Majority Leader, Representative] Dick Armey said very bluntly to that group that he didn't think the IMF was putting out fires, he thought they were the arsonist. I don't think Dick Armey is the kind of person who would be persuaded because the Council on Foreign Relations sees an important role for the IMF. Many of us have heard [Federal Reserve Chairman Alan] Greenspan in a speech say to the effect that Mexico was the first crisis of the new global economy, Asia was the second crisis, and he predicted there would be a third, because he said we have not yet solved the problems in the global financial arena. I think Russia probably qualified as the third, and then the Long-Term Capital Management [hedge fund] debacle on the heels of that.

My point is that we've been very lucky. We've almost forgotten how bad it was a year ago and how serious the implications were. Greenspan did lower interest rates, we've gotten through this it seems, but who knows what could happen? I'm not saying this is likely, but let me throw something out. What if

China became hostile toward Taiwan? What if they decided to devalue the yuan against the dollar as a political decision, because I think it's a political decision not to do it now, more than an economic one. So, my sense is that the reforms outlined here are not just mild, they're meaningless. To try to make a distinction between pegged rates versus saying that the IMF won't support those, but they're in favor of managed floating, there's not that much of a distinction. I mean managed floating is the same game – the government has an implicit peg, they accumulate reserves, and if they get close to losing that peg, they start intervening in the markets. The difference is they just don't show their cards, they keep changing it [the exchange rate] and letting it move downward as necessary. But it's the same idea in principle. What worries me is that it's the old story of when there's a thunderstorm going on, you can't go up on the roof to fix it. But when it stops raining, there's no need to fix the hole in the roof. I think we have an opportunity to make some fundamental changes to avoid even more serious crises in the future, because if we don't, I think the global economy is very much in jeopardy.

DAVID ANDREWS: I think Judy raises some very interesting points, whereas Jeffrey thinks that we're remodeling, moving a few walls, Judy seems to believe that we're shifting deck chairs on the Titanic. I'm actually inclining towards Judy's view, because of the shape of international monetary relations as I see them emerging. Jeffrey has argued, I think persuasively, that there is no yen block emerging. As a consequence we have two major currency blocks, the dollar zone and the euro zone, which are largely economically self-contained. Therefore, monetary policies will take only marginal account of the exchange rate.

Pursuing policies of benign neglect towards the exchange rate is likely to be fine for the citizens of the United States and of the European Union. But what about countries that have trade that is highly diversified between both these blocks? In the world that Bob Solomon was describing of high trade interdependency, massive capital flows, and financial interdependence, what happens to countries that aren't well suited to tying their currencies either to the dollar or to the euro exclusively? I don't think that there's been sufficient attention to the plight of these countries and how the architecture might be more seriously modified to address what looks to be a perennial problem.

ROBERT MUNDELL: In today's paper there's an article entitled "The IMF Criticized," and it says a few interesting things. [Bundesbank Deputy Governor] Jürgen Stark said the International Monetary Fund should shift its focus from lending toward crisis prevention. He said that there is too much overlap and duplication between the IMF and the World Bank, and that the IMF should focus on monetary, fiscal, and exchange rate policies, as well as reforms of banking in the financial sector. The IMF should lend less and concentrate more on crisis prevention. A rising need for IMF financing reflects poorly on the Fund's surveillance efforts. Generally speaking, the more successful the surveillance, the less required the IMF financing. I agree with that.

I think that the IMF has to take a certain amount of criticism because of their bungling of surveillance efforts that failed to anticipate the crises in the 1990s. But I don't regard that as a change in the architecture. It's just another maneuver.

On the same page is a long discussion of a new policy in Brazil which has indexed ten billion dollars of its debt in dollars on the gamble that the *real* will hold its own against the dollar and that this will save the Brazilian government a lot of money by reducing its budget deficit. This is a step in the wrong direction. I've suggested several times before that if I were able to make one single change, it would be to have legislatures forbid governments from borrowing in foreign currencies. It would force countries to restore stability in their own capital markets and monetary systems. I realize it sounds utopian today, but if any of the big powers in the nineteenth century or earlier in this [the twentieth] century ever had to give a guarantee on its currency, it would be looked upon as a great insult.

At a Treasury Consultant's meeting on January 12, 1971 – the day John Connally was being confirmed as U.S. Treasury Secretary – and both Paul Samuelson and Bob Solomon participated in that meeting – the majority insisted that the Treasury should impose a gold guarantee on all U.S. dollar balances. I was appalled at that recommendation. It sounded plausible in the short run because it would make countries happier with their dollar balances. I argued that it would be a disastrous mistake in the long run because the U.S. dollar represented the center of the international monetary system. Just imagine what would have happened if the U.S. had given a gold guarantee on dollar balances and then later found the price of gold soaring above $850 an ounce (as it did in 1980). Indexing debt or money or borrowing in foreign currency takes the pressure off policymakers to restore monetary stability. I think we need to increase the focus on things that will restore monetary stability.

The international monetary architecture endorsed at Bretton Woods resulted in a system of fixed exchange rates based on the dollar, with the latter committed to buy and sell gold freely at the legal price of $35 an ounce. This arrangement was a practical accommodation to the reality that the U.S. economy had become the superpower in the world economy, several times larger than its nearest rival. A symmetrical international gold standard of the pre-1914 variety would no longer work: its effectiveness would simply depend upon the policy of the Federal Reserve System. But it broke down in

1971 because the $35 gold price had been made obsolete with World War II and post-war inflation and the mounting antagonism on the part of European countries to U.S. policies during the Vietnam War. Rather than change the price of gold, the international monetary authorities destroyed the architecture. Now there is a hunger for a new archtecture.

It may be too early to talk about a new architecture for the international monetary system in 1999. We are in the midst of a revolutionary change in Europe. The euro has come into being but it will not circulate until 2002. In the interim, Europe is not likely to want to think about a new architecture. The best time would be after the euro gets solidly entrenched. For that reason I do not think there is going to be any revolutionary developments in the system over the next few years. We are heading for a world monetary structure characterized by three major currency blocs. The dollar, euro and yen blocs comprise 60 percent of world GDP and would be the main players at the center of the system. I believe that the future direction of reform will be based on the reality of these three blocs, and a mechanism for stabilizing, or at least mitigating the instability of dollar–euro, yen–dollar and yen–euro exchange rates.

But this is not enough. A system in which the smaller countries of the world have to choose either the dollar or the euro or the yen if they want to move toward a stable exchange rate arrangement is not particularly attractive. These blocs are always subject to political pressures. One member of the dollar bloc is Panama. Remember what happened in the Noriega period when the United States blocked balances with Panama, exerting political pressure. The U.S. may have been completely right, maybe General Noriega was a bad guy, but the fact that its policy can be politicized means that there needs to be some alternative to the dollar. It is my hope that the member nations of the International Monetary Fund could produce a world currency, built perhaps on a platform of a dollar–euro–yen fixed exchange rate monetary union. We may be a long way from that development today but, as the Chinese say, a journey of a thousand miles starts with a single step.

What I do think is possible, though, is a neutral bloc that is not a national currency – a gold bloc. The great genius of the international gold standard (and, for that matter, bimetallism) of the nineteenth century was that it facilitated monetary unity without political integration. Political integration in the world today is not sufficient to achieve monetary union on the basis of overvalued paper currencies. It is in that respect that gold, which is still the second most important international reserve, may have a monetary future. Other advantages of gold include its historic prestige, its ability to hold its value in the long run, and the fact that, unlike foreign exchange, it is no country's liability.

There is, nevertheless, a great deal of opposition to gold; chrysophobia remains rampant. I don't know, however, whether a consensus can ever be achieved to rebuild a kind of gold standard or, more likely, a kind of "gold bloc" currency area that would compete with the dollar, euro and yen areas. A necessary condition for a renewed use of gold would be that it be "decriminalized" by lifting the taxes that are currently a barrier to its circulation as money.

HERBERT GRUBEL: I will take an extreme position – let's get rid of the IMF. Now, I want to justify this. I have a great deal of difficulty emotionally to do so, because in the 1970s I had a very successful textbook published by Penguin that went through four editions and a Spanish edition and sold over 100 000 copies worldwide. I also was twice on a panel of economists sitting around the table at the executive room of the IMF with the executive directors listening to us regarding what they should change. So I have a great love for the IMF. But I heard a powerful speech about a month ago at the Mont Pelerin Society – Robert Bartley was there, too. The speech was given by George Shultz. Now you might remember that George Shultz is a man with outstanding experience. He is a professional economist from MIT. He has been Secretary of Labor, Secretary of the Treasury, Secretary of State and Head of the Office of the Management of Budget. He is the only man who has ever held four cabinet positions. He followed [MIT Economics Professor and former IMF First Deputy Managing Director] Stan Fisher, who had just given a speech in the most beautiful elegant bureaucratic way. He gave all the reasons defending the IMF that Robert just summarized. And then came George in his inimitable way, speaking very slowly and without emotion. I will briefly summarize what he said as I understood it.

The first reason given for why we need the IMF is because there is always this contagion following crises. There is this risk that unless the government, the collective, does something, the system will break down and humanity will really suffer. Shultz described when he was Secretary of the Treasury and one of the big banks in New York failed. They came to him and asked the Treasury to bail out their bank, claiming that otherwise the American banking system would crash. He said "No." Now we let banks fail all the time and nothing happens. He also related that before his appointment to the first Nixon cabinet, there was a national railroad strike that December. Instead of settling it, the Democrats invoked the Taft–Hartley Act. When he was sworn in in January, everybody said the economy would crash unless he invoked the Taft–Hartley Act again and used all of the influence of the government to impose a settlement. But Shultz said, since he was a labor economist, let them fight it out, and he didn't invoke the Taft–Hartley Act. The economy didn't crash, the strike settled, and since then there haven't been anymore recommendations about using the Taft–Hartley Act. The hard consequences that were predicted didn't come about.

At another Mont Pelerin Society meeting there was a young Russian who got up and said the IMF has done irreparable harm to Russia. He said that Russia had to impose taxes in order to get the state to function. Then, the IMF naïvely said they would lend Russia money to finance the government while they were implementing the tax system. What happened? Russian bureaucrats took all the money and they didn't put the tax system in place. This Russian said that if the IMF had not given Russia the money, they would have had to establish a tax system. He claimed that if Russia didn't have the IMF, they would not have had all the economic problems that they have had.

The second reason given for the IMF is a new role that they have adopted to go in like a military force and say, "We know what's good for you, Indonesia, and we're going to bail you out only if you do what we tell you." Shultz said he understood the great interdependencies in the political system of Indonesia. It was functioning properly, it was stable. The IMF, backed by the United States, would go in and destroy much of the political system rather than allow it to develop. The catastrophes that might befall the people of Indonesia from a breakup of the political system imposed from the outside cannot be foreseen. Indonesia may even dissolve. For the IMF to go and say, "You must do this," using lending as a lever, is counterproductive. They have to do it themselves. It's essentially an internal problem.

Finally, Al Harberger says that we need the IMF for humanitarian grounds, because there are all these awful shocks. Very few of them have actually ever been realized as far as I'm concerned, Arnold, but countries claim they need resources so they can adjust more gradually and reduce human suffering. But what the heck is the private capital market doing? If a country is doing the right thing, private capital will come and help.

In conclusion, there may be benefits that the defenders of the IMF bring up, but there is also the other side of the coin. What I wanted to illustrate is the costs of the other side of the coin, as seen by someone who has been in the middle and has practical experience [as an elected member of the Canadian Parliament].

FAUSTO ALZATI: I will be very short. The international financial system is evolving incredibly rapidly, and the practitioners are always going to be one step ahead of the international organizations and the governments that are supposed to regulate them. It's very hard to hit a moving target like that. I think that the first and the most important step is to increase transparency at all levels of the international financial system.

ROBERT SOLOMON: I don't like the notion of new world financial architecture, because it sounds so grandiose. It also sounds like there's going to be a lot of tinkering going on, a lot of central planning of world financial flows and whatnot. I also think that the Council on Foreign Relations, of which I am duly a member, exists in order to record the conventional wisdom. I'd be more impressed that George Shultz, and former Treasury Secretary William Simon, and the former Chairman of Citibank Walter Wriston, are all contemplating abolishing the IMF. I think that's an important fact. I'm not quite ready to join them in abolishing the IMF, because I agree with Arnold, that over the years, it's probably done more good than harm. It seemed to work pretty well when [Jacques] de Larosière was IMF managing director, and it doesn't seem to me to be working very well with [Michel] Camdessus there.

The IMF is basically a fig leaf for the U.S. Treasury. The Treasury has an overwhelming say and influence in the policies that are implemented, and I think that the Treasury hasn't been doing very well. We have had three big crises recently. Something has gone wrong. I have a lot of personal respect for [former Treasury Secretary Robert] Rubin, and I think he had showed an elegant sense of timing in departing from a discredited administration. But, I keep wondering if things will get better with a new Treasury and a new President who has more credibility. We cannot dismiss the fact that we've had three big crises, and something has gone wrong with the operation of the international financial structure. Whether that means a new architecture is needed, or simply some small changes, remains an open question.

JEFFREY FRANKEL: I just wanted to respond to Herb Grubel's mention of George Shultz. In the international debt crisis in the 1980s, when Shultz was Secretary of the State in the Reagan Administration, he was part of the strategy dealing with the debt crisis. This involved IMF bailouts of Mexico and many other countries at a time when those countries had poor monetary policies, big budget deficits, a high degree of state control, and import substitution economics. In the 1990s, when he's out of office, we have the East Asian crisis. The countries that we tried to help in Asia are countries that are following more sound monetary policies, more sound fiscal policies, have much more privatized economies, and much more open economies than the countries that he bailed out in the 1980s. And now he says the IMF should be abolished. It's easy for him to say this because he's not in office. Usually, you don't have a test case, but since he was in office, we know what he did when he was there.

HERBERT GRUBEL: Maybe he learned something.

SVEN ARNDT: All good things must come to an end and so must this session and this conference. I want to just quickly take this opportunity to thank the participants for allowing me to hound them and to pressure them and push them, I've enjoyed it immensely. I think it's been a good conference. I'd like to thank Bob Mundell, Paul Zak, and Luzma Brayton for organizing it.

ROBERT MUNDELL: Thank you, Sven, for a very able and fair job as chairman. It's almost as inappropriate and unnecessary to thank Luzma Brayton, because she has been so visible, and everyone knows that she has been the sparkplug putting this whole operation together as well as the organizing genius who spent long, long hours over the last summer in making everything work out. So Luzma, thank you very much. And of course, our host, Fausto Alzati. And finally, to the participants around the table: while we fight over issues, we do so in good fellowship as part of the same republic, the republic of learning, and the motto of that republic is excellence. So thank you all very much.

Index

accession countries 6
Alzati, F. 35, 58, 112, 157–8, 165
  avoiding adjustment using exchange
    rate 55
  bailouts 64
  discretion vs. rules 134–5
  gradualism 74–5
  market failure and state intervention
    121–2
  NACU 82
  policy 98–9
amero *see* North American monetary
  union
anchor of stability 66–7
Andrews, D. 49, 56, 127–9, 161
Appalachia 50
Argentina 18, 50, 55, 92, 110
  currency board 36, 59, 76, 77, 81,
    124, 126
  exchange rate policy 94, 95
  mismanagement 71–2
  provincial money 107
  real exchange rate 96, 97, 101–103
  tequila crisis compared with Mexican
    crisis 61–5, 67–9, 77
Armey, D. 160
Arndt, S. 41, 46, 58, 61, 84, 112, 155–6,
  166–7
Asia 130
  economic policy in East Asia 137–52
Asian crisis 9, 34–5, 60, 66, 166
  exchange rate movements as cause
    140–43
asymmetric shocks 53–7, 131–3

Baila, I. 129
bailouts 63–4, 157
balance of payments 31–2
bancor 15
Bank of Canada 54
Bank of Japan 50–51, 139, 140, 149, 152

Bank of Mexico 135
banks 98, 103, 107, 164
Baquiero, A. 77, 83, 119–21, 135
Bartley, R. 50–51, 83, 99–100, 108, 114,
  133
  Malaysia 146–7
  monetary policy and economic
    growth in Latin America 59–77
    passim
Belgium 33
Beltran, A. 42, 58, 69, 83, 121, 146
  Mexico's search for stability 118–19
Bergsten, F. 40, 153, 155
Black, C. 45
black market 98
Blair, T. 45–6
Blanchard, O. 37
Brady bonds 61
Brazil 55, 60, 91–2, 94, 101–102
Bretton Woods system 2, 4, 11, 14, 20,
  162–3
  US and 5, 15, 136
Britain 6, 15, 38, 44, 45–6
bubbles 27–8, 35
budget deficit 42, 125
Bundesbank 49, 73

Camdessus, M. 60, 166
Canada 78–87 *passim*
  Bank of Canada 54
capital
  controls 26–7, 32–4, 97–8, 147–8
  inflows 90, 95–6, 96–7
  mobility 17, 158–60
  tax on short-term inflows 32–3, 93–4,
    97, 98, 154, 158, 160
Carter, J. 100
Cassel, G. 3
Cavallo, D. 62, 68, 126
central banks 47–8, 69
  see also under individual names

Central and Eastern European countries
44–5
CFA (Communauté Financière
Africaine) 125
Chile 91, 92–4, 98
tax on short-term capital flows 32–3,
93–4, 97, 98, 154, 158, 160
China 140–41
Citibank 30
Clinton, W. 76, 159–60
Colosio, L.D. 117, 126
Comisión de Cambios 127
community/local currencies 107–108
competitive devaluation 134–5
compulsory surrender of export proceeds 97–8
Connally, J. 136
Connally, M. 41, 42, 58, 69
possibility of monetary stability in
Latin America 101–16 *passim*
contagion 154–5, 164
convergence 35–7
corners hypothesis 143–5, 160
corruption 18
Council on Foreign Relations 114,
153–5, 159–60, 166
Courchene, T. 85
credibility, policy 120
crises 154–5, 160–61, 164
Asian crisis *see* Asian crisis
debt crises *see* debt crises
crony capitalism 34–5, 151
Crow, J. 54
cultural sovereignty 80–81
currency areas 6–9, 10–11
currency boards 10, 17, 19, 69, 76,
124–6
Argentina 36, 59, 76, 77, 81, 124, 126
customs unions 101–102

David, L. 51, 84
debt, foreign 92–4, 98, 162
debt crises 96, 166
comparison of Mexico and Argentina
61–5, 67–9, 77
deflation 3–4
Delors Commission 79
demand and supply 88–90
Denmark 6
devaluations 64–5, 68, 90–91, 103, 113

competitive 134–5
Thai devaluation 141–2
developing countries 153
supply of funds to 92–4
dollar 2, 4, 15, 39–40
currency bloc 7–9, 10–11, 145–6, 163
dollar-euro rate 25–7, 40, 55
dollar-yen rate 9, 25, 138–40, 141,
149–50
effect of euro on dollar as reserve
currency 46, 155
G-3 monetary union 10–13
possible future problems 16–17
prestige 86
dollarization 68, 75–6, 109–110, 124
Dominguez, K. 139
Dornbusch, R. 19, 147–8
Dow Jones index 24, 28
Duisenberg, W. 43

Eastern and Central European countries
44–5
Ecuador 61
Eichengreen, B. 110, 142, 143
El Salvador 75–6, 94, 130
entrepreneurship 134
euro 36–7, 79, 145–6, 155, 163
dollar-euro rate 25–7, 40, 55
in Europe and the world 38–58
G-3 monetary union 10–13
significance in international economy
6–9
Euro-11 38–9
Euro System 44
European Central Bank (ECB) 43, 44–5,
48–9, 55–6
European Monetary Union (EMU) 5, 6,
12, 134, 143
development of 18–19, 127–9
expansion 44–6
see also euro
European System of Central Banks 44
exchange rate regimes 65–6, 73–4,
106–107, 154–5
fixed exchange rates *see* fixed
exchange rates
flexible exchange rates 2, 5–6, 65–6,
70–71, 113, 115–16, 130–31
future of international monetary
system 158–60

intermediate regimes 143–5, 146, 148
pegged exchange rates 40–41
possibility of monetary stability in
    Latin America 112–16
sliding pegs 27
exchange rates
among G-3 currencies 8–10, 12
Argentine crisis 64–5
Canada 80
central banks' control over 135
dollar-euro 25–7, 40, 55
dollar-yen 9, 25, 138–40, 141, 149–50
Mexico 19–20, 64–5, 112–13, 122–6
movements as cause of East Asian
    crisis 140–43
overvalued 122–3, 135
policy in Latin America 88–100
role of euro 40–41, 52–8
exports 88–90
compulsory surrender of export
    proceeds 97–8

factor mobility 17, 54, 86–7, 158–60
Federal Reserve system 2–3, 11–12, 32,
    73, 81, 86
Fernandez, R. 62, 126
Fetcher, W.R. 45
fiats 33
financial markets 24, 27–9
fiscal policy 42
Fisher, S. 164
fixed exchange rates 9–10, 65–6,
    130–33
and Asian crisis 142
Latin America 94, 114–15
Mexico 112–13, 123–6
see also currency boards;
    dollarization; monetary union
flexible exchange rates 2, 5–6, 65–6,
    70–71, 113, 115–16, 130–31
Flores, A. 77
Ford Motor Company 80
forecasting, short-term 29–30
foreign exchange reserves 7, 39, 114
Fraga Neto, A. 60
France 125
Frankel, J. 46–7, 56–7, 66, 75–6, 80,
    111–12
economic policy in Japan and East
    Asia 137–52 *passim*

Friedman, M. 57, 115

G-3 monetary union 10–13
G7 140, 159
G22 159
GDP 38–9
Germany 43, 128–9
Bundesbank 49, 73
Giscard d'Estaing, V. 50
gold 4–5, 20–21, 162–3
gold bloc 163–4
gold standard 2, 3, 8, 10, 162
gradualism 69, 74–5
Greenspan, A. 30–31, 100, 160
Greenwood, J. 70, 72
Grubel, H. 147, 151
abolition of the IMF 164–5, 166
exchange rate regime 113, 132–3
monetary policy in the NAFTA area
    and the possibility of monetary
    union 78–87 *passim*
politics 47–8, 52
Guatemala 94

Haberler, G. 27
Hague, W. 44
Harberger, A. 106–107, 108–109,
    130–31, 156–7
exchange rate policy in Latin America
    88–100 *passim*
Mexican and Argentine crises 61–2,
    63, 67–8
policy as servomechanism 29
shocks 49–50, 133
Harris, R. 85
Hausmann, R. 110
Hayek, F.A. von 80, 99
hedge funds 27
Hinshaw, R. 37, 88
Hirschman, A.O. 112
Holland 33
Honduras 94
Hong Kong 69–70, 72–3, 81, 105–106
Hong Kong Monetary Authority
    105–106

imports 88–90
import restrictions 89, 90
income distribution inequality 133, 134
Indonesia 76

inflation 24
    Hong Kong 69–70, 72–3
    Latin America 90–91
    Mexico 119–20, 125
innovation 1–2
institutional frameworks 83, 84, 85, 109
interest rates 42, 83, 85, 120
intermediate regimes 143–5, 146, 148
international currency (INTOR) 13–16
International Monetary Fund (IMF) 13,
    151, 156–7
    default on Brady bonds in Ecuador 61
    proposal to abolish 164–5, 166
    role 60, 154–5, 160, 161–2
international monetary system
    future of 153–67
    reform of 1–23
    state of the world economy 24–37
internationalization ratio 39
intervention 11–12, 139–40
    state intervention and market failure
        121–2
    sterilized intervention 93–4, 107,
        139–40
INTOR 13–16
investment decisions 34–5
Italy 36, 42, 47–8, 53

Jamaica 95–6
Japan 34–5, 72
    Bank of Japan 50–51, 139, 140, 149,
        152
    economic policy 137–52
    G-3 monetary union 10–13
    monetary union with US 150
    yen *see* yen
Johnson, C. 68, 106, 134, 145–6
    euro in Europe and the world 38–58
        passim
    fixed exchange rates and reserves 114
    monetary union in NAFTA area 82, 83
    productivity 104
    US balance of payments 31

Keynes, J.M. 3, 4, 9–10
Kohl, H. 76, 129
Korea, South 29, 141–2
Krugman, P. 147, 152

labor mobility 54, 86–7

Larosière, J. de 166
Latin America
    exchange rate policy 88–100
    monetary policy and economic
        growth 59–77
    possibility of monetary stability
        101–16
    see also under individual countries
leadership 126
lender of last resort 158–60
local/community currencies 107–108
Long-Term Capital Management
    (LTCM) 29, 160

Maastricht Treaty 5–6, 49
Mahathir Mohamad 146, 148
Malaysia 33–4, 146–7, 148
Malpass, D. 59
Manley, M. 95
market crash, 1987 30–31
market failure 121–2
mechanism of adjustment 63
Menem, C. 77, 126
Mercosur 101–102
Mexico 18, 19–20, 58, 59–60, 75, 97,
    114–15, 141–2
    Bank of Mexico 135
    crisis compared with Argentine crisis
        61–5, 67–9, 77
    currency union with US 117–18,
        128–9
    exchange rate policy 70–71
    factor mobility between US and 54
    monetary policy and economic
        performance 117–36
    monetary union in the NAFTA area
        82–3
    structural reforms 76–7
mini-devaluation policy 91
Mises, L. von 3
Modigliani, F. 28
monetary union 114
    EMU *see* European Monetary Union
    G-3 10–13
    Japan and US 150
    Mexico and US 117–18, 128–9
    North America 78–87, 117–18, 119,
        124, 127–9
money illusion 50
monistic models 30

Monnet, J. 42
moral hazard 142
Morita, A. 149
Mundell, R. 25–6, 37, 41, 56, 81, 84–5,
   96, 167
   anchor of stability 66–7
   asymmetric shocks 131–2
   community currencies 107–108
   expansion of EMU 44–5
   Federal Reserve 73
   future of international monetary
      system 161–4
   Japan-US monetary union 150
   Mexico and Argentine crises 62, 63
   monetary stability in Mexico 123–6
   real exchange rate economics
      104–106, 112–13
   reform of the international monetary
      system 1–23 *passim*
   stability of flexible exchange rate
      systems 52–4
   yen-dollar rate 149–50
Murdoch, R. 44, 45

NAFTA 60, 128
   monetary policy in the NAFTA area
      78–87
natural resources, prices of 80
Niinisto, S. 43
non-traded goods 111–12
North American monetary union 78–87,
   117–18, 119, 124, 127–9

opt-out mechanisms 51–2
optimum currency areas 46–7, 53, 56,
   57–8, 148
overshooting 95

Panama 94–5, 96–7, 163
pegged exchange rates 40–41
Plaza Accord 149
policymakers 98–9
political integration 42, 43
politics
   Latin America 61, 71, 73, 77
   role in EMU 47–9
population growth 118
price-earnings ratios 28
prices
   natural resources 80

stability 8
   unemployment and 102–103
   US price level 4–5
Prodi, R. 45
productivity 104, 105, 110, 134
protectionism 134–5

Quebec 85–6

Reagan, R. 99, 100
real exchange rate
   exchange rate policy in Latin America
      88–100
   possibility of monetary stability in
      Latin America 101–16
Rees, A. 79
reserves
   devaluation and 141–2
   foreign 7, 39, 114
   Mexico and accumulation of 117,
      120–21, 122, 127
risk premium 129–30
Rist, C. 3
Robbins, L. 1, 20, 41
Rodriguez, C. 126
Roman monetary standard 14–15
Rubin, R. 73–4, 138, 158, 166
Russia 60–61, 157, 165

Sachs, J. 147–8
Salinas, R. 65–6, 70–71, 84, 109–110,
   126–7, 132
Samuelson, P.A. 79
   state of the world economy 24–37
      passim
sanctions 42–3
Scaruffi, G. 15
SDR 14
Seaga, E. 95–6
Segerson, N. 47
seigniorage 41, 43, 82
Sera, Mr. (Mexican Finance Minister)
   115
servomechanism 29
Sanchez, C. 133–4
Shelton, J. 34, 73–4, 117–18, 135–6,
   160–61
shocks
   asymmetric 53–7, 131–3
   euro and 47, 49–50, 51–8

fixed exchange rates and 115, 126, 130–33
short-term capital inflows, tax on 32–3, 93–4, 97, 98, 154, 158, 160
short-term forecasting 29–30
Shultz, G. 164–5, 166
silver 20–21
Simon, W. 166
single (world) currency 8, 13–16, 17–18, 35–7, 41, 163
sliding pegs 27
Sojo, E. 76–7, 122–3
Solomon, R. 32–3, 42, 57–8, 65, 73, 114–15
    asymmetric shocks 54–5
    European System of Central Banks 44
    future of the international monetary system 153–7 *passim*, 165–6
Solow, R. 35
sovereignty 50
    cultural 80–81
Sprinkle, B. 99–100
Stark, J. 161
state intervention, and market failure 121–2
statistical taxes 101–102
sterilized intervention 93–4, 107, 139–40
structural reforms 64, 118–19
Summers, L.H. 33, 41, 68, 74, 138, 144
supply and demand 88–90
Sweden 6

Taft-Hartley Act 164
targets 101–104
    commitment to 135
taxes 103, 104, 110
    Argentina 71–2, 101–102
    tax on short-term capital flows 32–3, 93–4, 97, 98, 154, 158, 160
    Tobin tax 33, 154
terms of trade 108–109, 111
    shocks 53–4, 57
tesobonos 60–61, 61–2
Texas 111
Thailand 28–9, 60, 152
    devaluation 141–2
time inconsistency 145
Tobin tax 33, 154

trade 39, 153
    real exchange rate economics 88–90, 92
    surpluses in Mexico 127
transparency of pricing 17–18
tripartite world currency system 145–6

unemployment 102–103
unhedged (dollar) liabilities 142–3
United States (US) 24–5, 36, 37, 86, 135–6, 151–2
    Appalachia 50
    asymmetric shocks 131
    balance of payments 31–2
    and Bretton Woods system 5, 15, 136
    Carter inflation and Reagan disinflation 100
    currency union with Mexico 117–18, 128–9
    dollar *see* dollar
    dollarization 68, 75–6, 109–110, 124
    factor mobility between Mexico and 54
    Federal Reserve System 2–3, 11–12, 32, 73, 81, 86
    and fixed exchange rate 123
    G-3 monetary union 10–13
    inflation and developing countries' inflation rates 70, 72–3
    in international monetary system 2–5, 15–16
    local community currencies 107–108
    monetary union with Japan 150
    and North American monetary union 81
    price index 94–5
    Taft-Hartley Act 164
    Texas 111
    Treasury 125, 166
Uruguay 95, 96, 124

verifiability 144–5
Viner, J. 115
Volcker, P. 16

wages 102–103
Wallich, H. 26
World Bank 156–7
world currency 8, 13–16, 17–18, 35–7, 41, 163

World War I 3
Wriston, W. 166

yen 137–8, 151–2, 163
   currency bloc 7–9, 10–11, 137–8,
     145–6

G-3 monetary union 10–13
yen-dollar rate 9, 25, 138–40, 141,
   149–50

Zak, P. 51, 55–6, 82, 104, 129–30
Zedillo, E. 70